COUNSELING THE ALCOHOL AND DRUG DEPENDENT CLIENT

COUNSELING THE ALCOHOL AND DRUG DEPENDENT CLIENT

A Practical Approach

ROBERT J. CRAIG

Illinois School of Professional Psychology
West Side VA Medical Center, Chicago

Boston New York San Francisco
Mexico City Montreal Toronto London Madrid Munich Paris
Hong Kong Singapore Tokyo Cape Town Sydney

Executive Editor: *Virginia Lanigan*
Editorial Assistant: *Rob Champagne*
Marketing Manager: *Tara Whorf*
Production Editor: *Paul Mihailidis*
Editorial Production Service: *Matrix Productions*
Composition Buyer: *Linda Cox*
Electronic Composition: *Peggy Cabot, Cabot Computer Services*
Manufacturing Buyer: *Andrew Turso*
Cover Designer: *Kristina Mose–Libon*

For related titles and support materials, visit our online catalog at
www.ablongman.com.

Library of Congress Cataloging-in-Publication Data

Craig, Robert J.
  Counseling the alcohol and drug dependent client : a practical approach /
  Robert J. Craig.
    p. cm.
  Includes bibliographical references and index.
  ISBN 0-205-35916-7
    1. Substance abuse—Treatment.   2. Substance abuse—Patients—Counseling
  of.   I. Title.

  RC564.C733 2004
  616.86'06—dc21
                                                          2003040310

Printed in the United States of America

10 9 8 7 6 5 4 3 2 1   HAM   08 07 06 05 04 03

CONTENTS

Preface   xiii

About the Author   xv

CHAPTER ONE

The Extent and Cost of Substance Abuse on Society   1

SOURCES OF EPIDEMIOLOGICAL DATA   2
Alcohol Sales Data   2
Population Surveys   2
Death Records   2
Drug Abuse Warning Network   3
Treatment Surveys   3
Arrestee Urinalysis Data   3
Drug Seizure Data   3
Ethnographic Research   3
High School Senior Survey   3
National Household Survey on Drug Abuse   4

EXTENT OF THE PROBLEM   4
Alcohol   4
Cocaine   5
Ecstasy   7
Heroin   7
Hallucinogens   7
Marijuana   8
Nicotine   8

COST OF THE PROBLEM   10

COST-EFFECTIVENESS OF TREATMENT   11

CHAPTER SUMMARY   13

SOURCES OF INFORMATION   13

CHAPTER TWO

Etiology of Substance Abuse   15

   RISK FACTORS FOR INITIAL SUBSTANCE USE   16

   RISK FACTORS FOR SUBSTANCE ABUSE AND DEPENDENCE   16
      Genetic and Biological Risk Factors   17
      Psychological Risk Factors   17
      Psychopathology   17
      Environmental and Societal Risk Factors   18
      Familial Risk Factors   18
      School Risk Factors   18

   THEORETICAL MODELS   18

   PSYCHOLOGICAL MODELS   19
      Social Learning and Behavioral Theories   22
      Expectancy Theories   23
      Biological and Genetic Models   23
      Sociological Models   28
      Family Theory Models   29

   CHAPTER SUMMARY   32

   SOURCES OF INFORMATION   32

CHAPTER THREE

Drugs and Their Effects   35

   CHARACTERISTICS OF DRUGS   35
      Dosage   35
      Main Effects   35
      Peak Effects   36
      Potency   36
      Safety   36
      Route of Administration   36
      Drug Interactions   37
      Pharmacokinetics   37
      Neurotransmitters   38

   CLASSIFICATION OF DRUGS   40
      Drug Schedules   40
      Alcohol   41

Amphetamines   43
Methamphetamines   46
Barbiturates: Minor Tranquilizers   46
Caffeine   48
Cocaine   49
Hallucinogens   51
Heroin   52
Marijuana   55
Club Drugs   62
Nicotine   63

CHAPTER SUMMARY   67

SOURCES OF INFORMATION   68

CHAPTER FOUR
Assessment and Diagnosis   71

ASSESSMENT PROBLEMS AND ISSUES   71

PURPOSE OF ASSESSMENT   71

METHODS OF ASSESSMENT   72
Clinical Interviews   72
Recommended Interview Format   74

SCREENING INTERVIEWS   81
Addiction Severity Index   81
Comprehensive Drinker Profile   84

MOTIVATIONAL INTERVIEWING   84

LABORATORY TESTS   88
Toxicology Urine Screens   88
Hair Testing   91
Blood Alcohol Levels   92

PSYCHOLOGICAL TESTS   92
Minnesota Multiphasic Personality Inventory-2   94
Millon Clinical Multiaxial Inventory-III   94
Michigan Alcoholism Screening Test   95

DIAGNOSIS AND TREATMENT   95

PRESENTING ASSESSMENT RESULTS   95

CHAPTER SUMMARY   110

SOURCES OF INFORMATION   110

CHAPTER FIVE

Treatment Principles and Modalities   113

PRINCIPLES OF TREATMENT   113

PROBLEMS IN COUNSELING PATIENTS WITH ACTING-OUT DISORDERS   115

PREPARING TO COUNSEL   117

FORMULATING A TREATMENT PLAN   118

COUNSELING TECHNIQUES   118
Active Listening   118
Accurate Empathy   119
Giving Advice   120
Confrontation   120
Education   121
Exploration   121
Humor   121
Interpretation   122
Paraphrasing   122
Questioning   122
Reassurance   123
Reflection   123
Self-Disclosure   123
Silence   124
Summarizing   124

GENERAL TREATMENT CATEGORIES   124
Social Therapies   124
Behavioral Therapies   127
Medical Therapies   136

TREATMENT MATCHING   139

BRIEF INTERVENTIONS AND BRIEF THERAPIES   141
Stages of Change   142

HOW PATIENTS SABOTAGE TREATMENT   143
Acting Different   143
Defocusing   144
False Compliance   144

Family Rescuer   144
I've Got a Secret   145
Negotiating   145
Self-Pity   145
Addict Games   145

CHAPTER SUMMARY   147

SOURCES OF INFORMATION   147

APPENDIX: EXAMPLE TREATMENT PLANS   151

CHAPTER SIX

Group Counseling Techniques   155

CURATIVE FACTORS IN GROUP THERAPY   156

TYPES OF GROUPS   158

MODELS OF GROUP COUNSELING   159
Developmental Groups   159
Educational Groups   161
Focused Change Groups   161
Individually-Oriented Change Groups   162
Interpersonal or Interactional Groups   162
Object Relations or Systems Model   162
Problem-Solving Groups   163
Process Groups   163

FACTORS TO CONSIDER IN DEVELOPING A GROUP   164
Patient Selection   164
Inclusion and Exclusion Criteria   164
Selection Procedures   165
Group Structure   165
Limit Setting   165
Open or Closed Groups   165
Physical Setting   166

GROUP INTERVENTIONS   166

SPECIFIC PROBLEMS   167
Dropouts, Absences, and Tardiness   167
Confidentiality   168
The Intoxicated or High Patient in Group   168
Suspected Illicit Use without Acknowledging It   168

Continued Use with No Intention to Stop   168

CHAPTER SUMMARY   169

SOURCES OF INFORMATION   169

CHAPTER SEVEN
Counseling the Family of Substance Abusers   171

FAMILY SYSTEMS THEORY   172

FAMILIES OF SUBSTANCE ABUSERS   173
Family Structure   174
Abusive Relationship Patterns   175
Family Rules   176

ENABLING BEHAVIORS   176
Types of Enablers   177
Counseling the Enablers   177

CODEPENDENCE   178
Origins of Codependence   178
Codependent Traits   179
Codependent Roles   182
Counseling the Codependent   183

CHILDREN OF ALCOHOLICS   184
Roles   185
Treatment   187

ADULT CHILDREN OF ALCOHOLICS   187
Treatment   189

CHAPTER SUMMARY   189

SOURCES OF INFORMATION   189

CHAPTER EIGHT
Working with Special Populations   193

ADOLESCENTS   193
Stages of Adolescent Drug Use   194
Problems with Diagnostic Criteria   194
Interviewing Adolescents   196

Problems in Treating Adolescents   196
Monitoring Use   198
Legal Issues   198

WOMEN   198
Etiology   200
Treatment   200

MINORITIES   201
African Americans   201
Hispanics   202
Gays and Lesbians   203
Geriatric Populations   205
Native Americans   207

MILITARY PERSONNEL   207

PEOPLE WITH DUAL DIAGNOSES   208
Related Dual Diagnoses   208
Assessment   208
Treatment   209
Goals   209

CHAPTER SUMMARY   209

SOURCES OF INFORMATION   209

CHAPTER NINE

Public Policy   211

NATIONAL POLICY   211

INTERNATIONAL POLICY   212

SOCIAL INTERVENTIONS   212
Urine Testing   212
Over-the-Counter Drug Testing   213
Media Representation of Substance Abusers   214
Medical Use of Marijuana   214
Eliminating Happy Hours   215
End "Ladies' Nights"   215
Ban the Sale of Alcohol at Sporting Events   216
Ban College Campuses from Operating Bars or Selling Liquor   216
Ban Smoking by Actors in Movies and Television   217
Not Insure Tobacco-Related Illnesses   217

Fire Workers Caught Using Drugs   218
Eliminate Public Pay Phones   218
Pay Addicts Not to Get Pregnant   219

LAW ENFORCEMENT INTERVENTIONS   219
Legalization and Decriminalization   219
Videotape Suspected DUIs   220
Confiscate Cars   221
BALs to Start Cars   221
Over-the-Counter Nicotine Sales   222
Drug Roadblocks   222
Mandatory Sentencing   223
Interdiction   223
Seizing Assets   224
Money Laundering   224
Treatment   225

GOVERNMENT INTERVENTIONS   225
Food and Drug Administration Regulation of Tobacco as a Drug   225
Higher Taxes on Alcohol   226
Higher Legal Drinking Age   227

SOURCES OF INFORMATION   227

Author Index   229

Subject Index   235

PREFACE

The genesis for the ideas presented in this book brewed and percolated during the 28 years I have assessed and treated substance abusers, managed inpatient and outpatient substance abuse treatment programs, taught graduate courses on substance abuse, read salient substance abuse literature, spoken with scores of substance abuse personnel, and counseled innumerable patients. The final product presents the essence of this distillation. It details the mainstream of current thought on treating substance abuse and includes ideas gleaned from the clinical care of patients.

Substance abuse treatment personnel are among the most intensely dedicated and committed mental health professionals I have been fortunate to know. However, many often counsel without the benefit of recent research-based information or awareness of current trends and thinking within the substance abuse field. Our field is replete with counselors who are in recovery themselves. Recovering alcoholics or drug addicts can have a powerful influence and effect on those they counsel. They represent significant role models for those who are still in the early stages of recovery and for those who have not yet made the commitment to stop abusing substances. Unfortunately, many have a commitment to a particular type of intervention and believe that theirs is the only path toward abstinence and sobriety. For example, many recovering alcoholics believe that the principles and traditions of Alcoholics Anonymous (AA) are the only way to achieve treatment goals. Former addicts who have been through therapeutic community treatment often believe that really is the best way to stay off drugs. Both groups may denigrate methadone maintenance or the use of psychotropic drugs as part of an individual's treatment plan. This book is meant to broaden knowledge, skills, and attitudes regarding the best ways to assess, conceptualize, and treat substance abusers by treatment specialists who are not psychologists or psychiatrists. We hope to complement and not drastically change ideas about recovery.

Finding the right politically correct terminology is difficult in a period of changing racial identity specifications. In using these various terms, I mean no disrespect to those who would prefer some terminology other than the one used in a particular context. Throughout the chapters I use terms such as "substance abuser," "drug or alcohol abuser," "drug addict," "alcoholic," and "chemically dependent" interchangeably. Whenever these words appear, the reader should construe the meaning of the term as applicable to anyone who has a problem with licit (e.g., alcohol) or illicit (e.g., drugs) substances that is serious enough to cause distress in the abuser or concern among those who care about him or her. Similarly, I use the terms "African Americans," "Blacks," and "Black Americans," and the terms "Hispanic" and "Latino."

At the end of each chapter I list the informational sources for that chapter. In some cases I used these sources as references in the body of the text, but in many cases I did not, although they provided source material for the discussion of facts and ideas in that chapter. References are sources that I referred to in the body of text. Sources of influence are sources that influenced my thinking in one way or another, although I may or may not have used them in a particular chapter. I hope this practice becomes more common in scientific citations.

ACKNOWLEDGMENTS

The author would like to thank the following reviewers for their input and suggestions concerning this text: Jennifer R. Adams, The University of Tennessee at Chattanooga; Scarlett A. Benjamin, Keuka College; Peggy D. Campbell, Florence Darlington Technical College; Chandra M. Donnell, The University of Memphis; and Cheryl D. Dozier, University of Georgia.

ABOUT THE AUTHOR

Robert J. Craig, Ph.D., ABPP is a clinical psychologist and the Director of the Drug Dependence Treatment Center at VA Chicago Health Care System—West Side Division, serving as administrator, teacher, researcher and practitioner for 28 years. He is Board Certified in Clinical Psychology and Administrative Psychology, and a Fellow in the American Psychological Association, in the American Academy of Clinical Psychology, and in the Society for Personality Assessment. He serves as a consulting editor to the *Journal of Personality Assessment* and has done many ad hoc reviews for journals in psychology and psychiatry. He is a recent recipient of the Martin Mayman award for Distinguished Contributions in the Literature on Personality Assessment and is a professor at the Illinois School of Professional Psychology, where he teaches courses on testing, ethics, and substance abuse. He recently received the School's Outstanding Psychologist Faculty Recognition award. This is his third book on substance abuse.

COUNSELING THE ALCOHOL AND DRUG DEPENDENT CLIENT

■ ■ ■ ■ ■

CHAPTER ONE

THE EXTENT AND COST OF SUBSTANCE ABUSE ON SOCIETY

In this text, *epidemiology* is the study of the incidence and prevalence of disease and *incidence* is the total number of new cases developed within a defined period of time, and *prevalence* is the total number of cases (usually in the same period of time). Thus prevalence of alcoholism in the United States for this year would be the prevalence of alcoholism last year plus the incidence of alcoholism this year. The science of epidemiology has been extremely important, as it often identifies the extent of the problem, but also points to areas where research into disease etiology needs to be focused.

This chapter examines the extent and the cost of substance abuse in the United States today. How can we measure this? The U.S. government uses "leading economic indicators" to gauge the economic status of the nation. This index includes such indicators as the number of new housing starts, rate of unemployment, new factory orders, and the degree of consumer confidence, among others. The government issues reports on these data and economists use these figures to make projections and plans for their employers. The Federal Reserve uses these data to help fight inflation through the raising or lowering of interest rates it charges to member banks.

The government also provides indices that measure the current extent of substance abuse. Policy makers use these data to make recommendations regarding laws and policies to deal with the problem. For example, studies that reported that many of our soldiers in Vietnam were addicted to opium led Congress and then-President Richard Nixon to authorize the Veterans Administration (VA) to treat heroin addiction. Prior to this change in policy, VA hospitals treated only the medical consequences of narcotic addiction, not addiction itself. When the cocaine epidemic developed and studies demonstrated the extent of the problem and that many addicts were engaged in crime to support the habit, Congress allotted substantially more money to build more prisons, established drug courts, and, in some cases, mandated drug abuse treatment for those who were incarcerated. These are but a few examples of how the study of epidemiology can influence the direction of intervention in a given area, as well as public policy.

A variety of indices commonly is used to assess the extent of substance abuse in the nation. No single index is perfect and each has advantages and limitations. Each provides a different perspective on the problem and each complements others.

SOURCES OF EPIDEMIOLOGICAL DATA

Alcohol Sales Data

Sales data are derived from tax collection reports, which are carefully monitored and accurate. Alcohol sales data reveal the types and amount of alcohol consumed or purchased in a defined period of time. These data show whether alcohol consumption is increasing or decreasing and are useful for observing the effects of increasing taxation on alcohol consumption.

Population Surveys

Population surveys are the most common way of ascertaining the extent of drinking and drinking patterns within a defined population. Population surveys typically ask respondents to identify the kind of alcohol consumed (e.g., beer, wine, spirits), the amount used, the context of drinking, and any problems resulting from alcohol use. However, there are limitations to these data. Obviously, the accuracy and reliability of this index relies on the truthfulness of respondents. Surveys are costly and tend to underestimate consumption, compared to beverage sales (NIAAA, 1990). Surveys that rely on telephone responses miss chronic alcoholics who live on the street, or heavier drinkers who may not be available to answer questions. They also miss users in jails, hospitals, homeless shelters, and others without stable residences, as well as those in treatment programs at the time of the survey.

Death Records

The National Center for Health Statistics (NCHS) collects data pertaining to alcohol-related mortality from three major sources.

1. The NCHS files and tracks death certificates that list alcohol as a contributing cause of death.
2. The National Hospital Discharge Survey tracks deaths from diseases associated with alcohol. These data come primarily from community hospitals, and their accuracy depends on the physician completing the death certificate to properly code alcohol as a contributing cause of death.
3. The National Highway Traffic Safety Administration records every death from traffic accidents on public roads within 30 days of the accident. Alcohol-related deaths are determined by blood alcohol levels or by documentation provided by the investigating officer.

Multiple sources provide drug-related death statistics. Medical examiner offices report to the National Institute on Drug Abuse (NIDA), the Drug Abuse Warning Network (DAWN) project, coroners, and state public health agencies.

Drug Abuse Warning Network

Initiated by NIDA in 1972, DAWN is designed to be an early-warning index of the nation's drug abuse problem. Data are collected from 20 selected major U.S. metropolitan areas. Any drug-related visit to selected emergency rooms is reported to the DAWN project.

Treatment Surveys

Clinicians in many treatment-based surveys report the primary substance of abuse at admission to a drug treatment program. For example, the National Drug and Alcoholism Treatment Survey is completed by all treatment programs that receive federal funds. Since 90% of all treatment programs receive federal funds, this report is very exhaustive when completed accurately.

Arrestee Urinalysis Data

The Drug Use Forecasting System of the National Institute of Justice receives reports from police districts that test urine of arrestees. Arrestee Drug Abuse Monitor (ADAM) data are collected from the 25 largest U.S. cities. This type of data is somewhat skewed. Police districts periodically do sweeps and sting operations designed to reduce illicit drugs in a given area and to improve their own statistics of narcotic arrests, and these periodic initiatives influence statistics.

Drug Seizure Data

The Drug Enforcement Administration (DEA) and state and local enforcement agencies seize illicit drugs and analyze them for purity. They obtain information about the cost of street-level drugs. They send confiscated drugs to special labs for analysis of purity levels. They use these data as an index of drug availability.

Ethnographic Research

Criminal justice and correctional resources, public health surveys, and other sources that are unique to local communities also provide data.

High School Senior Survey

This annual survey, coordinated through the University of Michigan, samples drug use prevalence and patterns for high school students annually. Referred to as *Monitoring the Future,* the survey was initiated by and funded by NIDA in 1975. Eighth grade and tenth grade students have been included in the annual survey since 1991. About 45,000 students are selected randomly from representative samples from public and private schools yearly. Because these data have been collected using essentially the same methodology for almost three decades, they provide an excellent picture of trends in the use of legal drugs (alcohol, nicotine) and illegal drugs by minors over time. Because some questions pertain to attitudes toward use, research can correlate and predict future trends to the extent that more permissive attitudes are correlated with future use. Many substance abusers have dropped out of high school by their senior year and are not captured with this methodology.

National Household Survey on Drug Abuse

One population that is missed by previous methods is people whose substance abuse is confined to the home. This population primarily abuses prescription drugs. Researchers have collected data on this hidden population since 1972 and now conduct this research on an annual basis. The last published survey studied drug use trends in people 12 years old and older and sampled 70,000 randomly selected respondents.

These data sources provide the background for exploring the extent of the substance abuse problem in the United States. Although these data have built-in inaccuracies, they should reflect a good approximation of the extent of the problem.

EXTENT OF THE PROBLEM

The alcohol and drug abuse statistics in this section come from the most recent data available at this writing. The Web sites of the National Institute on Drug Abuse and the National Institute on Alcoholism and Alcohol Abuse contain the most recent data. Search for "NIAAA" or "NIDA" or use the entire names of these organizations to access their sites.

Alcohol

Table 1.1 reports the results of alcohol use by high school seniors from 1975 to 2001—a 27-year period. The data suggest that high school seniors report reduced prevalence of alcohol use over the 27-year span in the categories of lifetime use, annual use, and use in the past 30 days. Daily use increased with statistical significance (perhaps because of the extremely large sample sizes that allow statisticians to detect even minute differences) by 0.7% from 2000 to 2001. Alcohol remains a widely- and prevalently used drug by U.S. youth.

TABLE 1.1 Prevalence of Alcohol Use Among High School Seniors, 1975–2001

GRADUATING YEAR	PERCENT REPORTING ALCOHOL USE			
	LIFETIME	ANNUAL	30 DAYS	DAILY
1975	90.4	84.8	68.2	5.7
1976	91.9	85.7	68.3	5.6
1977	92.5	87.0	71.2	6.1
1978	93.1	87.7	72.1	5.7
1979	93.0	88.1	71.8	6.9
1980	93.2	87.9	72.0	6.0
1981	92.6	87.0	70.7	6.0
1982	92.8	86.8	69.7	5.7
1983	92.6	87.3	69.4	5.5
1984	92.6	86.0	67.2	4.8
1985	92.2	85.6	65.9	5.0
1986	91.3	84.5	65.3	4.8
1987	92.2	85.7	66.4	4.8
1988	92.0	85.3	63.9	4.2
1989	90.7	82.7	60.0	4.2
1990	89.5	80.6	57.1	3.7
1991	88.0	77.7	54.0	3.6
1992	87.5	76.8	51.3	3.4
1993	87.0	76.0	51.0	2.5
1994	80.4	73.0	50.1	2.9
1995	80.7	73.7	51.3	3.5
1996	79.2	72.5	50.8	3.7
1997	81.7	74.8	52.7	3.9
1998	81.4	74.3	52.0	3.9
1999	80.0	73.8	51.0	3.4
2000	80.0	73.2	50.0	2.9
2001	79.7	73.3	49.8	3.6

Source: Johnson, O'Malley, & Bachman, 1998, 1999, 2002.

Cocaine

Almost 2 million people in the United States use cocaine (see Figure 1.1). Cocaine use peaked at 5.7 million users in 1985. About 600,000 Americans try cocaine for the first time each year and 1.7 million Americans use cocaine at least once a month. The average age of using cocaine for the first time was 20.3 in 1997 (see Figure 1.2). Cocaine is widely available in most American metropolitan areas but may be leveling off.

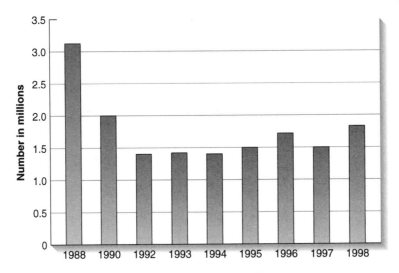

FIGURE 1.1   Monthly Cocaine Use in Millions

Sources: National Drug Control Strategy, 2000; NIDA Web Site Statistics, June 2002.

Data from the DAWN project suggest that cocaine-related deaths or trips to emergency rooms generally were stable from previous years. The percentage of treatment admissions for cocaine abuse declined or remained stable from 1993–2002. The percentage of high school seniors who tried cocaine in 1999 was 9.8% compared to 5.9% in 1994. Current monthly use of cocaine by seniors decreased from a peak of 6.7% in 1985 to 2.6% in 1999. Fewer than 1% of

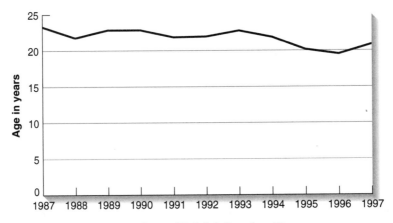

FIGURE 1.2   Average Age of Initial Cocaine Use

Sources: National Drug Control Strategy, 2000; NIDA, Web Site Statistics, December, 2000.

college students report cocaine use in the past month. Most cocaine abusers are older, inner-city African Americans, although some cities report different demographics.

Ecstasy

Ecstasy (MDMA/methamphetamines) is most often used by young adults and adolescents in "raves" (large, all-night dance parties) and by young adults at rock concerts. The 1998 National Household Survey reported a lifetime prevalence rate of 1.5% for people over age 12 (3.4 million) using MDMA at least once. Between ages 18–25, 5% had tried this drug. The rate increased to 8% in 1999. Use during the past year increased from 3.6% in 1998 to 5.6% in 1999 among 12th graders, and from 1.5% in 1998 to 2.5% in 1999 among 12th graders reporting use in the past month. Emergency room mentions of this drug increased from 68 in 1993 to 637 in 1997.

In 1997, 4.4% of high school seniors had used crystal methamphetamine at least once, an increase from 2.7% in 1990. Use in the past year increased from 1.3% in 1990 to 2.3% in 1997. According to the 1999 study, use among high school seniors decreased to 1.9%. According to the 1996 National Household Study, about 5 million people beyond the age of 12 had tried methamphetamines at least once. Use of this drug is more common in the Western United States, where the estimated number of hard core users is 356,000 (Office of National Drug Control Policy, 2000).

Heroin

In 1999, the lifetime use of heroin for 8th and 10th graders was 2.3% and for high school seniors, 2%. Less than 1% reported using heroin in the past 30 days at any grade level. In the National Household Survey of 1998, 130,000 respondents admitted to using heroin in the past 30 days and 2% of them admitted to lifetime use. Hard-core users (not sampled by either of these two data sources) are estimated to be about 980,000 in the United States. The average age of initial heroin use continues to decrease and was 17.6 in 1997 (see Figure 1.3). In 1998 more then 77,000 visits to emergency rooms were attributed to heroin. NIDA reports that heroin use has stabilized and shows low prevalence rates. Heroin-related deaths have increased in selected cities, but use patterns, emergency-room episodes, and purity levels vary by city (Office of National Drug Control Policy, 2000). However, the number of new heroin users seems to be increasing, especially among those under the age of 26.

Hallucinogens

These drugs most often are used in combination with other drugs. A frequently reported combination is "blounts" or "sherman sticks," marijuana dipped in PCP. Lifetime use inscreases with age: 8th graders report a 4.1% lifetime use, 10th

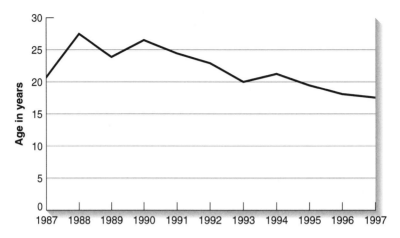

FIGURE 1.3   Average Age of Initial Heroin Use

Sources: National Drug Control Strategy, 2000; NIDA, Web Site Statistics, December, 2000.

graders report 8.5% lifetime use, and 12th graders report a 12.2% lifetime use in the 1999 survey. Annual use of LSD (a drug sampled separately from other hallucinogens) had a 2.4% use among 8th graders and 6% use for 10th graders. High school seniors report a past-month use of LSD at 2.7%, down from 3.1% in 1997. Among the 18–25 population, LSD lifetime use was reported at 13.9%.

Marijuana

Data in Table 1.2 indicate that more than half of U.S. youth have tried marijuana at least once: Roughly 23% of high school seniors and 11% of adults reported using marijuana within the past month. The average age at which adults first try marijuana is now 17.1 years (see Figure 1.4). An estimated 2.1 million people tried marijuana for the first time in 1998 and 73 million Americans have tried it at least once in their lifetime. The rate of emergency room mentions of marijuana also is increasing. Depending on the city cited, up to 50% of juveniles arrested test positive for marijuana. It is the most widely used illicit drug. However, the data in Table 1.2 also suggest that as people mature, their use of marijuana tends to subside.

Nicotine

In 1999, the annual youth survey indicated that 44.1% of 8th graders had tried cigarettes, 57.% of 10th graders, and 64.6% of 12th graders had tried cigarettes. Use among these groups in the past 30 days was 17.5%, 25.7%, and 34.6%. Among those smoking a pack a day, 3.3% were 8th graders, 7.6% were 10th

TABLE 1.2   Prevalence of Marijuana Use at Selected Grade Levels 1990–2001

	GRADE 8		GRADE 10		GRADE 12		ADULTS
	EVER	PAST MONTH	EVER	PAST MONTH	EVER	PAST MONTH	PAST MONTH
1990	—	—	27.9	13.5	42.2	18.5	10.9
1991	10.1	3.2	23.4	8.7	36.7	13.8	10.4
1992	11.2	3.7	21.4	8.1	32.6	11.9	9.7
1993	12.6	5.1	28.8	10.9	35.3	15.5	9.6
1994	16.7	7.8	30.4	15.8	38.2	19.0	10.1
1995	19.9	9.1	34.1	17.2	41.7	21.2	9.8
1996	23.1	11.3	39.8	20.4	44.9	21.9	10.1
1997	22.6	10.2	42.3	20.5	49.6	23.7	11.1
1998	22.2	9.7	39.6	18.7	49.1	22.8	11.0
1999	22.0	9.7	57.6	19.4	47.6	23.1	—
2000	15.6	9.1	32.2	19.7	36.5	21.6	—
2001	15.4	9.2	32.7	19.8	37.0	22.4	—

Sources: National Drug Control Strategy, 2000; NIDA Web Site Statistics, June 2002.

graders, and 13.2% were 12th graders. Cigarettes consistently have been the drug used by the greatest number of high school students daily. In the United States, 1998, an estimated 60 million smoke on a regular basis, representing 28% of the population above the age of 12. The rate of cigarette smoking among women is also increasing.

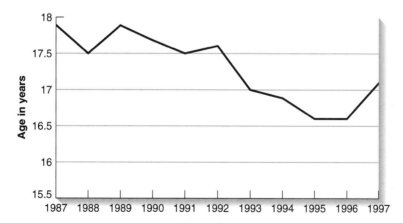

FIGURE 1.4   Average Age of Initial Marijuana Use

Sources: National Drug Control Strategy, 2000; NIDA, Web Site Statistics, December, 2000.

COST OF THE PROBLEM

A Columbia University report (Author, 1994) indicated that the cost to Medicare for the use of alcohol, drugs, and tobacco was $20 billion for hospital stays in 1994. They predicted, at the time, that the cost would rise to $170 billion in the next 7 years and to more than 1 trillion dollars during the next 20 years.

The most current data from NIDA and NIAAA, reported in late December 2000 for the year 1992, looked at health care costs, premature deaths, impaired productivity, motor vehicle crashes, crime, and social welfare costs. They estimated the economic costs to society from alcohol and drug abuse at slightly less than $250 billion dollars. Alcohol-related costs were about $148 billion and drug abuse costs accounted for the remainder. Health care costs for medical consequences of alcohol problems were $18.8 billion and of drug abuse were $9.9 billion. Treatment for alcoholism accounted for $5.6 billion and treatment for drug abuse for $4.4 billion.

Lost productivity cost $67.7 billion for alcoholism and $14.2 billion for drug abuse. Costs attributed to alcohol-related motor vehicle crashes were about $24.7 billion, including vehicle and property destruction. Crime associated with or attributed to alcohol was about 19.7 billion and crime associated with drug abuse was estimated at $59.1 billion. Alcohol was involved in 25%–30% of violent crimes and drug abuse in 25%–30% of income-generating crime. Alcohol-abuse crimes cost the Criminal Justice System $6.2 billion; drug abuse crimes cost $17.4 billion. Victims lost $2.1 billion in stolen cash or property.

The Office of National Drug Abuse Policy studied how much U.S. money went for illegal drugs, money, which, had it not been diverted, could have been used for savings or expenditures to benefit the overall economy. Between 1988 and 1995, U.S. citizens were estimated to have spent $38 billion on cocaine, $9.6 billion on heroin, $7 billion on marijuana, and $2.7 billion on other illegal drugs, including the misuse of legal drugs, totaling $57.3 billion dollars. This estimate does not include the costs of nicotine. This financial loss occurred despite the federal government seizing (in 1999) 1.175 metric tons of marijuana, 132 metric tons of cocaine, 1.09 metric tons of heroin, and 2.64 metric tons of methamphetamines (National Drug Control Strategy, 2000). 1998 saw 1.56 million arrests for drug abuse violations and 679 drug-related murders, and 1997 saw 15,873 drug-induced deaths.

Figures 1.5 and 1.6 depict the economic costs of alcohol and drug abuse from 1985 to 1995. For fiscal year 2001, the requested federal budget for national drug control was $19.2 billion.

The general public—mostly those who do not abuse alcohol or drugs—bears the economic burden of paying these costs though taxation. Government and private insurers directly pay these costs and society indirectly suffers the consequences of the problem. NIDA and NIAAA estimate that, when the 1995 costs are finally available, alcohol costs will have burgeoned to $166.5 billion and drug abuse costs to $109.8 billion.

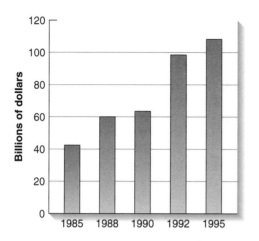

FIGURE 1.5   Economic Costs of Alcohol Abuse

Sources: National Drug Control Strategy, 2000; NIDA, Web Site Statistics, December, 2000.

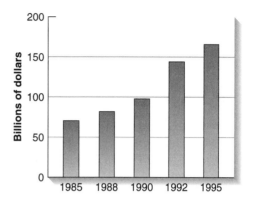

FIGURE 1.6   Economic Costs of Drug Abuse

Sources: National Drug Control Strategy, 2000; NIDA, Web Site Statistics, December, 2000.

COST-EFFECTIVENESS OF TREATMENT

Although the costs of addiction to society are staggering, the cost benefits of treating substance abuse are impressive, according to studies that examine the cost effectiveness of this treatment. The treatment of substance abuse takes a two-tiered approach, publicly funded programs and private programs. The research cited pertains to publicly funded programs, which tend to serve socially impoverished disadvantaged abusers, who have severe manifestations of substance use disorders. The extent to which these findings generalize to patients treated in private programs is a matter for research, but because patients in these programs generally have more resources, patients might do even better.

Although addiction and substance abuse are viewed as chronic and relapsing conditions, outcome data from many sources suggest that even a single episode of treatment can reduce drug and alcohol use, reduce family problems, reduce criminality, reduce health consequences of abuse, and increase workplace productivity. Researchers rarely take a longitudinal approach to this issue, focusing, instead, on average costs for an identified period of time. Addiction is a dynamic process—its costs wax and wane with the disorder itself. A more longitudinal view of addiction and recovery, using data from several years prior to recovery and several years after recovery, can provide researchers an accurate picture of the true costs. The selected reports that follow suggest that treatment for substance abuse is effective.

Annual costs to treat individual substance abusers range from $3,000 to almost $15,000 a year, depending on the nature of the treatment, the severity of the problem, and the area of the United States in which treatment occurs. Annual costs to incarcerate an individual substance abuser range from $30,000 to $50,000. Annual costs to treat an individual with AIDS are about $100,000. The data also demonstrate that clients who stay in treatment longer have better outcomes than those with shorter treatment stays (Hubbard et al, 1989).

The California Department of Alcohol and Drug Programs in 1994 conducted a cost-effectiveness study whose results attained national attention. They studied 97 providers, including outpatient programs, therapeutic communities, residential, and methadone maintenance programs. They concluded, after the two-year study, that every dollar spent on treatment saved the State of California seven dollars. Although treatment cost California $209 million dollars in public money, it saved taxpayers $1.5 billion dollars. Some of the key findings were:

1. Crime declined $1.3 billion after considering the costs of treatment.
2. Criminal activity declined by two thirds after treatment. Alcohol and drug use declined 40% after treatment. Hospitalizations declined one third after treatment.
3. Longer time in treatment was associated with greater reduction in crime. (Lasimes, 1994)

The National Association of State Alcohol and Drug Abuse Directors (1994b) released a state-by-state report on the effectiveness of treatment. Iowa reported a 12% decrease in hospitalizations. Minnesota found that 64% were abstinent after treatment and calculated that this saved taxpayers $22 million in health care costs. Ohio found a 66% decline in hospital admissions following treatment, an 89% decrease in absenteeism, a 92% decrease in tardiness, and a 57% decrease in job-related injuries. Colorado calculated that employment increased following treatment from 36% to 61% and average monthly income increased by $330. Maine found that 79% had not been arrested one year after treatment.

NIDA (1994) again in 1994 released results of a study demonstrating the long-term benefits of methadone treatment, showing that an untreated drug abuser costs society about $21,500 annually, but the cost of treating a drug abuser costs $1,750 during a six-month period. The study also showed a dramatic increase in employment during treatment.

Oregon, in 1996, released the results of a study documenting that every dollar spent on treatment saved the Oregon taxpayer $5.60 in reduced welfare, food stamps, Medicare, crime and its prosecution, and incarceration. (Substance Abuse Report, 1996)

These data are encouraging. Treatment is cost effective in an economic sense, but also in reducing and eliminating human suffering—both in those with the disorder and in those affected by the disorder.

CHAPTER SUMMARY

This chapter presented some basic concepts in the study of epidemiology and applied those concepts to alcohol and drug abuse. It presented statistics on the incidence and prevalence of the use of various drugs, including alcohol, and demonstrated the probable costs to society. It concluded with the cost-effectiveness of treatment for substance use disorders.

SOURCES OF INFORMATION

Abadinsky, H. (2000). *Drugs: An introduction*. Belmont, CA: Wadsworth.

Alcohol, Drug Abuse, and Mental Health Administration. (1991). *Drug abuse treatment: An economical approach to addressing the drug problem in America* (DHHS Publication No. ADM 91-1834). Rockville, MD: Alcohol, Drug Abuse, and Mental Health Administration.

Author. (1994). *The cost of substance abuse to America's health care. Report 2: Medicare Costs*. New York: Columbia University.

California Department of Drug and Alcohol Programs. (1994a). *The California Drug and Alcohol Treatment Assessment*. Sacramento, CA: Author.

National Association of State Alcohol and Drug Abuse Directors. (1994b). *Invest in treatment: It pays*. Washington, DC: Author.

Hubbard, R. L., Harwood, H. J., & Rachal, J. V. (1989). *Drug abuse treatment: A national study of effectiveness*. Chapel Hill, NC: University of North Carolina.

Johnson, L. D., O'Malley, P. M., & Bachman, J. G. (1998). *National survey results on drug use from the Monitoring the Future study, 1975–1997. Secondary School Students*. Rockville, MD: National Institute on Drug Abuse. Publication No. 98-4345.

Johnson, L. D., O'Malley, P. M., & Bachman, J. G. (2001). National survey results on drug use from the Monitoring the Future study, 1977–2001. *Secondary School Students*. Rockville, MD: National Institute on Drug Abuse.

LA Times, Tuesday, September 6, 1994: "A Boost for Treatment in the Drug War."

McLellan, A. T., Arndt, I. O., Metzger, D. S., Woody, G. E., & O'Brien, C. P. (1993). The effects of psychosocial services in substance abuse treatment. *Journal of the American Medical Association, 269*, 1953–1959.

National Institute on Alcohol Abuse and Alcoholism. (1990, January). *Alcohol alert*. U.S. Department of Health and Human Services. (PH278, No. 7, pp. 1–4). Washington, DC: Author.

National Institute of Drug Abuse. *NIDA notes*. U.S. Department of Health and Human Services, National Institutes of Health. *9*, 4. Rockville, MD: Author.

NIDA. (1994). Research demonstrates long-term benefits of methadone treatment. *NIDA Notes, 9*, 1–4.

Office of National Drug Control Policy (2000). *National drug control strategy: 2000 annual report*. Washington, DC: U.S. Government Printing Office.

Substance Abuse Report: "Oregon Studies Show Treatment Saves Taxpayers Money." April 1, 1996. Boston, MA.

. . . . . ──

CHAPTER TWO

ETIOLOGY OF
SUBSTANCE ABUSE

Various theories seek to explain why some begin to use alcohol and drugs and why some advance into addiction. It is important to have a working knowledge of the major theories presented here, and it is also important to realize that no one factor causes substance abuse or addiction. No one path, no reliable set of composite factors inevitably leads to substance abuse. Instead, substance abuse develops from multiple influences and numerous etiological factors (Glantz & Pickens, 1992).

Evaluating the accuracy of any theory as an explanatory construct demands an understanding of how various theories address the salient aspects of addictive behavior: Specifically, (1) What factors explain initial use? (2) What distinguishes initial use (experimentation) from continued use? (3) What explains transition from use to abuse? (4) Why do some people reach abstinence and some remain addicted? (5) Why do some people relapse? Does the theory explain shifts from one substance to another (e.g., why does a person stop using alcohol and switch to cocaine?), and explain shifts in epidemiological patterns over various time spans (why was there an increase in heroin use in America in the 1970s and an increase in cocaine use in the 1980s?). Finally, does the theory explain differential drug use in population subgroups? Various theories seem to explain one or more of these processes, but no one theory explains all of them comprehensively.

Remarkably, research shows that *variables that explain when a person becomes at risk for drug use seem not to predict transition into substance abuse*. That is, variables that suggest vulnerability to substance use essentially are distinct from variables leading to substance abuse (Glantz & Pickens, 1992). Some individuals appear to possess attributes, attitudes, and traits, or are in environments that increase their probability of transition from use to abuse—*risk factors*. Other people appear to possess attributes, attitudes, and traits, or are in environments that protect them from the probability of transitioning from use to abuse—protective favors. These protective variables may negate predispositional factors for developing substance abuse problems.

Etiological variables may be exogenous, or external, and endogenous, or internal. The salient exogenous variables associated with models of addiction include variables that are *ecological*—deviant environments, poverty, social deprivation, and discrimination; *developmental*—failure at transition points in the life cycle; *learning and conditioning*—acquisition of ineffective behaviors; and *psychodynamic*—unconscious processes that influence behavior. The salient endogenous variables are *genetic, internal environments*—biochemistry, metabolism, and physiology, and *neuropsychological*—defective brain functioning.

RISK FACTORS FOR INITIAL SUBSTANCE USE

The factors responsible for initial substance abuse were believed generally to be different from the factors responsible for continuing to abuse substances. A summary of the risk factors that seem to contribute to initial substance use follows.

- Drug availability (Individuals may have every risk factor that predicts substance abuse, but if they never have contact with alcohol or drugs, addiction will never occur.)
- Friends who use drugs
- Peer influences (This is different from friendship networks. Peer pressure constitutes a separate risk factor for initial use.)
- Bad conduct
- Unconventional behavior
- Poor academic achievement
- Parents with substantial problems (Parents who are wrapped up in their own troubles may have little time to nurture and monitor their children.)
- Poor relationship with parents
- Low involvement with traditional institutions with traditional values—nuclear family, religious institutions, school activities

One of these factors or a combination of several puts individuals at risk for initial drug use. Accordingly, if individuals possess none of these factors, the risk for initial drug use is low.

RISK FACTORS FOR SUBSTANCE ABUSE AND DEPENDENCE

Research has established certain features that are causally related to the development of substance abuse or dependence. They are categorized as genetic and biological, psychological and psychopathological, environmental and social, family, and school risk factors. Certain demographic variables also have an effect.

Genetic and Biological Risk Factors

Evidence that some form of alcohol abuse may be a genetically or biologically-based disease is presented later in this chapter. Research evidence is much stronger for implicating these factors in the development of alcoholism than it is for other forms of drug abuse. However, the influence of biological and genetic factors on a variety of behaviors, including substance abuse, cannot be discounted. Little is known of these possible causes, and the biological basis of alcoholism still has neither been proved nor established.

Psychological Risk Factors

Psychological factors that indicate risk for substance abuse include:

- Aggressive behavior
- Alienation
- Depression
- Fear of rejection
- Hyperactivity
- Low self-esteem
- High tolerance for deviance
- Impulsivity
- Need for immediate gratification
- Passive and dependent personality traits
- Poor coping skills
- Problems with authority or with intimacy
- Rebelliousness
- Rejection of socially approved goals and values
- Resistance to authority
- Self-destructive behaviors

Psychopathology

Psychiatric disorders strongly associated with substance abuse include:

- Antisocial Personality Disorder
- Attention-Deficit Disorders (ADD) (in childhood)
- Bipolar Affective Disorder
- Childhood behavior problems
- Conduct Disorder (in adolescence)
- Dysthymic Disorder
- Major Depressive Disorder
- Posttraumatic Stress Disorder

Environmental and Societal Risk Factors

Although internal conflicts and processes predict later substance abuse, certain environmental aspects associated with risk of substance abuse include:

- Amorality
- Criminality
- Delinquency
- Deviant subculture
- Economic advantages for selling drugs
- Growing up in a poor neighborhood
- Low involvement in structured, supervised organizations
- Peers who use drugs
- Poverty
- Social milieu that condones or permits drug use

Familial Risk Factors

Certain family characteristics that are associated with developing substance abuse problems include:

- Family antisocial behaviors
- Family disruption: divorce
- Family history of current or previous psychopathology
- Overindulgent parenting
- Physical, sexual, or psychological abuse or neglect
- Poor limit setting
- Poor parental attachment
- Family substance abuse

School Risk Factors

School-related factors that are associated with substance abuse include:

- Dropping out of school
- Sexual acting out
- Teen pregnancy

Theoretical Models

In a monograph, *Theories of Drug Abuse* (1980), NIDA presented 43 theories that purportedly account for aspects of addictive behavior. Why so many theories? No one theory can account satisfactorily for all aspects of the abuse and addiction continua. The value in knowing these theories is that one or more may provide salient understanding and explanation of individuals' substance abuse that are missed by other theories. Those that follow have become popular among substance abuse professionals of various disciplines.

Psychological Models

Psychological models of substance abuse emphasize something within people that largely accounts for the development of substance abuse problem. Psychological models can be categorized into three main theoretical approaches, personality models, which include psychoanalytic models and power motivations, social learning theories or behavioral approaches, and expectancy theories, which emphasize attitudes, beliefs, and attributions (Blane & Leonard, 1987).

Personality and Psychoanalytic Models.

The Addictive Personality.   According to this theory, addiction is not rooted in the chemical effect of the drug, but rather in the psychological structure of the patient. Analyst Sandor Rado (1957) argued that it is not the drug that creates an addict but *the impulse to use it*. Thus an addictive personality exists long before drugs and alcohol enter the picture. Drugs, except for hallucinogens, have only two effects—the reduction of pain (analgesics, sedatives, hypnotics), or the production of euphoria (alcohol, stimulants, opiates). Premorbid addiction begins with a high degree of tension, intolerance for pain, and depression. Drugs temporarily increase self-esteem and produce a return to the infantile narcissistic state in which all needs are satisfied.

An objective review of the evidence fails to confirm this theory. First, no study has verified a common set of personality traits inextricably related to the onset of abuse. When one study reveals such a pattern, subsequent studies fail to confirm these findings, and often present a different set of traits. Second, although drug addicts (Craig, 1979a,b) and alcoholics (Barnes, 1979), may evidence a common set of traits, these traits probably resulted from substance abuse and did not precede it. A few people may exhibit an addictive personality, in that they show excessive and dependent behaviors to a variety of substances or activities, these are probably the exception and not the rule.

Classical Psychoanalytic Models.   Freud viewed addiction as a substitute for masturbation and considered the impulse to drink—"dipsomania"—a substitute for a sexual impulse. Addictive problems—"primal addiction"—are a substitute for sexual satisfaction. Addicts and alcoholics, he proposed, are fixated at the erotogenic oral stage of psychosexual development and demonstrate developmental arrest. Thus addiction is rooted in oral dependence, which leaves the addict passive, with little interest in achieving anything other than immediate pleasure or relief. Addicts are unable to tolerate pain, frustration, anxiety, or depression, and use denial to escape reality. Ingesting alcohol or drugs is akin to infantile sucking. Alcohol and drugs become substitute love objects (Yorke, 1970). Rado (1957) developed these ideas, referring to addiction as "pharmacogenic orgasm," which competes with the regular ways for attaining sexual gratification. Other analysts agreed with Rado that addiction is an impulse neurosis used to satisfy sexual longings. Unconsciously repressed, these longings are inevitably incestuous. These theorists invariably relied on clinical rather than on research evidence to support their views.

Some analysts emphasize the distorted sense of self—low self-esteem—that frequently accompanies substance abuse. According to this view, narcissistically disturbed patients yearn for praise and adoration from an idealized support object (e.g., mother) because they are unable to provide self-approval. Substance abuse seems to cure the central defect in sense of self. It becomes the substitute love object that failed them in childhood. Ingesting a drug soothes both symbolically and physically and provides the lacking self-esteem. Drugs make addicts feel accepted and worthwhile. The personality disorders so frequent in this population (borderline, antisocial, and narcissistic) all suggest various degrees of grandiosity, identity diffusion, problems with control of affect, and distorted object relations. The focus of treatment therefore needs to shift from substance to personality (Blaine & Julius, 1977).

Self-Medication Hypothesis.   The notion of an "addictive personality" has been reformulated and renamed the "self-medication" hypothesis. Also called the pharmacodynamic theory of addiction, the theory argues that certain personality types abuse certain drugs to treat underlying psychiatric conditions, and painful affects and emotions. Their choice of drugs is not random, not related to drug fads or epidemics, and not related to peer influences, but results from an interaction of the pharmacological actions of the drug and underlying personality issues. Narcotic addicts prefer opiates because these drugs control their underlying affects of anger, rage, and aggression. Cocaine addicts choose a stimulant drug to relieve underlying depression (Khantzian, 1985).

While some patients choose drugs for their self-medication properties, the theory has not been substantiated for the majority of addicts. For example, whenever studies compare addicts on certain variables, sophisticated statistics clearly show that subgroups are formed not on the basis of drug of choice, but on the basis of personality type (Craig, Bivens, & Olson, 1997; Craig & Olson, 1990; Craig, Verinis, & Wexler, 1985; Moss & Warner, 1992).

Power Motivation.   People drink to increase power, according to this theory. Power is defined as a desire to make an impact through strong action, through reputation, or through arousing and focusing on strong emotions in others. Researchers report that alcohol increases thoughts of sex and aggression and decreases thoughts of nonphysical aggression. Heavy drinking is a quest for magical potency and an expression of impulsive power concerns that occur when there are strong demands for male assertiveness, low support for the male role, and a lack of socialized power outlets. The power motivation theory would be applicable only to male alcoholics. It can be extended to other forms of addiction: for example, on psychological tests, addicts often score in the clinically deviant ranges on tests that assess a desire to be free from restraints, rules, and conventions. Their strong needs for aggression and autonomy are consistent with power motivation.

Personality factors probably interact with other determinants to influence substance abuse decisions. Most of these theories essentially are untestable and confound the effects of drugs with personality manifestations. Any personality traits observed in the current clinical context may be the result of substance abuse and not the cause of it. The only way truly to test these theories is to assess a large number of people before they develop a substance abuse problem, then to follow these cohorts over time and determine which ones develop the problem and which ones do not, and then to compare these two groups on their premorbid personality functioning. A reliable set of personality traits or factors associated with the group who become addicted offers support for the theory that these personality factors are related causally to the etiology of the problem.

Most personality theorists in this area emphasize the concept of depression as central to understanding addiction. They argue that depression is related to infantile feelings of deprivation, a reaction to excessively punitive parental standards, and feelings of worthlessness. To defend against the effects of anger, resentment, and aggressive impulses, individuals use drugs to withdraw from these painful states into self-induced chemical bliss (Blatt, McDonald, Sugarman, & Wilber, 1984). During the infant's psychological development, a narcissistic injury occurs in the infant's attempt to incorporate a frustrating love object (e.g., mother) and the infant experiences hostility. This leaves the infant vulnerable to the pleasurable effects of drugs, which alleviate its depression and guilt. Drugs stave off depression that eventuates into a craving for the drug. The origin of this narcissistic injury, personality theorists allege, stems from maternal neglect or inadequate parental support, because of parental ambivalence about having the child. Substance abuse binds the tension aroused from these impulses and serves a defensive function by controlling sadistic impulses. An archaic ego structure, early damage to self-esteem, maternal neglect or overindulgence of dependency needs, and arrested psychological development are the central psychoanalytic and psychodynamic processes that explain addictive behavior.

Clinical evidence supports the notion that depression is central to many addictive behaviors. Psychodynamic theorists believe that depression has two sources. Anaclitic depression stems from concerns about the loss of love, feeling uncared for and rejected in the first year of life. Addictive depression stems from feelings of guilt, shame, and self-criticism. These two kinds of dynamically related depression occur at different levels of psychological development, involve different psychodynamic issues, and have different phenomenological experiences. Research evidence suggests that addictive depression is centered around feelings of shame, guilt, and worthlessness for past behaviors, not from feelings of neglect, deprivation, and lack of parental affect (Blatt, McDonald, Sugarman, & Wilber, 1984).

Depressive affective states frequently are seen among substance abusers, but the majority of research suggests that this depression is the result of chronic abuse of substances and not the other way around (Rounsaville, Kosten,

Weissman, & Kleber, 1985). This type of depression is a substance-induced mood disorder.

Social Learning and Behavioral Theories

Learning and conditioning unquestionably play a role in the development of substance abuse. The issue is the degree of importance of these variables in the final pathway to addiction. The theories reviewed in this section place the major emphasis on learning and environmental conditioning as causative.

Conditioning. Wikler (1973) argues that drug use initially is socially reinforced and that this reinforcement eventually is replaced by pharmacological reinforcement through suppression of withdrawal. The desire for positive reinforcement may diminish as dependence and tolerance increase and alcohol and drugs then are used to avoid punishment (withdrawal). Drug use becomes conditioned with contiguous environmental interoceptive (internal) or exteroceptive (environmental) stimuli, increasing the probability of the reoccurrence of desire for drugs in the presence of the environmental clues, long after the individual has abstained. Using more drugs reinforces the instrumental drug seeking behavior and wards off repetition of the withdrawal syndrome. The conditioned response is almost qualitatively similar to the actual drug effects.

■ *Reinforcement Theory.* Drugs are powerful reinforcers of behavior (Crowley, 1972). Alcohol and drugs produce pleasurable sensations. According to the laws of reinforcement, whenever a stimulus (e.g., using alcohol or drugs) is followed by a reward (e.g., feeling good), that connection is reinforced, increasing the probability of repeating that behavior (using alcohol or drugs) the next time that stimulus is presented.

■ *Primary reinforcers*—food, water, sex—strengthen behavior independently. *Secondary reinforcers* are learned. Money, for example, has no intrinsic value. It is mere paper or metal, on which are printed words and pictures. Money has no inherent reinforcing properties. People have assigned value to possessing money and it has become a secondary reinforcer. Alcohol and drugs are primary reinforcers.

■ A *negative reinforcer* is aversive. If a stimulus is followed by a response that is punishing, the probability of that response upon presentation of that stimulus should decrease. This is a principle behind the use of Antabuse (disulfiram). Alcoholics who take Antabuse experience no ill effects. If, however, they drink alcohol when Antabuse is in their system, they become violently ill. Thus, alcohol use should decrease in frequency because of the connection between taking alcohol and being negatively reinforced.

A given behavior should not be presupposed to be rewarding or punishing. Consequences that to some appear aversive, to others may be rewarding. Withdrawal might be thought to be an aversive consequence of drug use that would stop the behavior. But the addict learned that taking more alcohol and or drugs stops the discomfort and the inclination to take more drugs is strengthened.

Expectancy Theories

Studies based on *balanced placebo designs* have demonstrated that what people believe can influence their feelings and behaviors as if what they believe were true. In this methodology, the sample is divided into four groups. Two groups are told that they will receive alcohol, but only one receives it. Two groups are told they will not receive alcohol, but one does receive it. After consuming a beverage, the subjects perform a variety of tasks. They may watch a pornographic movie and then rate their degree of sexual arousal or watch a violent movie and then rate their level of felt aggression. Sometimes they are given physical tasks, such as moving a stylus around a board or driving a simulation machine. If alcohol effects are pre-potent, then groups that received alcohol, whether or not they believe they have used alcohol, will have significantly different scores from groups that did not receive alcohol. If expectancy effects are pre-potent, then scores of groups that believed they did or did not receive alcohol will be significantly different from scores of the groups that did or did not receive alcohol.

Results show, in general, that alcohol effects are pre-potent in physical and physiological assessments. However, when studies assess psychological processes, such as social anxiety, aggression, delay of gratification, assertiveness, sexual arousal, and mood, or cognitive processes, such as attention and recognition memory, expectancy effects predominate (Hull & Bond, 1986). These effects occur at low to moderate doses: eventually, dose overcomes all beliefs and exerts the main behavioral effects.

Biological and Genetic Models

The Disease Concept of Alcoholism. In the1950s, the American Medical Association declared alcoholism to be a disease, without offering scientific arguments or evidence to explain the designation. Other social behaviors also have been considered diseases. For example, in the antebellum South, a runaway slave was considered afflicted with a disease for which the treatment, on return, was lashing. Whether alcoholism is or is not a disease hinges on the definition of alcoholism. Various authoritative examples that attempt to define alcoholism follow:

- *American Medical Association.* Alcoholism results in significant impairment that is directly associated with persistent and excessive use of alcohol. The impairment may involve physiological, psychological, or social dysfunction.
- *American Psychiatric Association.* Alcoholism is a disease typified by impaired control over drinking, preoccupation with alcohol, continued use of alcohol in the face of adverse consequences, and distorted thinking.

■ *American Society of Addiction Medicine.* Alcoholism is a primary, chronic disease with genetic, psychological, and environmental factors that influence its development and manifestations. The disease often is progressive and fatal. It is characterized by continuous or periodic impaired control over drinking, preoccupation with the drug alcohol, use of alcohol despite adverse consequences, and distortions in thinking, most notably denial.

E. M. Jellinek is considered the father of the disease concept of alcoholism and often is cited as an authoritative source. Jellinek (1946) wrote about five "species" or types of patterned drinking (i.e., alcoholism). The *alpha alcoholic* does not lose control and has no physical dependence, no withdrawal, and no disease progression. In fact, this species is not a disease at all. The alpha uses alcohol for psychological relief. The interpersonal domain may be the area most affected in this type of alcoholism.

The *beta alcoholic* is characterized by medical problems associated with chronic drinking, but is neither psychologically nor physically dependent and does not experience withdrawal. This drinking pattern may be sanctioned socially and culturally. Prototypical examples of this species are the French, who often consume wine as part of their meals. Over time, this custom might result in medical complications associated with frequent drinking, but users would not be considered alcoholics.

The *gamma alcoholic* is the species most prevalent in the United States. Characterized by physical dependence with craving and withdrawal and loss of control, the gamma has the greatest degree of impairment to interpersonal relations and health, vocational deficits, and social deterioration. The gamma alcoholic is characterized by four distinct stages, referred to as the "progression of the disease." In the *pre-alcoholic* stage, drinkers experience some relief from drinking and experience increased tolerance to alcohol, allowing them to drink more. The onset of *blackouts* heralds the *prodromal* stage. Drinking may assume a surreptitious quality; guilt feelings, denial, and increasing dependence on alcohol ensue. *Loss of control* signals the *crucial phase*. Efforts to control drinking fail persistently as the ability to stop drinking decreases, family, work, and legal problems may develop, morning shakes may appear, physical status begins to decline, promises and resolutions to stop fail or cease to exist, and drinking is associated with myriad excuses. The *chronic phase* is associated with binges and benders, obsessive drinking, moral deterioration, drinking with "social inferiors," impaired thinking, and total defeat. The individual has "hit bottom" (Jellinek, 1946).

Delta alcoholics can abstain from alcohol for a specific period of time or for a specific occasion, just to demonstrate that they are not alcoholics. A delta may go to a wedding and not drink at all, but once the point is "proved," alcoholic behaviors resume.

Epsilon alcoholics are able to abstain for weeks and even months at a time, but drink periodically and to excess and according to an unpredictable pattern. Binge drinking is often a part of the clinical picture.

Jellinek's data sources for these types of drinking patterns were derived from male, mostly gamma-type alcoholics attending AA. Applied generally, his work suggests that (a) alcoholism is variable and associated with several different types of patterns, and (b) not all forms of problematic drinking are diseases.

Evidence for the Disease Concept.   What is the evidence for the theory that alcoholism is a disease? Notice that I have used the word "theory," many in this field take alcoholism as disease as an article of faith. I believe that the *essential hallmark of alcoholism is loss of control.* Until the biological mechanism has been discovered that results in loss of control, this remains a theory and not a fact. The disease theory of alcoholism has converging lines of evidence.

1. Animal studies demonstrate that a strain of rats can become physically alcohol-dependent: Their offspring over time and successive generations are born with an apparent predisposition to physical dependence on alcohol upon exposure. Researchers can also breed a strain of rats that are averse to alcohol. This suggests that physical dependence on alcohol can be genetically transmitted and inherited.

2. In studies of the familial incidence of alcoholism, alcoholics were more likely to have a near relative who was alcoholic than any population of nonalcoholics. From 2% to 50% had fathers who were alcoholics and 5% had mothers who were alcoholic. The rates of sibling alcoholics consistently were higher than all types of other relationships and all types of nonalcoholics. Studies show a persistent low frequency of parental alcoholism in families of nonalcoholics. Alcoholism is more prevalent among near than distant relatives. However, 47% to 82% of alcoholics do not come from families in which one or both parents were alcoholic. These studies demonstrate that alcoholism tends to run in families (Cotton, 1979; Goodwin, 1984).

3. In general, monozygotic (identical) twins show higher concordance rates for alcoholism than dizygotic (fraternal) twins. However, twin studies have not been consistent in determining the relative contribution of genetics and environmental influences. Some studies report a sizable effect; other studies do not.

4. Although alcoholism runs in families, not everything that runs in families is biologically based—speaking Chinese tends to run in families but obviously is socially learned! Adoption studies could separate the effects of environment versus heredity. Studies by Goodwin (1979; 1983) are cited often as the definitive evidence on this subject. Goodwin studied alcoholic families in Scandinavia. (Twin and adoption studies often are conducted in Scandinavia, because those countries allow researchers access to patient medical records and keep good data on many diseases.) Goodwin studied 55 sons whose fathers (85%) or mothers (15%) had been hospitalized for alcoholism, and 78 sons of nonalcoholics who had been adopted by nonalcoholic families within the first six weeks of life. The rate of alcoholism in this sample was almost four times higher (18%) among sons of alcoholics compared to controls (5%), whether or not they were raised by their biological or adopted parents. A separate study found no differences between the rates of alcoholism in daughters of alcoholics, whether or not they were adopted. Goodwin argued that these results suggest at least one type of family alcoholism has a genetic base. It is characterized by early age of onset, is severe enough to require treatment, is always confined to men, often is associated with antisocial personality disorder, and is not associated with any other form of psychopathology. Note however, that biology is not destiny. Among males in this sample who were at high risk for developing alcoholism, 82% did not!

The Task Force on Substance Abuse that revised the diagnoses in DSM-IV wanted very much to include a diagnosis of "familial alcoholism," which, presumably, was genetically based. After reviewing the scientific evidence, they concluded that other influences often can account for the data, or, at least, could not be ruled out. Hence, they concluded that insufficient evidence existed at the time to make such a formal diagnosis, although it might eventually be proved.

5. *High risk* studies compare patients with alcohol-positive family histories to others with alcohol-negative family histories on a variety of biological, behavioral, and psychological dimensions. The studies look for *biological markers* or for *psychological markers* known or suspected to be biologically controlled. Differential findings between groups would suggest a possible genetic base for alcoholism.

For the most part, *biological markers* have been elusive. The rate of metabolism is genetically controlled but there is no correlation between metabolism rate and the development of alcoholism. Ethnic differences in biochemical sensitivity and reaction to alcohol exist among many Asians, who experience a facial flush in response to alcohol that might be a protective barrier to becoming alcoholic, but it is unrelated to developing alcoholism. One report revealed that alcoholics have abnormally low levels of monoamine oxidase (MAO), a brain chemical that is found in small blood cells called platelets (Tabakoff, Hoffman, Lee, Saito, et al, 1988). Work on the significance of these findings continues.

A variety of *neuropsychological* and *cognitive markers* have been explored to no avail. Many confounding and uncontrolled factors exist: when these variables are properly controlled, previous differences between groups disappear. For example, children of alcoholics are six times as likely to suffer physical abuse from an alcoholic father than are offspring of nonalcoholics. Any group differences in neuropsychological or cognitive functioning could be attributed to physical abuse and thus be independent of heredity (Pihl, Peterson, & Finn, 1990).

One *psychological marker* holds promise. Sons of alcoholics differ in their sensitivity to the subjective effects of alcohol. They feel less intoxicated than the family history negative group, even though their blood alcohol levels are identical. This means that sons of alcoholics may not feel they are getting drunk, which allows them to drink more (Shuckit, 1987).

Henri Begleiter and staff (Begleiter, Porjesz, Bihari, & Kissen, 1984) reported that preadolescent sons of alcoholics exhibit a decrease of the P 300 brain wave—an EEG reading—following a visually evoked potential. They always show slow alpha wave in response to small doses of alcohol. This *electrophysiological marker* may be the site researchers have been seeking. However, because it can take decades for alcoholism to develop, it will take decades to determine if this is the biological marker that can predict alcoholism. Recent evidence suggests that other factors also can contribute to this brain wave pattern and that it may not be a reliable predictor for alcoholism in high-risk patients (Polich, Pollack, & Bloom, 1994).

In 1990, a national newspaper reported about an article in the *Journal of the American Medical Association* announcing that the "alcoholism gene" had been discovered. Researchers had concluded that the dopamine D2 receptor gene was associated with alcoholism in 77% of the cases they studied (Tabakoff, Hoffman, Lise, Saitu, Willard, et al., 1988). The *JAMA* editorial stated that the findings were "promising but needed replication." The findings were promising because the research might have opened the way to subclassifying alcoholism on the basis of genes, using a simple blood test. Subsequent research that failed to confirm these original findings was not highly publicized (Gelernter, 1991). The general public has accepted the notion that the alcoholism is a disease and any findings that seem to support this possibility receive much attention. However, the idea that alcoholism is a disease remains one theory among many, for the source of this disease remains elusive. The disease concept of alcoholism remains a theory.

Biology and Opiate Dependence.   Although biochemical and physiological approaches explaining opiate dependence continue to form the bases of many research efforts (Berkowitz, 1976), among many physicians, the theory that *heroin addiction is a metabolic disease* (Dole & Nyswander, 1967) has been the most popular explanation of heroin dependence. This was an *ex post facto* explanation of the success of methadone maintenance—a heroin substitute treatment— among many addicts. Clinicians argued that heroin use over time created an altered response to narcotics at the cell level resulting in a "metabolic deficiency" that was satisfied and "balanced" with the introduction of the narcotic drug, methadone. While not arguing that a metabolic deficiency existed prior to the development of addiction, they argued that heroin abuse created such a deficiency and that methadone maintenance was equivalent to giving insulin to diabetics.

Laboratory studies of addiction have been more successful in determining abuse potential of psychoactive drugs (Johanson, Woolverton, & Schuzter, 1987) than in supporting a preexisting physiological base for opiate addiction. In laboratory research, caged monkeys learn to press a lever to receive a preselected dose of a particular drug. If the drug is addictive, then the animal will continue to press the lever to get the drug. Such research has been used to argue that addiction is biological, for these animals have no personality problems and no psychopathology, nor did they come from an impoverished environment. In fact, all this research demonstrates is that if you place an animal in a cage, restrict its movement, reduce its normal level of activity, and then provide it with an addicting drug, the animal will take it. Other research shows that rats addicted to heroin in the laboratory and then returned to their normal habitat with heroin available, return to their normal habits and do not use heroin.

Sociological Models

Role Theory.   Sociological models of addiction stress the role of the environment in the development of an addictive disorder. Winick (1974) argued that the incidence of substance abuse will be high in groups with (1) access alcohol and illicit substances, (2) disengagement from the negative proscriptions against their use and abuse, and (3) role strain or role deprivation. He defines a role as a set of expectations and behaviors associated with a specific position in a social system.

The theory explains prevalence rates in several groups:

Soldiers in Vietnam were under considerable role strain, and many units actively condoned use of opiates among the troops. Officers, however, had no role strain (they were doing what they had been trained to do), and using drugs would have interfered with their careers. Fellow officers also exerted considerable negative attitudes toward the use of drugs.

Physicians with considerable role strain (surgeons and psychiatrists) have higher rates of alcoholism and drug abuse than physicians with routine practices and little stress (dermatologist and radiologists). Drug use tends to increase among physicians with ambivalence about being doctors during the last year of residency and prior to taking board exams.

The theory explains high drug use among musicians, who, as a group, have more tolerant attitudes about using drugs, play in venues where drugs frequently are available, and experience role strain with shifting music preference patterns (e.g. transitions from Dixieland to swing, jazz to rock, rhythm and blues to the British Sound, folk rock to hard rock, rap to Latino).

Drug use is frequent in college, according to this theory, because of role competitiveness, disillusionment over conventional societal roles, positive attitudes towards experimentation, and drug availability.

Thus, the theory is able to apply to a broad range of situations, is parsimonious—requiring only a few variables to explain multiple cases—and has direct application to intervention and health approaches.

Association Theory.   There is an old saying: Tell me who you're with and I'll tell you who you are! Association theory simply concludes that people use and abuse illicit substances based on their associates. It argues that such factors as peer pressure would be primary in the development of addiction.

Status Theory.   According to this theory, a certain degree of status is conferred in using or abusing chemical substances. Drugs and heavy consumption of alcohol provide users with a sense of identity, with a purpose in life, and with a certain status within the drug subculture. This theory may be more applicable to abusers from inner cities, where selling drugs can temporarily elevate economic status, and provide sellers and users with a different status level among their drug-using peers.

Maturation Theory. Winick has also developed a microtheory that attempts to explain why some people stop using drugs (Winick, 1962, 1964). Noting that studies demonstrate that addicts start using drugs in their teens and early 20s, Winick surveyed data from federal sources and looked at ages at which individual addicts no longer appeared in their data base. He observed a noticeable drop-off in prevalence of addiction beginning around the age of 40 and steeply declining thereafter. Winick argued that addicts mature out of their addiction, because the stresses and strains that originally lead a person to start using drugs have become stabilized or no longer exist. Hence an addict can now face life without using drugs. Of course, the de-addiction also may be caused by factors such as the effects of treatment, the effects of incarceration, difficulties of maintaining a substance-abusing lifestyle, family and community pressure, and so forth, as much as "maturation." Under maturation theory, treatment is likely to be maximally efficacious at the point in the life cycle when the individual is likely to "mature out" anyway: perhaps more concentrated efforts need to be exerted at that point. This theory does not apply to alcoholics, because there is no evidence that alcoholics routinely stop using alcohol in their 40s, 50s, and beyond.

Family Theory Models

Addicts may come from a variety of environments, including impoverished ones, and they may have certain personality traits or various kinds of compromised biology, but family theorists argue that the real pathology lies within the family. Most assert that substance abusers come from unstable families that provide a poor role model. The patient becomes a scapegoat for problems in the parental relationship. The patient's role is to divert attention from this marital conflict so parents can relate over the abuser's problem behavior. This theory will be developed more in Chapter 7.

Many family theories argue that the development of a symptom must be taken in the context in which it occurs. Family members have an investment in maintaining the symptom, which develops because families are unable to adjust to transitional periods and crisis points in the family life cycle. In the typical family structure of an abuser, one parent is intensely involved with the patient and the other is punitive and distant or absent. The abuser stays involved to provide a channel for parental communication, to prevent further conflict, or to receive child-like parental attention. Family ties prevent abusers from developing appropriate outside relationships. The euphoria of drugs is secondary to the function that drug use serves within the family, according to this theory.

Three case histories follow to demonstrate how these theories can be applied to individuals. Counselors might consider several theories to determine which fits a case best.

Case History 1.   The patient is a 39-year-old, married, white male who was self-referred for help with "an alcohol problem." His presenting complaints were "emotional stress and alcoholism." He reported a drinking history since age 16 and problematic drinking for about the last two years. He drinks only on weekends—a half pint of vodka. He said that alcohol "acts like medicine" and calms him down. He reported that he was unable to go to a party without having more than three drinks, and he said the next day he needs to drink upon awakening. He denied tolerance to alcohol and alleged that he can no longer drink as much as he once could. He denied history of blackouts, DTs, memory problems, hepatitis, or diminished sexual drive or functioning. He reported mild "shakes" that dissipate when drinking. When asked if he was physically dependent on alcohol he said, "Probably." He reported early morning awakenings and tossing and turning in his sleep. He denied any depression, said his appetite was good and denied use of other drugs.

He was treated once before in a 28-day inpatient alcohol rehabilitation program about two years ago. He attended AA for three months but discontinued it because he said he didn't need it. His therapist, whom he had seen for four months, had sent him there. Recently a physician had prescribed a tranquilizer, but the patient did not fill the prescription because he feared becoming dependent on drugs.

He is an officer in an engineering company. He does not believe his peers or his boss know about his drinking. He said his past performance evaluations were high, but they see him sweating at work and he has had some absenteeism, particularly at the early part of the week, which they are beginning to notice. He denied using vodka to avoid detection at work, and seemed genuinely naïve about this.

He has been married for four years. His wife thinks he drinks too much so he has been hiding his drinking because he doesn't want to get into arguments with her about this. He alleges no marital problems. He does not have a legal history and denied DUI arrests, charges, or even driving when he is drunk.

Family history includes a mother who did not drink and a father who "drank too much" but was never treated for a drinking problem. Patient's sister does not drink.

When pressed about his "emotional stress," which he said precipitates his drinking, he was unable to elaborate or specify. He complained about the long drive home from work each night, some job pressures, which were "not too great," and said he drinks more in happy times (e.g., birthdays, holidays, etc.). During the interview the patient sweated frequently, using tissue to wipe his face. No other symptoms were noticeable. He last drank a half pint of vodka two days ago.

Case History 2. The patient is a 23-year-old, single, unemployed African American male who abuses PCP. He's had three bad trips on this drug, producing psychotic reactions requiring hospitalizations of one week each. He claims that when he uses heroin with PCP he does not get bad reactions and lists PCP as his main drug.

The patient's father is Black and currently in jail for making and distributing PCP. He had a successful business until "the Whites drove him out of business" and he turned to making PCP. The father made quite a fortune doing this and raised his three children in a wealthy white neighborhood until he was caught and jailed. The patient's mother is White and all of the children are light-skinned. The patient's sister passes for White, married a White man, and identifies primarily with the White culture. The patient's brother tries to date White women, but has been unsuccessful. He is able to get dates with Black women, but has trouble relating to them and prefers White women. The parents separated over the father's imprisonment.

The patient states that he hates his mother and blames her for all his troubles. They have had many family quarrels, usually over issues of racial identity. He strongly identifies with his father and, at age nine, was already making PCP with his father. He reports a history of getting high from the fumes while making PCP and beginning to use it regularly during adolescence (age 16). He was 18 when his father was sent to prison and the family fortune disintegrated. By then he had dropped out of school.

He is militantly antiWhite to the point of nonviolent hatred. He reports that his mother tried to get him to enter the White culture, but he refuses to have anything to do with her side of the family. When the father went to jail, the patient moved in with a girl who is Black, but who could pass for White, although she identifies with the Black culture. She does not use drugs and hassles him about his own use of drugs. They have no plans for marriage. Patient continues to take PCP but now has switched to daily heroin use. He is awaiting his father's release from jail in a year or two, at which time they plan to open a restaurant. If that fails, they plan to return to making PCP.

Case History 3. The patient is a 25-year-old, single, unemployed White male who was referred for treatment by his mother. Patient drinks alcohol usually on weekends, usually getting drunk. During these times he often gets belligerent, occasionally gets into barroom fights, and has several disorderly conduct charges. He lives with his parents. His father is described as passive, dependent, and thoroughly dominated by his wife, whom the patient described as "a bitch," making "excessive demands" on all of his four brothers, his father, and himself. She is adamant about the patient getting a job but makes no threats to throw him out. His father wants the patient to cut down on his drinking, while mother insists on complete abstinence. His father has been on Valium® for four years. One day, in a rage, the patient flushed all his father's pills down the toilet. When asked why he did that, he replied "maybe then my father will stand up to my mother."

CHAPTER SUMMARY

This chapter presented some of the more popular theories that explain drug-using behavior and evidence to support them. Psychological, sociological, familial, and biological/genetic models have been invoked to help us understand addiction. No single theory seems sufficient to explain all patterns of addictive behavior. Risk factors for developing initial drug use and for transitioning to substance abuse and dependence were highlighted.

SOURCES OF INFORMATION

National Institute of Alcohol Abuse and Alcoholism. (1985). *Alcoholism: An inherited disease.* Rockville, MD: National Institute of Alcohol Abuse and Alcoholism.

Barnes, G. (1979). The alcoholic personality: A reanalysis of the literature. *Journal of Studies on Alcohol, 40,* 571–634.

Begleiter, H., Porjesz, B., Bihari, B., & Kissen, B. (1984). Event-related brain potentials in boys at risk for alcoholism. *Science, 227,* 1493–1496.

Berkowitz, A. M. (1976). Biochemical and physiological approaches to opiate dependence. *International Journal of the Addictions, 11,* 989–1008.

Blain, J., & Julius, D. (Eds.). (1977). *Psychodynamics of drug dependence.* NIDA Research Monograph #12. DHEW Publication No. (ADM) 77-470. Rockville, MD: National Institute on Drug Abuse.

Blane, H. T., & Leonard, K. E. (Eds.). (1987). *Psychological theories of drinking and alcoholism.* NY: Guilford Press.

Blatt, S. J., McDonald, C., Sugarman, A., & Wilber, C. (1984). Psychodynamic theories of opiate addiction: New directions for research. *Clinical Psychology Review, 4,* 159–189.

Cotton, N. S. (1979). The familial incidence of alcoholism: A review. *Quarterly Journal of Studies on Alcohol, 40,* 89–117.

Craig, R. J. (1979). Personality characteristics of heroin addicts: A review of the empirical literature with critique—Part I. *International Journal of the Addictions, 14,* 513–532.

Craig, R. J. (1979). Personality characteristics of heroin addicts: A review of the empirical literature with critique—Part II. *International Journal of the Addictions, 14,* 607–626.

Craig, R. J., Bivens, A., & Olson, R. (1997). MCMI-III derived typological analysis of cocaine and heroin addicts. *Journal of Personality Assessment, 69,* 583–595.

Craig, R. J., & Olson, R. E. (1990). MCMI comparisons of cocaine abusers and heroin addicts. *Journal of Clinical Psychology, 46,* 230–237.

Craig, R. J., Verinis, J. S., & Wexler, S. (1985). Personality characteristics of drug addicts and alcoholics on the Millon Clinical Multiaxial Inventory. *Journal of Personality Assessment, 49,* 156–160.

Crowley, T. J. (1972). The reinforcers for drug abuse: Why people take drugs. *Comprehensive Psychiatry, 13,* 1–7.

Dole, V. P., & Nyswander, M. E. (1967). Heroin addiction—a metabolic disease. *Archives of Internal Medicine, 120,* 19–24.

Editorial. (1990). *Journal of the American Medical Association.* April 18, V. 263, No. 15.

Gelernter, J. (1991, October 15). No association between an allele at the D2 Dopamine receptor gene (DRD2) and alcoholism. *Substance Abuse Report, 3.*

Glantz, M., & Pickens, R. (Eds.). (1992). *Vulnerability to drug abuse.* Washington, DC: American Psychological Association.

Goodwin, D. W. (1979). Alcoholism and heredity: A review and hypothesis. *Archives of General Psychiatry, 36,* 57–61.

Goodwin, D. W. (1983). The genetics of alcoholism. *Hospital and Community Psychiatry, 34,* 1031–1034.

Goodwin, D. W. (1984). Studies of familial alcoholism: A review. *Journal of Clinical Psychiatry, 45,* 14–17.

Hull, J. G., & Bond, C. F. (1986). Social and behavioral consequences of alcohol consumption and expectancy: A meta-analysis. *Psychological Bulletin, 99,* 347–360.

Jellinek, E. M. (1946). Phases in the drinking history of alcoholics: Analysis of a survey by the official organ of Alcoholics Anonymous. *Quarterly Journal on the Study of Alcohol, 7,* 1–88.

Johanson, C. E., Woolverton, W. L., & Schuster, C. R. (1987). Evaluating laboratory models of dependence. In H. Y. Meltzer (Ed.), *Psychopharmacology: The third generation of progress* (pp. 1617–1625). New York: Raven Press.

Khantzian, E. J. (1985). The self-medication hypothesis of addictive disorders: Focus on heroin and cocaine dependence. *American Journal of Psychiatry, 142,* 1259–1264.

Lettieri, D. J., Sayers, M., & Pearson, H. W. (1980). *Theories on drug abuse: Selected contemporary perspectives.* Rockville, MD: National Institute on Drug Abuse.

Moss, P. D., & Warner, P. D. (1992). An MMPI typology of cocaine abusers. *Journal of Personality Assessment, 58,* 269–276.

Pihl, R. O., Peterson, J., & Finn, P. (1990). Inherited predisposition to alcoholism: Characteristics of sons of male alcoholics. *Journal of Abnormal Psychology, 99,* 291–301.

Polich, J., Pollock, V. E., & Bloom, F. E. (1994). Meta-analysis of P300 amplitude from males at risk for alcoholism. *Psychological Bulletin, 115,* 55–73.

Rado, S. (1957). Narcotic bondage: A general theory of the dependence on narcotic drugs. *American Journal of Psychiatry, 114,* 165–170.

Rounsaville, B. J., Kosten, T. R., Weissman, M. M., & Kleber, H. D. (1985). *Evaluating and treating depressive disorders in opiate addicts.* Rockville, MD: National Institute on Drug Abuse.

Salmon, R., & Salmon, S. (1977a). The causes of heroin addictions—A review of the literature. Part I. *International Journal of the Addictions, 12,* 679–696.

Salmon, R., & Salmon, S. (1977b). The causes of heroin addictions—A review of the literature. Part II. *International Journal of the Addictions, 12,* 937–951.

Schuckit, M. A. (1987). Biological vulnerability to alcoholism. *Journal of Consulting and Clinical Psychology, 55,* 301–309.

Shaffer, H., & Burglass, M. (Eds.). *Classic contributions in the addictions.* NY: Brunner/Mazel.

Tabakoff, B., Hoffman, P. L., Lee, J. M., Saito, T., Willard, B., & DeLeon–Jones, F. (1988). Differences in platelet enzyme activity between alcoholics and nonalcoholics. *New England Journal of Medicine, 318,* 134–139.

Vaillant, G. E., & Milosky, E. S. (1982). The etiology of alcoholism: A prospective viewpoint. *American Psychologist, 37,* 494–503.

Wikler, A. (1973). Dynamics of drug dependence: Implications of a conditioning theory for research and treatment. *Archives of General Psychiatry, 28,* 611–616.

Winick, C. (1962). Maturing out of narcotic addiction. *Bulletin on Narcotics, 14,* 1–7.

Winick, C. (1964). The life cycle of the narcotic addict and of addiction. *Bulletin on Narcotics, 16,* 2–11.

Winick, C. (1974). A sociological theory of the genesis of drug dependence. In C. Winick (Ed.). *Sociological aspects of drug dependence* (pp. 3–13). Cleveland, OH: CRC Press.

Yorke, C. (1970). A critical review of some psychoanalytic literature on drug addiction. *British Journal of Medical Psychology, 43,* 141–159.

Zucker, R. A., & Gomberg, E. S. (1986). Etiology of alcoholism revisited: The case for a biopsychosocial process. *American Psychologist, 41,* 783–793.

CHAPTER THREE

DRUGS AND THEIR EFFECTS

This chapter addresses the issue of drugs and their effects, beginning with basic information on characteristics of drugs.

CHARACTERISTICS OF DRUGS

A drug is any substance that alters the structure or function of some aspect of the person. This definition does not apply specifically to drugs of abuse, but rather to all drugs.

Dosage

Drugs have primary and secondary, or side, effects. The nature of these effects depends on the drug itself and on the amount taken. For example, at low doses, alcohol produces a state of relaxation, but at higher doses it produces intoxication and at extremely high doses it can produce coma. The relationship between a drug and its response is called the dose–response relationship, and usually is graphed in a dose–response curve. Figure 3.1 portrays an example of a dose–response curve. Below a critical value, or threshold, a drug has little or no effect. Above the threshold, the drug exerts its main effects.

Drugs dose levels may be subclinical, therapeutic, or lethal. A sub-clinical dose is below the level necessary for it to produce desired effects. A therapeutic dose is the amount of a drug needed to produce the desired effect. A lethal dose is the poisonous level of a drug that results in death.

Main Effects

The primary effects of a drug act on the body in expected ways. For example, the main effect of analgesics is to alleviate pain, although they may also produce secondary or side effects, such as drowsiness.

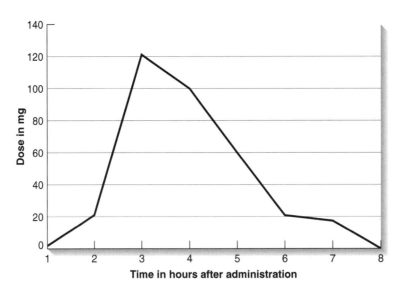

FIGURE 3.1   Sample Dose–Response Curve

Peak Effects

Drugs differ in duration of action. Some reach their main effects rapidly and have short duration (e.g., cocaine), whereas others last for hours (e.g., hallucinogens). The length of time a drug maintains its main effects is its peak effect.

Potency

The strength, or potency, of the drug determines the amount of a drug needed to reach its maximum effects. The more potent a drug (e.g. LSD), the smaller the amount of the drug needed to get the desired effect. Alcohol is a relatively less potent drug, because more of it is needed to reach the desired effect.

Safety

Drugs are safe only at certain thresholds. Above this point is overdose, resulting in adverse effects that may include death. The Food and Drug Administration (FDA) is responsible for determining the safety and efficacy of a drug before it is released for public use through physicians' prescriptions and through over-the-counter medications.

Route of Administration

Most drugs are taken orally, intravenously, or inhaled or insufflated (sniffed), but they also may be taken rectally, sublingually (under the tongue), vaginally, and topically. However, the first three routes are most common for drugs of abuse.

Oral drugs are convenient and generally are the least expensive. Their effects on the user may be chemically altered by the stomach and intestines and they may not be absorbed well by the body. Oral drugs have a delayed onset before they work their way through the digestive system and enter the bloodstream. Oral drugs may irritate the stomach. An overdose on oral drugs can be reversed with gastric lavage (stomach pumping).

Injecting drugs into a vein allows them to enter the bloodstream and reach the brain within seconds. Some people cannot tolerate a needle, and diseases and risks are associated with needle use, especially unsterile needles. Intravenous (IV) overdoses are difficult and sometimes impossible to reverse,

Inhaling (smoking) drugs allows rapid onset of their main effects, but can cause damage to the oral cavity, trachea, and lungs. Overdoses are difficult to reverse.

Snorting drugs is similar to inhalation and allows for rapid onset. However, snorting may cause damage to the nasal septum, and overdoses may be more difficult to reverse.

Drug Interactions

Drug interactions are of three basic types: Additive, synergistic, and antagonistic. Drug effects are additive when the combined effects of two separate drugs are equivalent to the effects of each drug singly (e.g., Doriden and Tuonol). Antagonistic drug reactions occur when separate drugs produce opposite physiological reactions. For example, heroin produces a high but a narcotic antagonist (naltrexone) taken concurrent with heroin inhibits the effect of the heroin and causes a state of withdrawal. Synergistic (sometimes called potentiating) effects occur when drugs interact with greater total effect that when they are taken separately (e.g., Demerol and Vistaril).

Pharmacokinetics

This branch of pharmacology deals with the absorption, distribution, metabolism, and excretion of a drug. Each has its own principles of action.

Absorption. Before a drug can exercise its effects, it must be absorbed into the bloodstream. The rate of absorption of a drug varies with route of administration. Drugs taken intravenously reach the blood stream and brain more rapidly than drugs that are taken orally. Drugs in higher doses are absorbed faster than drugs in lower concentrations. Absorption for drugs taken orally depends on several factors. Liquid drug preparations are more readily absorbed than drugs in capsule or tablet form. However, agents can be added either to enhance or to delay absorption. As a swallowed preparation travels through the stomach and intestines, the presence of food may delay the process of absorption. Acidity and alkalinity in the gastrointestinal tract can affect solubility and are themselves affected by certain foods and other drugs. Fat-soluble drugs enter the bloodstream faster than water-soluble drugs.

Distribution.   After absorption, a drug must travel through the body: The speed of this distribution depends on the status of the cardiovascular system, especially of the heart.

Metabolism.   The drug eventually arrives at the liver, which detoxifies and metabolizes the drug and makes it ready for excretion, although small amounts of drugs are metabolized outside the liver and small amounts are excreted without being metabolized. The rate of metabolism depends on several factors, including the health of the liver and the cardiovascular system. The half-life of a drug is the time it takes for the body to metabolize and eliminate half of the original dose. This is a measure of the duration of a drug's action on the body.

Excretion.   The final stage is the elimination of the drug from the body. The primary method of excretion for most drugs is through urination, hence urine testing to detect drugs. The kidney must be healthy, or excretion will be interrupted. Drugs can be excreted through perspiration, respiration (hence blood-alcohol testing using breathalyzers), and defecation.

Neurotransmitters

Each neuron (nerve cell) is made up of a nucleus, a cell body, an axon, and dendrites, or terminals. Between each neuron is an empty space, called a synapse. Although there may be 15 billion neurons in the brain, no two neurons touch each other. They must communicate by chemical messages. The electrical nerve message travels from the dendrites to the cell body, down the axon, and to the dendrites of the neighboring neuron. Before it can cross the synaptic cleft, vesicles in the nerve terminal release the neurotransmitters they store, which occupy the synapse, thereby stimulating the adjacent dendrite. Each neuroterminal releases only one neurotransmitter and the dendrite receptors are responsive to only one neurotransmitter.

It is speculated that there may be up to 200 different neurotransmitters, but only a few have been determined to be affected by psychoactive drugs. These are acetylcholine (used in learning and memory), dopamine (used in motor activity), serotonin (used in arousal and mood modification), and endorphins (used in pain relief).

Psychoactive drugs affect and disrupt this neural process. They can destroy neurons or neurotransmitters, alter their permeability, affect the enzymes that create the neurotransmitters, affect the release of neurotransmitters stored in the vesicles, affect the re-absorption of the neurotransmitters into the vesicles, block a receptor, and change the sensitivity of a receptor. Each affected process has deleterious effects on behavior.

However, three main factors affect perception of and response to a drug: (a) personal variables, (b) environmental variables, and (c) dose or amount of drug ingested.

Personal Variables.

■ *Age.* Body weight, physiological functions, and neurological processes change with age. Doses recommended for adults need to be modified in pediatric and geriatric cases.

■ *Gender.* Body weight (generally higher in men than women), body fat (generally higher in women than men), hormonal differences, and differences in male and female physiology cause drugs to affect men and women differently.

■ *Race.* Ethnic and racial factors are mediated largely by cultural and sociological differences rather than by race, thus race may be a minor factor in how drugs affect the body.

■ *Nutrition.* Impaired nutrition can cause a drug to have a deleterious effect on various body organs and processes.

■ *Disease.* Damage to organs, particularly from diseases of the nervous system, affects the pharmacokinetics of a drug.

■ *Genetics.* Genetic composition may affect how people respond to a drug. For example, Asians seem to have sensitivity to alcohol that has been traced to their genetic endowment. This is also a racial effect.

■ *Expectations.* What people believe a drug will do can affect how the drug actually does affect them. If they believe that alcohol will increase sexuality, then they may become more sexually aggressive and even more sexually capable for a while and with low alcohol doses. Placebo (i.e., inert substances) studies clearly show that beliefs can influence cognitive, emotional, sensory, and physiological reactions to a drug.

■ *Previous Drug Experiences.* First-time marijuana users have been known to experience panic attacks, because they are unaccustomed to the drug's effects, whereas long-time marijuana users never experience this reaction. Users learn to compensate for drug-induced changes and are able to cope with them better than novice users.

Environmental Variables.

■ *Physical Environment.* Rhesus monkeys were placed in a cage in which movement was restricted, then were allowed to inject cocaine by pressing a lever. The animals soon became addicted. This suggests that at the human level, introducing a state of boredom and restricting the usual social environment, then introducing a psychoactive drug can influence whether a person will take that drug.

■ *Social Environment*. People and circumstances can influence others' behavior and can determine if they do or do not take drugs. In a social group where drug use is condoned, when there is stress in an individual's life, and when the proscriptions against use have been lifted, the individual is more likely to use than if these variables are not present.

Biological Variables.

■ *Dose*. No matter what their beliefs, no matter what environment they inhabit, or who they are with, eventually the dose of a drug overcomes all other variables and, in effect, mostly determines the reaction they get from it.

CLASSIFICATION OF DRUGS

Psychoactive drugs commonly are classified by how they affect the central nervous system. The drugs and their main courses of action appear in Table 3.1.

Drug Schedules

The Drug Enforcement Administration (DEA) has produced a commonly used schedule of drugs based on degree of dependence or abuse and degree of usefulness in medicine.

TABLE 3.1 Classification of Psychoactive Drugs

CLASSIFICATION	EXAMPLE	ACTION
Cannabinoids	Marijuana and marijuana derivatives (THC)	Depressant with hallucinogenic
Depressants	Alcohol, barbiturates, tranquilizers	Slow the action of the CNS
Hallucinogens	LSD, mescaline	Produce hallucinations and visual distortions
Inhalants	Toluene, paint thinner	Volatile, affect the brain
Opioids	Heroin, morphine	Control pain
Phencyclidine	PCP	Animal tranquilizer with hallucinogenic properties
Stimulants	Cocaine, amphetamines	Arouse and excite the CNS

- Schedule I Drugs have no accepted medical use and have a high abuse potential. They include heroin, LSD, and mescaline. They cannot be prescribed.
- Schedule II Drugs have high abuse potential with severe psychological and physical dependence liability. They include morphine, codeine, Dilaudid, Demerol, and Dexedrine. They are available only through prescriptions.
- Schedule III Drugs have less abuse potential than those in Schedules I and II. They include Doriden, paregoric, and pentobarbital. They are available only through prescriptions.
- Schedule IV Drugs have less abuse potential than those in Schedule III. They include phenobarbital, chloral hydrate, Valium, Xanax, and Ativan. They are available only through prescriptions.
- Schedule V Drugs have less abuse potential than those in Schedule IV. Preparations contain limited quantities of narcotic and stimulant drugs (e.g., antitussives, antidiarrheals, and certain analgesics). They are available through prescriptions or over-the-counter.

As this section continues, it discusses major psychoactive drugs of use and abuse, highlighting their major properties and the medical, psychological, social, and public health problems that may be associated with their use and abuse.

Alcohol

Main Effects. In general, the effects of alcohol vary depending on the amount taken and the amount of alcohol in the blood. At low doses alcohol creates a feeling of relaxation. Increased blood alcohol is reflected in reduced alertness, slightly impaired judgment, reduced visual acuity, reduced mental and physical functioning, and lowered coordination.

Detection. Alcohol can be detected in blood and urine; the most popular way to detect alcohol use is the presence of alcohol on the breath. Blood alcohol level (BAL) testing is used in most substance abuse programs to determine levels of alcohol in the body.

Tolerance. Tolerance develops as the body adjusts to a given amount of drugs at any time. Drinkers eventually need more and more of the drug to get high, because tolerance quickly builds to repeated use of alcohol.

Intoxication. Alcoholic intoxication evolves through a series of stages that depend on the amount of alcohol ingested, the degree of tolerance, and the amount of food or other drugs in the alimentary canal. Emotional signs include slowed reaction times, loss of control over actions and behavior, impaired judgment and thinking, and erratic behavior. Other signs include mental confusion, staggering and loss of balance, slurred speech, and memory dysfunction. Vomiting and loss of consciousness may occur. An alcoholic coma may ensue that puts the individual at risk for death by overdose.

Dependence and Addiction.   Many people become physically dependent on alcohol and become addicted. Others seem to be able to drink socially and responsibly without becoming addicted.

Withdrawal.   Mild forms of alcohol withdrawal include headaches, nausea, vomiting, tremulousness, and the shakes. Symptoms occur from 6 to 48 hours after the last drink. A more severe withdrawal syndrome is *delirium tremens (DTs)*, characterized by visual hallucinations and profound confusion. The onset of DTs usually occurs from 7 to 10 days after the last drink, but may occur within 48 hours.

Medical Problems.   Because alcohol affects every cell of every tissue of every organ of every system in the body, a report on all of alcohol's effects on the body would be too lengthy. Only the more common problems will be highlighted.

■ *Birth Defects.* Alcohol crosses the placental barrier and can affect the embryo and fetus. Fetal Alcohol Syndrome affects newborns: Excessive alcohol use by their mothers during pregnancy causes affected infants to have facial abnormalities and mental retardation.

■ *Brain Diseases.* The cerebellum—the part of the brain that controls balance and coordination—can atrophy and degenerate, resulting in unsteady gait, slurred speech, and staggering ambulation. Strokes may occur because of hypertension associated with chronic drinking.

■ *Gastritis.* This inflammation of the lining of the stomach (which can become easily upset by excessive alcohol use) results in nausea, headaches, and vomiting.

■ *Heart Disease.* The heart may become enlarged because of alcohol abuse, resulting in shortness of breath, labored breathing, and other symptoms of cardiac disease.

■ *Korsakoff's Psychosis.* This vitamin deficiency disorder results from a deficiency of Vitamin B1 (thiamin). Alcohol interferes with digestion and the passage of nutrients from the intestines into the bloodstream. An alcoholic's liver has a decreased ability to convert and release nutrients for body availability. Processing alcohol requires thiamin, which it uses up. Alcohol in the body gets immediate attention, so other nutrients are left waiting, and may be washed out before the body can use them. The long-term result of Vitamin B1 deficiency is a psychotic condition, in which patients suffer a severe distortion of memory and confabulate—make up stories for things they cannot remember.

■ *Liver Damage.* The liver processes and metabolizes alcohol. Over time, excessive alcohol use can result in alcoholic fatty liver, hepatitis, and cirrhosis, a scarring of the liver that is usually fatal without a liver transplant.

■ *Pancreatitis.* Alcohol can inflame the pancreas over time.

■ *Ulcers.* The stomach and small intestine can become ulcerated with crater-like erosions and chronic stomach pains following ingestion of food.

■ *Wernicke's Encephalopathy.* Another vitamin deficiency disorder, it is characterized by rapid onset of headaches, ataxic gait, abnormal eye movements, mental confusion, and disorientation.

■ *Miscellaneous Cancers.* Alcoholics who also are addicted to nicotine are susceptible to the many cancers associated with tobacco chewing and smoking.

Public Health Problems.

■ *Highway Accidents.* About half of all highway accidents are estimated to be alcohol-related.

■ *Blackouts.* Alcoholics may lose consciousness but may remain awake and have total memory loss for all their behaviors during the drunken state. In a phenomenon called *state-dependent learning,* individuals will recall those behaviors when intoxicated but will be unable to recall them when sober.

■ *Violence.* Drinking may result in increased belligerence and end in barroom brawls, street fights, and arguments and fights with family and friends. Alcohol abuse often is implicated in domestic violence and spouse abuse.

Amphetamines

Stimulant drugs speed up CNS functioning. Stimulants have the potential for abuse and dependence. Physiologically, they trigger the release of catecholamines, neurotransmitters in the brain called (epinephrine, norepinephrine, and dopamine), blocking their re-uptake and the return to physiological equilibrium. This probably occurs by stimulating the reticular activating system, a brain center. In counseling, precise information on the physiological, chemical, and cellular mechanisms of stimulant drugs is not necessary because their physical, mental, and behavioral effects, not essential brain functioning, are the focus of treatment.

Caffeine and cocaine are naturally occurring stimulants that originate from plants and leaves, whereas amphetamine drugs are manufactured synthetically.

The effects of stimulant drugs depend on the particular drug, dose, pattern of use, and degree of tolerance. Because of this variability, the present chapter discusses commonly abused drugs separately.

Amphetamines and methamphetamines have actions similar to the naturally occurring hormone, adrenaline. Representative drugs in these synthetically produced preparations include Benzedrine, Methedrine, Preludin, and Ritalin.

Main Effects. Stimulant drugs enervate the CNS, resulting in increased blood pressure, heart and pulse rate, sweating, dilated pupils and bronchial tubes, and a lessened desire for sleep. At higher doses, users may experience dizziness, blurred vision, tremors, heart palpitations, dry mouth, and loss of coordination.

The psychological effects of amphetamines depend on the dose. Short-term effects include increased alertness, energy, and attentiveness, and loss of fatigue and appetite, with feelings of mild euphoria and increased mental and physical power, confidence, ambition, and persistence. At high doses users may experience hyperactivity; over-talkativeness; restlessness; anxiety; exaggerated feelings of power, superiority, and ability; and possibly aggressiveness and hostility. Some users describe a rush of orgasmic-like intensity. Loss of appetite is so compelling that food becomes unappealing. Emotions are intensified and extreme suspiciousness and paranoia may develop. An unusual effect of high dose amphetamine use is compulsive behavior—individuals engage in a repetitive task for hours.

Route of Administration.   Amphetamines and methamphetamines are available in tablets or capsules but can appear as powder or crystals. Users typically take them orally, sniff them, or inject them into their veins. Sometimes users inject amphetamines combined with heroin: *speedballing.*

Tolerance.   Tolerance to amphetamines develops in an unusual pattern. Tolerance does not develop at the same rate to all the effects of these drugs.

Dependence.   Stimulant drugs are capable of producing a range of dependent states from weak to very compelling. The World Health Organization (WHO) and the American Psychiatric Association (APA) define a formal diagnosis of amphetamine dependence.

Withdrawal.   Following cessation of heavy amphetamine use, profound sleep and marked depression may occur.

Detection.   Amphetamines commonly are detected through urine toxicology screens.

Medical Uses.

■ *Weight Control.* The appetite-suppressing effects of amphetamines have resulted in physicians prescribing them for patients who want to lose weight. Use in this manner is recommended for only very short periods of time, because users tend to rely on them and studies have shown that any weight loss while on amphetamines does not last long. The medical profession increasingly dissuades physicians from prescribing them for weight control.

■ *Insomnia.* Amphetamines once were used to treat insomnia. Better drugs, such as Trazadone, are now available for this purpose.

■ *Narcolepsy.* In this rare sleep disorder, a person falls asleep at odd times and without the intention of doing so. The stimulant action of amphetamines counteracts the desire to sleep but does not treat the underlying condition.

■ *Childhood Hyperactivity.* Hyperkinesis—childhood hyperactivity—often is treated with the stimulant, Ritalin.

■ *Amphetamine Models of Psychosis.* Some people experience a psychotic disorder after continuous use of amphetamines. This has occurred reliably under laboratory conditions in both animals and in humans. Amphetamine studies provide the closest drug model to paranoid schizophrenia.

Amphetamines have been used historically to reduce nasal congestion, as a bronchodilator to treat lung disorders, for depression, epilepsy, Parkinson's Disease, obesity, and as an aid in diet management. In reality, amphetamines are the treatment of choice in few medical disorders.

Adverse Reactions.

■ *Amphetamine Psychosis.* Chronic and heavy use of amphetamines can result in psychotic behavior that is indistinguishable from paranoid schizophrenia, except for the kind of hallucinations. Amphetamine studies have demonstrated qualitative differences, however: hallucinations in amphetamine induced psychosis primarily are visual, but in paranoid schizophrenia, they usually are auditory. This has occurred reliably under laboratory conditions in animals and in humans. Abusers realize that their paranoia is a drug effect and largely ignore it. However, as the paranoid state intensifies and becomes compelling, the user may act on the delusions. The delusions dissipate upon awakening after a deep sleep.

■ *State Dependent Learning.* Material learned during an amphetamine "run" often is lost to memory upon awakening but recalled upon re-administering the drug.

■ *Depression.* This is an extremely common adverse effect of chronic amphetamine use. After a run, users become profoundly depressed and may take more amphetamines to rid themselves of the depression, creating a vicious cycle.

■ *Violence.* Heavy users of amphetamines are prone to sudden, unpredictable, violent acts. Amphetamines can act on mental processes by creating suspiciousness, variable moods, intensified anger, and hyperactivity. Users react to minor provocations, resulting in aggression and violence.

■ *Malnutrition.* Chronic users do not eat properly because of the appetite-suppressing effects of amphetamines. Combined with hyperactivity caused by the drug, failure to eat properly puts the user at risk for developing vitamin deficiencies and malnourishment. Also, because of their generally run-down condition, poor diet and lack of sleep, and altered life style, abusers are at risk for other infectious diseases.

■ *Panic Reactions.* Two kinds of panic reactions may complicate amphetamine use. In the first, users experience rapid heart beat, anxiety, nervousness, heavy breathing, and heart palpitations and fear an impending heart attack. In the second, the symptoms are similar but users interpret them differently, believe they are going crazy, lose control, and go into full panic mode. These effects cease when the drug wears off.

Methamphetamine

Methamphetamine is a white, odorless, and bitter-tasting crystalline powder that is soluble in water and in alcohol. Also called "crank," "ice," or "crystal," it is smoked, injected, snorted, or taken orally. It produces all of the effects, side effects, and complications of amphetamines, but at a more intense level. Its high potency and purity levels increase its potential for tolerance and dependence. Its half-life is about 11 hours, prolonging the effects beyond those of cocaine or amphetamines. The drug may be detectable in urine for several days.

Look-Alike Drugs.   Initially these drugs were found in over-the-counter medications packaged to look like stimulants and formulated in larger doses to give them greater potency. Look-alike drugs were advertised in magazines and in underground newspapers. Because these drugs were legal, no laws prevented their sale. Eventually these "promotional practices spread to sedative-hypnotics and cocaine look-alikes.

The medications in these drugs were Phenylpropanolamine (PPA), a mild stimulant; ephedrine, which is about five times weaker than amphetamines, but has all the same CNS properties; and caffeine. The sedative-hypnotic look-alikes contain antihistamines to induce drowsiness. The cocaine look-alikes contain PPA, caffeine, ephedrine, procaine, benzocaine, lidocaine, and other stimulants.

Eventually the U.S. Food and Drug Administration (FDA) concluded that these preparations constituted new drugs and laws were changed to make them illegal.

Barbiturates: Minor Tranquilizers

Barbiturates, a class of drugs that are CNS depressants, sometimes are referred to as sedative-hypnotics. All have clinical utility in medical practice and most have abuse potential. They can be divided into *ultra short-acting* drugs, which are used to induce anesthesia (e.g., sodium pentothal); *short- or intermediate-acting* drugs, which last for about four hours and are used to treat insomnia (e.g., Seconal, Nembutal); and *long-acting* drugs (e.g., phenobarbital), which are used to treat epilepsy. The ultra short- and long-acting barbiturates are rarely abused; the short and intermediate-acting barbiturates are commonly abused.

Predominant Effects. When used as prescribed, barbiturates depress the CNS, resulting in states ranging from drowsiness through anesthesia. When used improperly, they can result in decreased breathing and slow heart rate and may cause cardiac arrest. (Some states use a lethal dose of barbiturates for state-ordered execution.) Barbiturates can produce a state equivalent to that produced by alcohol: Respiration slows, reflexes become sluggish, speech slurs, movement decreases, loss of balance may occur, various muscles feel numb, sensitivity to pain diminishes, and the user feels drunk or high.

Psychologically, barbiturates may produce a state of disinhibition, a sense of well-being, confusion, forgetfulness, reduction of worries and lessening of anxieties, decreased sexual performance, memory lapses, errors in judgment, difficulties in thinking and reasoning, and reduction of anger, hostility, and resentment.

Route of Administration. Barbiturates usually are taken orally, although some require intravenous administration under medical care.

Tolerance. Long-term use of barbiturates results in tolerance. If two or more barbiturates or barbiturate-like drugs are used at the same time, the drugs compete for metabolism within the liver. Neither is properly metabolized and toxic effects multiply, which can result in overdose and death. This is most likely to occur when users mix barbiturates with alcohol to produce a better high.

Dependence. Barbiturates, like all other CNS depressants, have the potential to produce drug dependence after several weeks of continuous administration.

Withdrawal. The severity of the barbiturate withdrawal syndrome varies according to the strength of the drug, the amount taken, and the length of use. Generally, the barbiturate withdrawal syndrome can occur as long as 10 days after cessation of use and is similar to withdrawal from alcohol. Withdrawal symptoms include restlessness, cramps, nausea, vomiting, dizziness, chills, runny nose, agitation, nervousness, insomnia, delirium, delusions, convulsions, and seizures. Withdrawal from barbiturates is more dangerous than withdrawal from alcohol and should always be done under medical supervision.

Detection. Barbiturates readily are detected with urine toxicology screens, as well as through blood tests.

Public Health Problems.

- *Suicide.* Barbiturates are the chemical agents most frequently used to commit suicide.
- *Accidental Deaths.* Alcohol combined with barbiturates puts users at risk for accidental fatal overdose.

■ *Street Diversion.* Automobile accidents may result because of the psychomotor retardation effects of barbiturates. Barbiturates are sold readily on the street.

■ *Seizures.* Abrupt cessation of barbiturate use without medical care can produce seizures and medical emergencies.

■ *Miscellaneous Hazards.* Difficulties in coordination, faulty judgment, and emotional states ranging from lethargy to lability put barbiturate abusers (under the effects of these drugs) and those around them at risk for accidents and injury.

Caffeine

Caffeine belongs to the Xanthines family of drugs, which have stimulant properties.

Route of Administration.   Caffeine is present in most coffees, teas, colas, and peppered beverages, unless it is extracted. It is present in some aspirin compounds, cold medications, and decongestants, and in chocolate and cocoa. Thus the normal route is oral.

Caffeine Overdose?   Don't laugh! Technically, caffeine overdose is possible, because all drugs have a threshold above which the drug becomes a poison. In fact, death from caffeine overdose is extremely rare.

Main Effects.   Caffeine stimulates brain centers in the cerebral cortex and in the medulla that regulate actions of the heart and other muscles, resulting in increase in heart rate, blood pressure, and pulse rate. Caffeine increases the output of stomach acid and stimulates the production and elimination of urine. Caffeine reduces sleep. Most of these effects usually are mild. Psychological effects include increased alertness, reduced fatigue, and improvement in psychomotor performance and concentration. Onset of caffeine effects begins within one hour and last from 3 to 4 hours.

Side Effects.   Some people experience fatigue, lethargy, irritability, gastric burning, and cardiac arrhythmias (irregular or skipping heartbeats). "Restless leg" syndrome, spontaneous twitching of the lower leg, has also been attributed to caffeine. Symptoms of excessive caffeine use are similar to those of generalized anxiety disorder.

Withdrawal.   Abruptly halting regular excessive use of caffeine can produce withdrawal symptoms of anxiety, irritability, depression, agitation, headaches, cardiac arrythmias, muscle twitching, insomnia, restlessness, and agitation.

Dependence.   Mild dependence can result from caffeine use. Generally a very mild withdrawal pattern may occur upon ceasing use after a history of regular consumption.

Tolerance.   Caffeine produces tolerance only to a slight degree. Consumption of more than seven cups of coffee a day is considered excessive use.

Medical Uses.   Most of the medical uses for caffeine occur in over-the-counter cold remedies. A controversial experimental use of caffeine was treatment for children with ADD with hyperactivity. Stimulant drugs have a calming effect in children and caffeine was tried in place of more potent anti-hyperactive medications, such as Ritalin. Results were mixed and caffeine's use in this manner is not routinely accepted medically.

Caffeine is generally a part of most people's diet in the United States. Despite this prevalence, serious problems from caffeine are rare: Little harm comes from low-to-moderate use of caffeine for most people and its abuse potential is particularly low. However, the use of caffeine has become classically conditioned to the ingestion of other drugs, particularly to nicotine in the form of cigars and cigarettes. Thus caffeine can become a risk factor for relapse among people trying to quit smoking. Substance abuse counselors may have to deal with caffeine use among alcoholics in recovery, who are notoriously heavy consumers of coffee at AA meetings.

Cocaine

Cocaine, a powerful CNS stimulant drug, is an alkaloid derived from the coca bush, which is native to the Andes countries. Coca thrives in the warm valleys above sea level. The shrub can produce its first harvest in 18 months and can yield its crop four to five times each year for the 40 years of its life expectancy. The coca plant contains at least 14 different alkaloids, with cocaine representing about 85% of the total alkaloid content. The coca plant, among the oldest drugs known to mankind, has been used for centuries: in religious rites and festivals in South America, and in the late 1800s, as the main psychoactive drug in a number of elixir preparations. It emerged as a popular drug of abuse in the 1980s and remains so today.

Main Effects.   Cocaine is a local anesthetic with stimulant properties and produces the same sensations as other stimulant drugs with few exceptions. (In experiments, users were unable to determine if they were given cocaine or amphetamines under blind test conditions.) Cocaine rewards the brain by increasing the release of dopamine, a brain neurotransmitter. Unadulterated cocaine appears as a white, crystalline powder. Street cocaine is diluted with various fillers. Upon ingestion of cocaine, the user's heart rate immediately rises. This is dose related and returns to normal within 40 minutes. The user's blood pressure increases, with peak effects occurring within 25 minutes. While the half-life of amphetamines is about four hours, the half-life of cocaine is about 40 minutes. Cocaine free-basers usually take a hit every 5 minutes until their supply is exhausted. Cocaine binges may last from 30 minutes to several days, depending on the supply. Socio-recreational users may start with a single hit, but moderate cocaine use often increases to daily use and then gets out of control. For a more detailed account on physiological effects, refer to the presentation on amphetamines in this chapter.

Psychological effects make cocaine a very popular drug. These effects are modified if the user chews coca leaves, as is the custom in South America, inhales it, uses it intraveneously, or smokes it, as is popular in the United States. In general, within 15 to 30 minutes, the user experiences of exhilaration and euphoria and an increase in energy with a positive mood intensifying to acute elation and feelings of competence and power. In animal studies, cocaine-dependent rats take cocaine to the exclusion of food, water, and sex until they eventually expire.

Free-basing cocaine refers to smoking a chemically treated form of cocaine powder. The drug is freed from its chemical base, a hydrochloride salt, by treating cocaine powder with sodium hydroxide, ether, baking soda, or various alcohols. The cocaine is filtered or skimmed off and dried. By this time, it looks like rock candy granules, and is called rock cocaine or crack. It is then heated in a pipe and smoked. Free base may be vaporized and inhaled. Free base cocaine is chemically different from cocaine hydrochloride and different from all other forms of cocaine. It is ineffective when snorted or taken in IV preparations and is only psychoactively potent when volatilized by smoking or inhaling.

Tolerance.   Tolerance to cocaine has been demonstrated in laboratory animals. Few experimental cocaine studies examine humans, and reports of tolerance to the drug have been largely anecdotal. Clinical users of the drug report that the first few hits at the start of a run are the best: they try to use more of the drug to repeat the initial sensation. Males have been known to spontaneously ejaculate when free-basing for the first time, but have little success when they try to recapture that initial drug-induced orgasmic experience.

Addiction.   Cocaine has been thought of as a drug that does not result in physical dependence. This seems to be true of chewing coca leaves. In free-basing cocaine, users continue to use the drug despite adverse consequences, increasing the risk of severe psychological dependence on the drug. If addiction is compulsive use in spite of adverse consequences, then cocaine can be considered very addictive.

Withdrawal.   There is no clear-cut withdrawal pattern from cocaine use. Some former users report lethargy, depression, and lassitude.

Detection.   Cocaine can be detected in urine and in blood. The short half-life of cocaine requires that urine specimens need to be collected within a shorter time from last use than other drugs of abuse.

Medical Uses.   Cocaine is used in medicine as a local anesthetic, particularly in dentistry. It is used in eye surgery and, because of its ability to deaden pain and constrict blood vessels, thus limiting bleeding in the anesthetized area, it has value in surgery involving the nose and throat.

Medical Problems.   Intravenous cocaine users are at risk for all of the complications associated with taking any drug under nonsterile conditions. Complications include hepatitis, abscesses, cellulitis, tetanus, collapsed veins, overdoses, lung abscesses, endocarditis, and generalized septicemia. Pulmonary deficits also have been found among cocaine free-basers. Perforation of the nasal septum is also a possibility. Tactile hallucinations ("cocaine bugs"), visual hallucinations ("snow lights"), chest pain, stroke, weight loss, and sexual dysfunction have also been reported. Neuropsychological deficits, including impairments in memory, visuospatial abilities, and problems with concentration have been found.

Many users take cocaine when having sex, but cocaine's reputation as a "love drug" is not supported. Users beliefs about the drug cannot be separated from the reduced inhibitions it causes. Males do report increased sexual endurance while using cocaine, but the effect dissipates after extended use of the drug.

Public Health Problems.

- *Crime and Violence.* To get money to support their dependence on cocaine, users steal and may commit violent crimes.
- *Fires.* Free-basers may accidentally start fires while lighting their pipes to smoke cocaine.
- *Maternal Complications.* Pregnant women who take cocaine are at risk for miscarriages, premature deliveries, stillbirths, and low birth-weight babies.
- *Learning Disabilities.* Children born to cocaine-using mothers have experienced many learning problems in school.
- *AIDS and Other Sexually Transmitted Diseases.* Users may trade sex for cocaine and engage in sexually risky practices that put them at risk for AIDS and other sexually transmitted diseases (SDSs).

Psychosocial Problems.   Cocaine use often results in loss of job, family, and friends. Psychological disorders can include cocaine-induced *paranoia* and *psychosis*.

Hallucinogens

Hallucinogens are a class of drugs that produce psychotic-like reactions, which wear off as the drug wears off. Include in this class are LSD, mescaline, psilocybin, and a range of other chemicals, such as MDA, PCP, PMA, TMA, and DMT.

LSD.   Lysergic acid, diethylamide is made from lysergic acid, found in ergot, a fungus that grows on grains. It may be taken orally, in capsules, or in liquid form. Often it is added to some type of absorbent paper, divided into small squares and sold in single doses.

Main effects of LSD often are unpredictable and can be affected by personality variables, mood, context or environment in which the drug is taken, and the amount taken. When LSD is orally ingested, main effects occur within an hour and can last from two to twelve hours. Physical effects can include dry mouth, increased heart rate and blood pressure, sweating, loss of appetite, and sleepiness. Psychological effects are more pronounced. They may include visual hallucinations, changes in feelings and normal sensations, distortion in sensory and time perception, rapid mood changes, and delusions. On a bad trip, the user may fear loss of control, insanity, and death. They experience terrifying thoughts and feelings and may cry profusely.

Psychological Problems.

- *Flashbacks.* The hallucinogenic experience may recur spontaneously in the absence of drug ingestion.
- *Psychosis.* Hallucinogens may precipitate a psychotic reaction that does not abate without treatment.
- *Severe Depression.* Even a chronic user may go into a deep depression.
- *Tolerance.* Resistance to the effects of these drugs can develop very quickly. Sensitivity to the drug will eventually return after a sufficient interval of non-drug use.
- *Addiction.* Hallucinogens do not produce physiological dependence but may produce psychological dependence.
- *Withdrawal.* There is no withdrawal pattern upon cessation of use.

Heroin

Heroin is in a class of drugs called *narcotics,* which occur in natural forms, such as morphine and codeine, and in synthetic forms, such as Demorol and Dilaudid. They are among the most effective analgesics. Heroin is the street narcotic most often abused. The other drugs have similar actions on the CNA and differ only in strength and duration. At the present time, heroin has no medicinal use, whereas morphine, codeine, and synthetic narcotics are routinely used in medical practice.

Heroin (diacetylemorphine) is produced from the plant *papivar somniferum.* Morphine from the poppy is treated with acetic acid to form heroin. Heroin effects last from 4 to 6 hours.

Routes of Administration.   Heroin may be snorted, injected under the skin (skin-popped), or taken intravenously. Sometimes it is taken with intravenous cocaine.

Effects.   Injections produce near-instantaneous effects, and snorting produces effects in 2 to 5 minutes. The high or euphoria can last from 10 to 30 minutes, and its other effects from 4 to 6 hours. Euphoria, lethargy, drowsiness, apathy, slurred speech, and difficulties in attention and memory characterize heroin intoxication. The pupils may become dilated due to lack of oxygen, causing addicts to need to wear sunglasses. Chronic use results in impairments in social and occupational functioning. Upon initial use, many people experience dysphoria, nausea, and vomiting rather than a heroin high.

Opioid receptors are found throughout the body. At least three types of opioid receptors, mu, delta, and kappa, bind to opiates. Each molecule of a drug, such as heroin must bind to a specific receptor to have an effect. One way of treating opiate addiction is to use drugs that occupy the receptor cell, thereby preventing the problem molecule from exerting its action. The drug is then metabolized and excreted harmlessly.

Tolerance. Tolerance builds up quickly with repeated use of heroin. The user needs more and more of the drug to achieve the same narcotic effects.

Dependence. Physical dependence results with repeated use of heroin. Upon cessation of use, the heroin dependent person will experience an opiate withdrawal syndrome. Attempts to use heroin without becoming physiologically dependent—chipping—is rarely successful.

Withdrawal. Opioid withdrawal occurs upon cessation of heroin use. Withdrawal symptoms are identical to a bad case of the flu: They include running nose, yawning, increased heart rate, insomnia, elevated blood pressure, irritability, muscle cramps, tremors, diarrhea, nausea, and vomiting. Sometimes the legs will shake and tremble, hence the term "kicking the habit." The syndrome is reversed by using more opiates or drugs taken under medical supervision.

Detection. Acetic acid is metabolized and urine screens detect the remaining morphine. General screens may report the results that are positive for heroin, while more specific drug screens will identify the exact drug, morphine. Sometimes heroin is taken in such small amounts that it is not detected in opiates screening, but other drugs, such as quinine, used to cut—dilute—the drug, can be detected. A quinine-positive urine screen is only presumptive evidence for heroin use, because a positive quinine can occur from drinking gin and tonic water, as well as from other sources. An opiate-positive urine screen is definitive evidence of narcotic drug use, but more specific tests must be ordered to separate positive morphine from other prescribed narcotic drugs, such as codeine.

Medical Consequences. The majority of medical complications associated with heroin abuse result from the conditions under which the drug is taken and not from the drug itself.

- ■ *Digestive System.* (1) Stomach: Rates of peptic or duodenal ulcers are no different for abusers and non-users; (2) Intestinal Tract: Obstruction can occur when addicts swallow drugs in a condom or balloon to avoid police detection or to smuggle drugs; (3) Rectum: Chronic constipation is a side effect of chronic opiate use.

■ *Endocrine System.* Decrease in the hormone ACTH occurs after morphine administration; diabetes may be less common among heroin addicts.

■ *Heart and Circulatory System.* Endocarditis—an inflammation in the lining surrounding the heart—is a risk factor for drug addicts. Septicemia may arise around injection sites. Heroin taken 24 hours before an electrocardiogram produces a 55% rate of electrical abnormalities.

■ *Lymphatic System.* Lymphadenopathy is often present. "Puffy hand syndrome" may occur as a result of lymphatic obstruction and the sclerosing actions of injections on the soft tissue and veins result in collapsed veins in hands, arms, and legs.

■ *Genitourinary System.* (1) Renal disease may occur in association with bacterial endocarditis. (2) Venereal diseases are common among heroin addicts.

■ *Hepatic System.* Viral hepatitis and hepatitis C+ are liver disorders that appear in high frequencies among heroin addicts. Most heroin addicts will show abnormal liver functions and elevated liver enzymes on blood tests.

■ *Integument.* (1) Skin lesions may be apparent. Also, "railroad track marks" in the bodies of heroin addicts occur as a result of the repeated puncture of the skin over accessible veins and subsequent scar formation. (2) Abscesses and cellulitis occur from injection. (3) Tattoos may be placed to obscure injection sites.

■ *Nervous System.* Heroin produces few direct neurological dysfunctions. However, neuropsychological studies show abnormal findings in 41% to 64% of polydrug addicts two months after cessation of drug use.

■ *Pulmonary System.* Emboli may result from endocarditis from the injection of inert substances or from bacterial infections. The incidence of tuberculosis is substantially higher among heroin addicts.

■ *Sexual Functioning.* Men report decreased sexual desire, difficulty in establishing and maintaining an erection, or delayed ejaculation. Both men and women report a decreased quality of orgasm. HIV disease and HIV positive status is also higher in heroin addicts.

Other Problems.

■ *Alcohol Abuse.* Heroin addicts have substantially higher rates of alcohol and polydrug abuse compared to the general population.

■ *Feigned Disorders.* Drug addicts manipulate and fake many kinds of symptoms to get opiate drugs.

■ *Neonatal Addiction.* Neonates from addicted mothers have higher rates of mortality and morbidity as a result of poor prenatal care and the abstinence syndrome. The drug dependent mother's child is born drug dependent and needs medical attention to treat opiate withdrawal.

■ *Overdoses.* Most heroin addicts eventually experience a drug overdose.

■ *Psychopathology.* Most heroin addicts have a variety of personality disorders, especially antisocial, narcissistic, histrionic, passive–aggressive, and dependent disorders. Substance-induced mood disorders are common, as are anxiety and affective disorders. A subsample experienced childhood hyperactivity.

■ *Mortality.* Heroin addicts die younger than the general population. Their deaths result from accidental overdoses, accidents, suicides, and murder.

Marijuana

Marijuana is derived from a mixture of leaves, stems, and flowers from the plant *Cannabis sativa,* a weed of the hemp family. Cannabis flourishes in hot, sunny climates, but can be grown in most places with little cultivation—some users even grow it in their bed rooms. Marijuana's psychoactive cousin, *hashish,* is derived from the resin scraped from the flowering top of the same plant.

Hashish is between 5 and 10 times as potent as marijuana. Some authorities believe there are qualitative differences in effects as well as differences in drug strength. Because hashish, compared to marijuana, is not much of a problem in the United States there is little research interest in scientifically establishing this point.

The cannabis plant contains at least 419 different chemicals, including hydrocarbons, sugars, and steroids: some 60 of these chemicals, referred to as *cannabinoids,* are unique to cannabis. In 1964, delta-9-tetrahydrocannabinol (THC) was identified as the principle psychoactive substance in marijuana. THC (pronounced "tick" or "tack") has since been synthesized and is sold on the street. The potency level of street marijuana varies regionally and at different times, but generally is from 1% to 5% of the total content of the product.

Main Effects. Euphoria and relaxation are the adjectives most often used to describe the common psychoactive effects of marijuana. In general, marijuana use produces effects similar to those produced by alcohol. Marijuana users may also become very giddy and experience a sudden increase in appetite. Physical effects include a reddening of the eyes, dryness of the mouth and throat, increase in pulse and heart rate, and a small decrease in body temperature. Marijuana does not produce changes in pupil size. Additionally, it causes problems in concentration, slows reaction time, reduces visual acuity and the perception of time, and disrupts learning. It also lowers testosterone levels, sperm count, and sperm motility.

Marijuana researchers recently have found a natural chemical in the brain (anandamide, from a Sanskrit word meaning bliss) that acts on the body like marijuana. This ligand binds to the same nerve cell receptors as THC. It may produce similar effects, such as pain relief, or may affect mood regulation.

Route of Administration. Marijuana generally is smoked, resulting in marijuana intoxication in 5 to 10 minutes in experienced users. Peak effects are reached within a half-hour and can last anywhere from 2 to 3 hours. When marijuana is orally ingested—as when it is mixed with food—the drug takes more time to work its way through the gastrointestinal system and to be absorbed into the bloodstream. Drug effects will begin in 45 minutes to 2 hours after ingestion, but the effects will last longer—from 2 to 6 hours.

Detection of Marijuana. Transforming THC into its metabolites for eventual excretion is a slow process. Estimates vary, but one week after a person smokes marijuana, up to 50% of THC remains in the body's cells: Traces of marijuana have been found in the urine eight days later. It may take 4 to 6 weeks to metabolize all of the THC from the system and marijuana can be detected in blood up to a month after the last use. Thus, a THC-positive urinalysis or blood test does not necessarily indicate recent use. Forensic specialists can test blood for recent or past marijuana use, but toxicologists do not routinely perform such tests.

Tolerance. Tolerance to the effects of marijuana has been established in animal research. Occasional and recreational use of marijuana does not produce tolerance. Among chronic and heavy marijuana users, tolerance to the effects of the drug has appeared and some users report a kind of reverse tolerance, in which regular users become more sensitive to the effects of the drug than novice or irregular users.

Addiction. No notable withdrawal signs occur after cessation of marijuana use among infrequent, occasional, or regular users. Heavy and chronic use of marijuana does produce symptoms of withdrawal. The National Institute of Drug Abuse (NIDA) defines heavy marijuana use as smoking 1–3 joints per day.

Marijuana Issues. Marijuana use has lead to such a variety of myths, speculation, and false beliefs that a review of these issues is critical for the scientific status of marijuana as a drug and for counseling the marijuana abuser. If the counselor conveys information that does not correspond with the life experiences of the marijuana abuser, effective counseling will not occur.

(A) Is Marijuana a "Safe" Drug? Absolutely not! The notion that marijuana is a safe drug developed in the 1960s, when hallucinogens were resulting in bad trips and visits to emergency rooms and marijuana overdoses were infrequent. Marijuana users were not experiencing bad trips or getting symptoms of withdrawal, so the idea spread that marijuana was safe and could be used without problems. This has placed us in a reverse position than is normally the case when a new drug is introduced. The FDA is responsible for determining the safety and efficacy of a new drug before it is permitted to be prescribed or sold over the counter. With the appearance of marijuana into our society, people were using marijuana and presumed it was safe, until it proved otherwise.

Using marijuana with alcohol is particularly dangerous. Too much alcohol turns into poison in the body. The body's natural defense against poison is to expel the substance by vomiting before it acts on critical body functions. Marijuana reduces nausea and suppresses the vomiting reflex, thereby increasing the chance of an accidental alcohol overdose and death.

Marijuana causes difficulty in concentration, slows reaction time, reduces muscle coordination and visual and time perception, and may create a sense of gaiety. This ego state does not support the safe operation of machinery, as in driving a car. Marijuana reduces glare recovery time, the ability of the eyes to adjust to sudden increases in light reaching the retina, as from a passing motor vehicle at night.

(B) Is Marijuana a Gateway Drug?   The "stepping stone" hypothesis proposes that marijuana use leads to use of hard drugs, especially heroin. Drug histories of heroin addicts indicated that marijuana was their first illicit drug, followed by amphetamines, and then by heroin, and scientists reasoned that marijuana was a stepping stone to heroin addiction. Today, most experts agree that no conclusive evidence demonstrates that the effects of marijuana are causally linked to the use of other drugs.

(C) Does Marijuana Lead to Criminal Behavior?   Marijuana use *is a crime* in most states, so technically, the answer to this question is yes. However, if acquisition, possession, and use are decriminalized, no reliable evidence suggests that marijuana causes crime or violent behavior. Marijuana use is underrepresented in studies of assaultive criminals. Animal studies on aggression and marijuana indicate that the drug reduces spontaneous aggression in a variety of social interactions. Animals do show an increase in aggression when stressed in an experiment and then given marijuana intravenously. Marijuana reduces predatory aggression in animals that are not stressed.

(D) Marijuana and Learning.   Under the acute effects of marijuana, learning is impaired. In animal experimentation, marijuana consistently disrupts the performance of previously learned tasks, slows the ability to learn new tasks, disrupts the ability to learn complex discrimination tasks, and interferes with short-term memory. When the marijuana user returns to the drugless state, learning capacity returns to normal levels. In general, few or no problems in learning have appeared with occasional or recreational use. However, more learning problems have appeared among chronic and heavy users. Recent evidence suggests that cognitive impairments linger in heavy marijuana users (Block & Ghoneim, 1993; Pope, Gruber, & Yurgelun-Todd, 1995; 1996).

(E) Amotivational Syndrome.   Some believe that marijuana affects motivation. The idea first was generated in the late 1960s and early 1970s when so-called "potheads" were observed to be dropping out of school. Allegedly, chronic marijuana use lead to their lack of interest in school.

The amotivational syndrome is not an official diagnostic label. Some of the symptoms that have appeared in the literature include:

- Loss of interest, general apathy, and passivity
- Loss of desire to work or to be productive
- Loss of energy and a general state of tiredness
- A moody and depressed state of mind, with an inability to handle frustration
- Inability to concentrate
- Decreased ability to master new material or organize multiple ideas
- Impairment in verbal facility
- Slovenliness in habits and appearance, including deterioration in hygiene

Loss of ambition, interest, and achievement may interact with some personality traits. The main problem in demonstrating that marijuana use is causative is separating the effects of predisposing personality problems from the effects of marijuana. Perhaps some people who turn to marijuana are experiencing problems in life and would be societal dropouts even if they did not use marijuana. Others may be socially deviant and marijuana use may be part of that deviance.

(F) Marijuana and Psychopathology.   Marijuana can produce a variety of psychiatric disorders. A psychotic reaction is a potential risk in using marijuana, but is rare and may appear only in individuals who are already at risk for developing psychosis. Acute panic reactions are more frequent, especially among novice users who are unfamiliar with the effects of the drug. Flashbacks also have been induced by marijuana among previous users of hallucinogens. In general, the more emotionally unstable the user, the greater the risk for experiencing a psychiatric disorder when taking marijuana.

(G) Marijuana and Physical Problems.

■ *Lung Damage.* Marijuana produces serious problems with the lungs because of the constituents of marijuana smoke and the manner in which marijuana is smoked.

First, all the negative aspects of using tobacco apply to marijuana. Marijuana has most of the constituents of tobacco, except nicotine, and has THC, which produces effects of its own. Second, the way marijuana is smoked is particularly damaging to the lungs. Typically, marijuana users inhale deeply and try to hold the breath to sustain the exposure of the marijuana and maximize the absorption of fumes. Furthermore, they use various paraphernalia designed to intensify the high by allowing more marijuana exposure into the lungs: "Power hitters," "buzz bombs," and "star war pipes" produce streams of smoke into the mouth, windpipe, and lungs. Gas masks prevent exhaled smoke from escaping, allowing the marijuana smoke to be inhaled again and again. Roach clips allow users to smoke the joint to the point where nothing is left. Third, marijuana contains more substances that are known to cause cancer than tobacco does. Marijuana contains more tar than tobacco and it stays in the body longer than other tobacco constituents. A rule of thumb is that smoking one joint is equivalent to smoking 16 cigarettes.

■ *Brain Damage.* The possibility that marijuana results in permanent or long-lasting changes in the brain cannot absolutely be ruled out, although research suggests that marijuana does not cause brain damage with infrequent use. It does produce a temporary impairment in brain functioning, cannabis intoxication, which is reversed when the effects of the drug wear off. However, no neurological study has demonstrated any permanent brain damage after marijuana use. Researchers have reported no differences on neurological and neuropsychological tests between groups of marijuana users and non-users. Implanting electrodes deep within the brains of monkeys and scalp recording techniques demonstrated changes in cell structures in animals that was related to marijuana smoke exposure equivalent to a daily joint for five days per week for up to six months. However, such microscopic changes were not noticeable at the behavioral level. Studies using computerized transaxial tomography (CAT scan) a technique for visualizing the anatomy and functioning of the brain, found no cerebral atrophy in men who used marijuana regularly.

■ *Chromosome Damage.* The issue of birth defects and of chromosome damage became prominent after the tragic international experience with thalidomide—a tranquilizer whose use by pregnant women resulted in many deformed babies. NIDA reports no convincing evidence that marijuana causes clinically significant chromosome damage, although, like other drugs, its use is contraindicated for pregnant women.

■ *Immune Response.* Scientists have also studied whether marijuana affects the body's ability to fight disease and infection by impairing the immune system. Earlier studies reported a suppression of the immune system in animals, but at higher doses than commonly used in the street. Later studies have not detected any consistent suppression of the immune system. Epidemiological studies comparing the incidence and prevalence of various diseases and infections between users and non-users, particularly at college health centers, have not shown higher rates of disease or infections than would be expected if the immune system were damaged. However, more lengthy studies are needed.

■ *Sexual Functioning.* Most scientists agree that any effects of marijuana on sexual activity are because of its action on higher brain centers causing a reduction in inhibitions. Marijuana does not directly affect the sexual apparatus or its emotional centers in the brain. Some in the general public believe that marijuana use results in promiscuity and loss of control over sexual impulses: It is interesting that the same drug that is alleged to result in a loss of drive, motivation, and energy and which can, in fact, result in passivity, is the drug alleged to lead to sexual aggressiveness.

Marijuana seems to intensify a variety of sensory experiences, prolongs the perception of the passage of time, produces disinhibited states, and may produce an increase in affectional bonding between people. It is understandable that increases in sexual desire have been reported under this drug-induced state. Surveys of marijuana users report that sexual activity correlate with degree and duration of marijuana use. Females report an increase in sexual desire toward familiar partners and males report an increase in desire toward familiar and unfamiliar partners. Marijuana may influence sexual activity, but its effects are mild and not compelling. Closer to the truth may be that marijuana's effects on sexual functioning depend more on the personality of the user and the expectations that the user has about marijuana's effect on sexual ability.

Marijuana does not produce longer duration of intercourse, it does not increase the number of orgasms, and it does not necessarily increase the frequency of sexual activity. It has not been shown to be causally related to the commission of sexually aggressive assaults, rapes, or other sexual crimes consistently.

■ *Endocrine and Reproductive Functioning.* Research is now shedding light on marijuana's role in the functioning of the gonadal-hormonal system. Compared to nonusers, chronic marijuana users have lower levels of testosterone (the male sex hormone), lower sperm counts, and lowered sperm motility. These conditions are reversed when users discontinue the drug. Chronic marijuana use in females has been associated with difficult menstrual cycles, failure to ovulate, or shorter periods of fertility. Animal studies suggest that marijuana affects estrogen, the principal female sex hormone, and progesterone, a reproductive hormone. This evidence suggests that marijuana should be avoided by sexually developing teen-age girls and women during childbearing years.

■ *Cardiac Functioning.* Marijuana increases heart rate as much as 50%. Tachycardia is the most prominent physiological response to an acute dose. This effect is temporary and of little consequence in a healthy adult. Patients who have already developed cardiovascular disease should refrain from marijuana use. They acquire chest pains—angina pectoris—more rapidly and with less effort when using marijuana than when using tobacco.

■ *Legalization and Decriminalization.* Legalizing marijuana would allow its distribution and sales in a manner similar to tobacco. Decriminalizing marijuana would change the penalties for small amounts of the still-illegal drug intended for personal use would be similar to a traffic fine.

(H) Marijuana and Medicine. Marijuana's potential role in the treatment of disease has been explored for many years. Recently, interest has intensified among politicians and researchers.

1. *Treatment of Nausea and Vomiting.* Perhaps the most important role for marijuana and its derivative, THC, is possible use for the treatment of nausea and vomiting that often accompany cancer chemotherapy. The drug has been given on an experimental basis to cancer patients who have responded unfavorably to the more traditional antinausea and antiemetic drugs. Preliminary evidence is inconclusive. It seems to work for some patients but not for others. Some patients do not like the accompanying drunken-like state, while others enjoy the tranquilization. Sometimes marijuana's side effects result in patients discontinuing the drug. Some patients even report tolerance: They no longer get high but do experience a reduction of nausea and vomiting.

A recent survey asked clinical oncologists—doctors who treat cancer—how useful they considered Marinol (the synthetic form of THC) in controlling nausea and vomiting. Marinol ranked ninth on a list of antiemtic drugs of oncologist's drug preferences for treating mild to moderate nausea or vomiting caused by chemotherapy, and ranked sixth for treating cases of severe nausea and vomiting (Schwartz, 1994).

Some patients argue that they get better relief from smokable marijuana than from oral Marinol, but they would have to smoke 4 to 6 joints daily, resulting in short-term memory problems and continuous intoxication.

2. *Treatment of Glaucoma.* Glaucoma is a disease of the visual system, often leading to blindness, and caused by a buildup of pressure in the eye. Marijuana reduces this intraocular pressure, either smoked or taken as THC. Problems exist, however, in determining the right dosage and in finding ways to reduce marijuana's other side effects. Glaucomas are most prevalent in the elderly, who often do not enjoy the drunken feeling produced by marijuana. THC eyedrops do not have similar system-wide effects, but users develop tolerance, making eye-drop preparations impractical for routine treatment of glaucoma. The long-term safety and efficacy of using marijuana to treat glaucoma has not been established.

3. *Treatment for Asthma.* Marijuana has some ability to dilate the lung's air passages (broncodilation). Marijuana cigarettes also irritate the lungs and chronic users sometimes report coughs and bronchitis. Oral THC avoids these irritants of the respiratory tract, but the possible medicinal effects are delayed as the drug awaits absorption in the gastrointestinal system: It is ineffective for rapid relief of asthmatic broncospasms.

4. *Treatment for Epileptic Convulsions.* Animal experimentation demonstrates that marijuana has paradoxical effects. It both increases and decreases seizure thresholds. This suggests that different ingredients in marijuana produce differential effects on seizure activity. THC has been shown to reduce seizure activity, leading to speculation that one or more of its constituents might have some utility in the treatment of epilepsy and related seizure disorders. Street marijuana would be of little value in this regard, because THC's cannabinol is present in infinitesimal amounts compared to laboratory studies, which give cannabinol in therapeutic doses.

5. *Treatment for Multiple Sclerosis.* A small number of studies have reported that marijuana resulted in lowered spasticity (involuntary muscle contractions) in paraplegics and in patients with advanced multiple sclerosis. The evidence is, as yet, inconclusive about marijuana's possible role in seizure-spectrum diseases.

6. *Treatment for Anorexia.* Anorexia or loss of appetite is a growing problem in the United States. Street-marijuana users often report an "attack of the munchies," or an increased desire for food. Some self-reports say that marijuana has enhanced the perceived quality of food eaten. Thus, marijuana may have some appetite-stimulating properties that would be valuable for treating loss of appetite, which can also appear in cases of severe depression. Reports of marijuana's appetite stimulation effects are largely anecdotal: Experimentation to date is insufficient to offer definitive conclusions.

In summary, there is little evidence that marijuana is useful in present-day medicine although experimentation may continue. Any applications probably will be through synthesized or chemically-related products, not street marijuana.

Club Drugs

A club drug is a vague term for a variety of drugs used at nightclubs or raves. Users of club drugs typically are in their teens or early twenties.

The main club drugs are MDMA, GHB, and rohypnol, ketamine, and methamphetamine.

MDMA.   Ecstasy is an amphetamine analogue with stimulant and hallucinogenic properties. Effects include an increase of affectional bonding between users, mild hallucinations, and a feeling of being at peace. These effects can last from 3 to 6 hours, while side effects, such as depression, confusion, anxiety, insomnia, and paranoia, can last up to two weeks, depending on the dose. Recreational dose is one or two 60mg to 120mg tablets.

MDMA blocks the re-uptake of the chemical transmitter serotonin, thereby interfering with neural impulses. This excess of serotonin at the synapse results in the psychological effects of the drug.

Short-term physical effects include increased heart rate, sweating, chills, increased blood pressure, blurred vision, muscle tension, and involuntary teeth-clenching—all amphetamine-related effects. Long-term effects have yet to be determined, because MDMA abuse is a relatively new phenomenon. While MDMA is not physically addicting, tolerance to this drug does develop.

GHB.   Liquid G is a clear, colorless, and odorless liquid, but it may come in tablet or pill form. It had been used in the 1960s as an anesthetic but its use was discontinued because of problematic side effects. It became a recreational drug in Europe in the 1990s and spread to the United States. The drug had been used by bodybuilders for increased muscle mass.

The recreational effects of GHB are similar to those of alcohol. GHB is quite dangerous. There is a fine line between recreational use and overdose, which cause coma and death, particularly when the drug is taken with alcohol.

GHB is a CNS depressant. Sexual predators spike a drink with this drug, causing the ingester to become intoxicated, sedated, and even unconscious. Frequent ingestion results in withdrawal effects, which include anxiety, sleep problems, and general drowsiness that could last for several days. Whether GHB is physically addicting is presently under investigation.

Ketamine.   Ketamine is a non-barbiturate anesthetic, and produces effects similar to LSD and PCP. It comes in a clear liquid, white powder, or pill form. It had been used mostly in veterinary medicine but began to be abused in the United States in the 1980s and 1990s. It is taken intramuscularly or intravenously, snorted, or in oral form. Psychologically the drug produces a kind of dissociative state with impaired perception, sexual stimulation, a feeling of relaxation, and an intensification of sounds and colors.

Side effects of ketamine include muscle numbness, slurred speech, feelings of invulnerability and exaggerated strength, and occasional aggressive and violent behavior. It also can produce a hallucinogenic effect akin to an out-of-body experience. Its anesthetic effects stops the user from feeling pain. More severe effects include loss of coordination, vomiting, and convulsions. Physical dependence and withdrawal are not common with this drug, but psychological dependence can develop.

All of these drugs become more dangerous when they are used with other drugs—especially with alcohol and marijuana.

Nicotine

Given the serious nature of other abused drugs with which substance abuse counselors have to deal, why are smoking-related problems included in this volume? *Nicotine,* the main psychoactive ingredient in tobacco, *is a drug.* Millions use this drug daily, want to quit, but have trouble doing so, and so keep using it. Most who do quit experience a *nicotine withdrawal syndrome,* which is reversed or reduced by taking more of the drug—another smoke. Continued use of this drug over time results in *tobacco-related disorders:* The APA has includes tobacco dependence and tobacco withdrawal in its manual of psychiatric disorders. Tobacco use demonstrates every aspect of the addiction cycle, including *dosage escalation* (i.e., smoking more and more until a comfortable level of the drug is reached), *drug use* to maintain the habit, *tolerance* to the drug (gradually built up over time), a *pattern of dependence,* and a *withdrawal pattern* that appears upon discontinuation of the drug. Finally, many people *relapse* after abstaining for varying periods of time.

There is no behavioral toxicity associated with smoking. The adverse effects of tobacco stem exclusively from chronic use, whereas other drugs of abuse may induce acute reactions upon a single administration. There are no reports of tobacco overdose, nor does it induce metal illness. Tobacco users do not engage in aberrant behavior and are not dangerous to others, except when their smoking interferes with others' breathing. Using tobacco does not result in lowered productivity—at least not until the health consequences of tobacco use begin to exert their toll.

This discussion focuses on smoking cigarettes, but most of the material applies as well to smoking cigars and pipes and chewing tobacco.

Effects of Nicotine.   Nicotine is a stimulant and behaves much like amphetamines, though it is not as strong. It increases blood pressure, heart rate, and provides a sense of increased energy.

While people smoke for nicotine, they die from *tar*—the total amount of particulate matter after subtracting nicotine and moisture. Tars represent millions of chemical particles and produce most of the tobacco taste. When they condense from smoke, they form a smelly, tar-like substance. More than 1,200 different toxic chemicals have been identified in tobacco or tobacco smoke, including some poisons that probably are assimilated into the tobacco products through the use of fertilizers and insecticides. Tar contains more than 30 chemicals known to cause cancer.

Carbon Monoxide.   Of the at least 20 noxious vapors in tobacco, the most deadly is the colorless, odorless carbon monoxide gas, the same gas that kills people when they operate a car in an unventilated space. Carbon monoxide prevents red blood cells from picking up enough oxygen and inhibits cells from giving up oxygen as fast as the tissues need it. This eventually results in shortness of breath from insufficient oxygen. While nicotine stimulates the heart to beat faster, requiring more oxygen, carbon monoxide results in the body having less oxygen than it needs. The long-term results are cardiovascular disease and coronary heart disease.

Withdrawal.   Some people experience no signs of withdrawal upon cessation of smoking, while others do experience the nicotine withdrawal syndrome: Nervousness, irritability, lightheadedness or dizziness, sleepiness and reduced energy, itching, or a feeling of excess weight in the chest are some of its symptoms. Not all of these symptoms will occur but one or more of them will be present in withdrawal.

Why Do People Start Smoking?   Motivations for the onset of tobacco use are unquestionably social and psychological in nature and origin: curiosity, rebelliousness, social pressure, modeling behaviors from peers, parents, and idols and the effects and influence of advertisements. Most smoking begins during adolescence where these variables are particularly potent.

Why Do People Continue to Smoke?   Researchers have identified variables associated with continuing tobacco use:

- *Stimulation.* Some experience energy and a sense of well being when they smoke.
- *Handling.* Some people need something to do with their hands and enjoy manipulating the tobacco products. They use unusual lighters, blow smoke rings, and experiment with how long they can hold smoke in their lungs.
- *Relaxation.* Smoking is associated with pleasurable effects and many find it relaxing. All smokers report a particular time when smoking is most enjoyable.

- *Crutch.* Smoking can act as a tranquilizer. Indeed the rate of smoking among psychiatric patients—especially alcoholics—is higher than that of the general population.
- *Craving.* Some smoke because they think they cannot get along without a cigarette and give in to every temptation to smoke.
- *Habit and Dependence.* Some smoke because they are addicted, and others out of habit. More and more evidence is accumulating that nicotine has more addictive properties than once believed. It is difficult to separate the effects of repeated positive reinforcement associated with smoking combined with the dependence-producing effects of nicotine. If a smoker inhales, nicotine reaches the brain in about 7 seconds, providing near-instantaneous reinforcing effects. A user who smokes one pack a day and gets 7 to 10 puffs per cigarette, gets about 50,000–70,000 "zaps" of reinforcement to the brain each year from cigarette smoking. That's more "zaps" than from almost any other known form of drug abuse. Thus, smoking appears to be a kind of over-learned habit associated with the addicting properties of nicotine.

Some exceptions emerge to the idea that nicotine is purely addicting. Injections of nicotine, nicotine chewing gum, and nicotine pills are not viewed as pleasurable by research subjects, whereas nicotine delivered via tobacco is perceived as pleasurable among tobacco users. On one hand, if nicotine were purely addicting, route of administration would make little difference to the user. On the other hand, smokers tend to regulate puff rate, puff size, and amount of inhalation, suggesting that they are regulating their blood nicotine levels. Nontobacco smoking products, such as cigarettes made from other materials, like lettuce, and low nicotine cigarettes are not popular and lose out in taste tests. This suggests that smokers smoke for nicotine and not simply out of habit.

The WHO has concluded that tobacco produces relatively little stimulation of the CNS. Compared to other dependence-producing drugs, tobacco causes little disturbance in perception, mood, thinking, behavior, or motor function. Recently, however, the Phillip Morris Company, a major U.S. producer of tobacco products, has admitted that tobacco is addicting.

Why Do People Want to Stop Smoking?

- *Health.* Some people want to quit smoking before they experience a serious health problem, others want to reduce the seriousness of a health problem or to prevent it from becoming worse, and still others want to reduce the risks of developing a smoking-related habit.
- *Financial.* Smoking is expensive and the costs of smoking escalate with inflation and taxes. When people add up the cost of their habit, they often reflect on what they could have done with this amount of money and decide to quit.
- *Social Pressure.* More and more limitations are being placed on smoking in public places. It has become socially acceptable to tell smokers that you do mind if they smoke.

- *Parental Example.* Parents who tell their children not to smoke yet light up themselves realize the hypocrisy of this behavior and want to stop to set a good example for their children.
- *Esthetics.* Smoking causes bad breath, produces an odor on clothes, and permeates rooms with tobacco smells. It stains the teeth and fingers. Ashtray residue is unsightly. Someone spitting chewing tobacco into bowls is a revolting sight. When people decide they want fresh breath, fresh-smelling clothes, and a fresh appearance, they stop smoking.
- *Personal Mastery.* Some stop smoking to demonstrate that they have personal control over their lives.

Why Do People Relapse?

- *Withdrawal Symptoms.* Some have trouble coping with the withdrawal syndrome and return to smoking to feel better.
- *Stress and Frustration.* If a person has learned that smoking helps them feel less stressed, encountering a stressful or frustrating situation acts as a trigger to return to smoking.
- *Social Pressure.* Some people taunt quitters to test their resolve. Also, if a user's social group or sexual partner continues to smoke, there may be real or implied pressure to return to former habits.
- *Alcohol Consumption.* Many associate smoking with drinking. When they take a drink, they experience a strong desire for a cigarette.
- *Conditioned Environmental Cues.* The pairing of alcohol with tobacco is but one example of a larger process in which certain cues in the environment stimulate the desire to smoke. When users are in that same environment and experience those same cues, they feel the urge to use—smoke.

Medical Problems.

- *Heart Disease.* While not all heart problems are smoking-related, tobacco use is a big risk factor in developing high blood pressure, after heredity and high cholesterol levels are taken into account. Coronary heart disease is a leading cause of death among smokers.
- *Respiratory Diseases.* Cigarette smoking is a major cause of chronic obstructive pulmonary disease, chronic bronchitis, and emphysema. Smoking inhibits the cilia, hair-like structures in the lungs, from cleaning the respiratory tract and gradually destroys them. Smoker's cough develops as the body's alternate method of attempting to rid the lungs of foreign material. As this process worsens and the cilia are destroyed, emphysema results, producing immense difficulties in breathing. Smoking also affects the lungs' ability to resist infections, so smokers have a higher incidence of lung infections.

- *Cancer.* Lung cancer is the biggest risk associated with smoking, but smoking is also implicated in cancers of the larynx, pharynx, oral cavity, lips, esophagus, pancreas, and bladder. The incidence of cancer rises in direct proportion to the number of cigarettes smoked.
- *Cigarettes and Pregnancy.* Nicotine and carbon monoxide from cigarettes retard the growth of the fetus, resulting in an infant with low birth weight, which in turn creates further medical problems. There is also a correlation between women who smoke and rates of stillbirths and spontaneous abortions.
- *Smoker's Wrinkles.* Smoker's wrinkles are ridges in the facial skin, particularly around the eyes, forehead, and cheeks. After controlling for the effects of age and an outdoor lifestyle, the severity of wrinkling is correlated with a history of habitual smoking.

Social Problems.

- *Fires.* Cigarette smoking is a leading cause of fires and deaths from fires. People fall asleep when smoking in bed, or flip not fully extinguished cigarettes into a trash container. Authorities recommend the manufacturing of a self-extinguishing cigarette that will die out after a brief period of time if it is not smoked.

- *Sidestream Smoke.* Sidestream or secondhand smoke is cigarette smoke exhaled into the air. Exposure to this kind of smoke also is referred to as passive smoking. When nonsmokers breathe this smoke-filled air, their blood pressure and heart rate increase, and the carbon monoxide gas reduces the oxygen levels in their blood, too. When nonsmokers leave a smoke-filled room, it takes hours for the carbon monoxide to leave their blood. Nonsmokers develop similar health risks to smokers when they are repeatedly exposed to sidestream smoke.

Most people are aware of many of these risks and dangers but continue to smoke. This is because the short-term consequences of smoking are rewarding, whereas the long-term consequences are aversive. The diseases associated with smoking take decades to develop, during which time the brain of the smoker is reinforced after each puff.

CHAPTER SUMMARY

This chapter introduced some main concepts in pharmacology and pharmacokinetics and a number of other variables that affect the drug user's psychological experience. It reviewed the major drug classes, presenting their main effects in the medical, psychological, and social domains. It cited public health problems. Knowledge of drugs and their effects helps counselors understand patients' drug use and leads to tailored treatment interventions. This is more fully addressed in the next chapter.

SOURCES OF INFORMATION

Abraham, H. D. (1983). Visual phenomenology of the LSD flashback. *Archives of General Psychiatry, 40,* 884–889.

Abraham, H. D., & Wolf, E. (1988). Visual function in past users of LAS: Psychophysical findings. *Journal of Abnormal Psychology, 97,* 443–447.

Adel, E. L. (1980). Fetal alcohol syndrome: Behavioral teratology. *Psychological Bulletin, 87,* 29–50.

Alarcon, R. D., Dickinson, W. A., & Dohn, H. H. (1982). Flashback phenomena: Clinical and diagnostic dilemmas. *Journal of Nervous and Mental Disease, 170,* 21–223.

Berry, J., van Gorp, W. G., Herzberg, D. S., Hinkin, C., Boone, K., Steinman, L., & Wilkins, J. N. (1993). Neuropsychological deficits in abstinent cocaine abusers: Preliminary findings after two weeks of abstinence. *Drug and Alcohol Dependence, 32,* 231–237.

Block, R. I., & Ghoneim, M. M. (1993). Effects of chronic marijuana use on human cognition. *Psychopharmacology, 110,* 219–228.

Carroll, C. R. (1985). *Drugs in modern society.* Dubuque, IA: Brown.

Cohen, S. (1980, January). Marijuana: Pulmonary issues. *Drug Abuse and Alcoholism Newsletter.* Vista Hill Foundation. *9.*

Cohen, S. (1982, October). Alcohol and malnutrition. *Drug Abuse and Alcoholism Newsletter.* Vista Hill Foundation. *11.*

Cohen, S. (1992, December). Marijuana and the public health: An analysis of four major reports. *Drug Abuse and Alcoholism Newsletter.* Vista Hill Foundation. *11.*

Cohen, S. (1983, May). Marijuana use detection: The state of the art. *Drug Abuse and Alcoholism Newsletter.* Vista Hill Foundation. *12.*

Cohen, S. (1983, June). The rise and fall of the look-alikes. *Drug Abuse and Alcoholism Newsletter.* Vista Hill Foundation. *12.*

Davis, B. L. (1982). The PCP epidemic: A critical review. *The International Journal of the Addictions, 17,* 1137–1155.

Decker, S., Fins, J., & Frances, R. (1987). Cocaine and chest pain. *Hospital and Community Psychiatry, 38,* 464–466.

Devane, W. A., Hanus, L., Breuer, A., Pertwee, R. G., Stevenson, L. A., Griffin, D., Gibson, D., Mandelbaum, A., Etinger, A., & Mechoulam, R. (1992). Isolation and structure of a brain constituent that binds to the cannabinoid receptor. *Science, 258,* 1882–1884.

Doweiko, H. E. (1996). *Concepts of chemical dependence* (3rd ed.). Pacific Grove, CA: Brooks/ Cole.

Dusek, D. E., & Girdano, D. A. (1993). *Drugs: A factual account* (5th ed.). New York: McGraw-Hill.

Estroff, T. W., & Gold, S. (1986). Psychiatric presentations of marijuana abuse. *Psychiatric Annals, 16,* 221–224.

Eyre, S. L., Rounsaville, B. J., & Kleber, H. D. (1982). History of childhood hyperactivity in a clinic population of opiate addicts. *Journal of Nervous and Mental Disease, 170,* 522–529.

Felder, C. C., Briley, E. M., Axelrod, J., Simpson, J. T., Mckie, K., & Devane, W. A. (1993). Anandamide, an endogeneous cannabimimetic eicosanoid, binds to cloned human cannabinoid receptor and stimulates receptor-mediated signal transduction. *Proceedings of the National Academy of Sciences, 90,* 7656–7660.

Fiore, M. C., Bailey, W. C., Cohen, S. J., et al. (2000). *Treating tobacco abuse and dependence: Clinical practice guideline.* Rockville, MD: U.S. Department of Health and Human Service. Public Health Service.

Fischman, M. W. (1988). Behavioral pharmacology of cocaine. *Journal of Clinical Psychiatry, 49,* 7–10.

Fishbein, D. H., & Pease, S. E. (1996). *The dynamics of drug abuse.* Boston: Allyn & Bacon.

Gawin, F. H., & Kleber, H. D. (1986). Abstinence symptomotology and psychiatric diagnosis in cocaine abusers: Clinical observations. *Archives of General Psychiatry, 43,* 107–113.

Goldberg, R. (1997). *Drugs across the spectrum.* Englewood, CO: Morton.

Graeven, D. B., Sharp, J. G., & Glatt, S. (1981). Acute effects of Phencyclidine (PCP) on chronic and recreational users. *American Journal of Drug and Alcohol Abuse, 8,* 39–50.

Grabowski, J., & Dworkin, S. I. (1985). Cocaine: An overview of current issues. *The International Journal of the Addictions, 20,* 1065–1088.

Grant, I., & Judd, L. L. (1976). Neuropsychological and EEG disturbances in polydrug users. *American Journal of Psychiatry, 133,* 1039–1042.

Grant, I., Mohns, L., Miller, M., & Reitan, R. M. (1976). A neuropsychological study of polydrug users. *Archives of General Psychiatry, 33,* 973–978.

Hall, W. C., Talbert, R. L., & Ereshefsky, L. (1990). Cocaine abuse and its treatment. *Pharmacotherapy, 10,* 47–65.

Halikas, J., Weller, R., & Morse, C. (1982). Effects of regular marijuana use on sexual performance. *Journal of Psychoactive Drugs, 14,* 59–70.

Householder, J., Hatcher, R., Burns, W., & Chasnoff, I. (1982). Infants born to narcotic-addicted mothers. *Psychological Bulletin, 92,* 453–468.

Itkomen, J., Schnoll, S., & Glassroth, J. (1984). Pulmonary dysfunction in "freebase" cocaine users. *Archives of Internal Medicine, 144,* 2195–2197.

Khantzian, E. J., & Treece, C. (1995). DSM-III psychiatric diagnosis of narcotic addicts: Recent findings. *Archives of General Psychiatry, 42,* 1067–1071.

Kinney, J., & Leaton, G. (1986). *Loosening the grip: A handbook of alcohol information.* St. Louis, MO: Times Mirror/Mosby College Publishing.

Kokkinidis, L., & Anisman, H. (1980). Amphetamine models of paranoid schizophrenia: An overview and elaboration of animal experimentation. *Psychological Bulletin, 88,* 551–579.

Kosten, T. R. (1990). Neurobiology of abused drugs: Opioids and stimulants. *Journal of Nervous and Mental Disease, 178,* 217–227.

Kosten, T. R., Rounsaville, B. J., & Kleber, H. D. (1982). DSM-III personality disorders in opiate addicts. *Comprehensive Psychiatry, 23,* 572–581.

Lichtenstein, E. (1982). The smoking problem: A behavioral perspective. *Journal of Consulting and Clinical Psychology, 50,* 804–819.

Lyden, S., Rounsaville, B. J., Eyre, S., & Kleber, H. D. (1983). Suicide attempts in treated opiate addicts. *Comprehensive Psychiatry, 24,* 79–89.

MacDonald, B. I., & Czechowicz, D. (1986). Marijuana: A pediatric overview. *Psychiatric Annals, 16,* 215–217.

McWilliams, S. A., & Tuttle, R. J. (1973). Long-term psychological effects of LSD. *Psychological Bulletin, 79,* 341–351.

NIAAA. (1989, August). Alcohol withdrawal syndrome. *Alcohol Alert.* Rockville, MD: National Institute on Alcohol Abuse and Alcoholism. 1–4.

NIAAA. (1993, January). Alcohol and the liver. *Al-cohol Alert.* Rockville, MD: National Institute on Alcohol Abuse and Alcoholism. *19,* 1–4.

NIDA Notes (1993). *Research advances.* Rockville, MD: National Institute on Drug Abuse. September/October. *12,* 5–7.

NIDA Notes (1996, March/April). *Facts about marijuana and marijuana abuse.* Rockville, MD: National Institute on Drug Abuse. *15,* 1–4.

O'Brien, C. P., Woody, G. E., & McLellan, A. T. (1984). Psychiatric disorders in opioid-dependent patients. *Journal of Clinical Psychiatry, 45,* 9–13.

Platt, J. J. (1986). *Heroin addiction: Theory, research, and treatment* (2nd ed.). Malabar, FL: Krieger.

Pope, H. G., Gruber, A. J., & Yurgelum-Todd, D. (1995). The residual neuropsychological effects of cannabis: The current status of research. *Drug and Alcohol Dependence, 38,* 25–34.

Pope, H. G., & Yurgelum-Todd, D. (1996, February 12). The residual cognitive effects of heavy marijuana use in college students. *Journal of the American Medical Association, 275,* 521–527.

Powell, D. J., & Fuller, R. W. (1983). Marijuana and sex: Strange bedpartners. *Journal of Psychoactive Drugs, 15,* 269–280.

Ray, O., & Ksir, C. (1993). *Drugs, society, and human behavior* (6th ed.). St. Louis, MO: Mosby.

Rounsaville, B. J., Jones, C., Novelly, R. A., & Kleber, H. D. (1982). Neuropsychological functioning in opiate addicts. *Journal of Nervous and Mental Disease, 170,* 209–216.

Rounsaville, B. J., Weissman, M. M., Kleber, H., & Wilber, C. (1982). Heterogeneity of psychiatric diagnosis in treated opiate addicts. *Archives of General Psychiatry, 39,* 161–166.

Rounsaville, B. J., Weissman, M. M., Wilber, C. (1982), & Kleber, H. D. (1983). Identifying alcoholism in treated opiate addicts. *American Journal of Psychiatry, 140,* 764–766.

Siegel, R. J. K. (1978). Cocaine hallucinations. *American Journal of Psychiatry, 135,* 309–314.

Smoking cessation: Information for specialists. (1996). Rockville, MD: U.S. Department of Health and Human Services, Agency for Health Care Policy and Research, Centers for Disease Control and Prevention.

Spotts, J. V., & Shontz, F. C. (1984). Drug-induced ego states. I. Cocaine: Phenomenology and implications. *The International Journal of the Addictions, 19,* 119–151.

Spotts, J. V., & Shontz, F. C. (1984). The phenomenological structure of drug-induced ego states. II. Barbiturates and sedative-hypnotics: Phenomenology and implications. *The International Journal of the Addictions, 19,* 295–326.

Starssman, R. J. (1984). Adverse reactions to psychedelic drugs: A review of the literature. *Journal of Nervous and Mental Disease, 172,* 577–595.

Vardy, M. M. (1983). LSD psychosis or LSD-induced schizophrenia?: A methodological inquiry. *Archives of General Psychiatry, 40,* 877–883.

Weddington, W. W., Brown, B. S., Haertzen, C. A., Cone, E. J., Dax, E. M., Herning, R. I., & Michaelson, B. S. (1990). Changes in mood, craving, and sleep during short-term abstinence reported by male cocaine addicts. *Archives of General Psychiatry, 47,* 861–868.

Winters, W., Venturello, P., & Hanson, G. (1992). *Drugs and society.* Boston: Jones & Bartlett.

Young, T., Lawson, G. W., & Gacono, C. B. (1987). Clinical aspects of phencyclidine (PCP). *The International Journal of the Addictions, 22,* 1–15.

CHAPTER FOUR

ASSESSMENT AND DIAGNOSIS

This chapter discusses ways to assess substance abuse and the substance abuser, covering three commonly used tools for this process: clinical interviews, screening tests, and laboratory tests. However, the best assessment tool is the counselor. Substance abuse counselors are in the best position to interpret the patient's responses, behaviors, and test results except for medical and psychological tests. Accordingly, properly trained and experienced counselors should have faith in their own assessment, keeping a healthy, skeptical eye open for being manipulated, tricked, and misled.

ASSESSMENT PROBLEMS AND ISSUES

Counselors must recognize certain problems inherent in achieving complete assessment accuracy. (1) Terms are not definitive. "Abuse" to one counselor may be considered "dependence" by another counselor. (2) The natural history—the ebb and flow of symptoms and problems of abuse and dependence over time—is difficult to ascertain. Abusers may, in fact, own multiple histories, because the substance abusing patient population is heterogeneous. Nurco, Cisin, and Balter (1981 a,b,c) have produced evidence for types of substance abusers who vary in their behavior, symptoms, treatment episodes, use, and abstinence across the life-span. (3) Co-morbidities can mask substance abuse problems, and vice versa. (4) Motivation of the patient, the family and even a program or facility can affect the nature and quality of the assessment. (5) Special populations of abusers—women, minorities, elderly, children. and adolescents—have unique issues. All of these factors can affect and influence assessment accuracy.

PURPOSE OF ASSESSMENT

Counselors assess patients, not in a vacuum, but for specific purposes: (1) to evaluate the severity of a problem, (2) to establish risk relationships (e.g., comorbidities), (3) to diagnose, (4) to provide feedback to program staff, (5) to characterize the problem as individual or family, and (6) to guide treatment planning. The assessment itself should be multimodal—covering several domains of functioning, uniform—examining all clients systematically in the same way, and comprehensive.

METHODS OF ASSESSMENT

Clinical Interviews

The clinical interview is the most common assessment tool counselors use. Clinical interviews can be performed under structured or semistructured models. In the structured clinical interview, the counselor asks questions from a prepared list. The questions are identical for every patient. In a semistructured interview, the counselor asks questions that cover certain domains of functions, but the questions may vary from patient to patient. The counselor is required to assess certain areas in a semistructured interview but is free to probe more deeply, depending on the answers of the patient. Using a semistructured interview format that assesses critical elements and functional domains allows the counselor to develop a comprehensive treatment plan that is targeted to specific problems and that addresses individualized needs. Such an interview will feel more comfortable to the patient.

Reliability of Substance Abuse Reports.   Can counselors rely on the information given to them by substance abusers, who are known, as a group, to be in denial and who lie, trick, and manipulate? The answer is a qualified yes—if certain conditions are met. A large body of research has found a high degree of correspondence between life history information and data from collateral sources such as family, criminal records, and other significant informants, and that provided by the individual patient. Discrepancies have been attributed to normal memory decay, with a few exceptions. Alcoholics underestimate or underreport the amount of alcohol ingested and drug addicts overestimate or exaggerate the amount of drugs taken and underreport the extent of criminal activity. Drug addicts may also mask specific crimes.

These conclusions are based on counselor-client relationships in which trust has been established and clients believe that the information will be kept confidential and will be used to benefit them. To reduce evasiveness and suspiciousness, counselors can tell patients that the information cannot be released, except as otherwise specified by law, without their written consent and that it will be kept confidential and released only on a need-to-know basis. Also, counselors should tell patients how the information will be useful to them. When these conditions have been met, substance abusers are likely to give reliable and valid life history information (Craig, 1988).

If patients' suspicions have not been satisfactorily addressed, the information they provide may be inaccurate. However, once patients see that their counselor is honest and speaks truthfully, they increasingly will provide more reliable information over time.

Confidentiality.   Counselors must be aware of the federal regulation governing alcohol- and drug-abuse patient records (U.S. Department of Health, Education, and Welfare, 1987). This law is among the most restrictive and protective of mental health records. These are the essential provisions of extremely cumbersome confidentiality of alcohol and drug abuse records.

- All patient records involved in the assessment and treatment of substance abuse are confidential, except under certain exceptions. These include the requirement to report child and elder abuse and neglect, protecting patients who are a danger to themselves or to others, and to intervene when the patient expresses serious suicidal intent.
- In general, information may not be released without obtaining signed informed consent. Exceptions are for medical emergencies, to carry out a court order, to report child abuse or neglect, to protect others from a client who is deemed dangerous, and for research, audit, or program evaluation. Personally identifying information may be released in the latter case.
- Undercover agents or informants may not be enrolled in a substance abuse treatment program, unless they are given permission by a court order.
- A program may not acknowledge to law enforcement personnel whether a person is or is not attending a treatment program.

An unusual feature of this law is the requirement that programs inform patients of their right to confidentiality prior to collecting substance abuse information. Also, specific information must be given to patients as detailed in Table 4.1. Programs may duplicate this statement and give it to prospective patients.

Taping Clinical Interviews.   Session may be taped for many reasons, most commonly for supervisory or training purposes. Counselors may want to review their interviews to see how they sound to clients. Sometimes taping is done for self-improvement. Tapes also may be required for submission to review bodies for counselor certification programs. Counselors must get clients' written permission to tape. Even so, when covering legal areas, counselors should ask clients if they want to have the tape turned off. This reinforces the presentation of the interview as confidential and helps to avoid any possible self-incrimination by clients. If the legal system becomes aware that a tape is available, this tape may be subpoenaed in evidentiary discovery. Having the tape turned off for the legal inquiry reduces the value of the tape for subsequent legal proceedings pertaining to criminal behavior and further protects the client and maintains the integrity of the counselor and program.

Countertransference.   Countertransference may be defined as feelings aroused in the therapist by the patient. Substance abusers have the capacity to

TABLE 4.1   Confidentiality Statement for Substance Abusing Clients

The confidentiality of alcohol and drug abuse patient records maintained by this program is protected by Federal law and regulations. Generally, the program may not say to a person outside the program that a patient attends the program, or disclose any information identifying a patient as an alcohol or drug abuser. Unless

1. The patient consents in writing
2. The disclosure is allowed by a court order
3. The disclosure is made to medical personnel in a medical emergency or to qualified personnel for research, audit, or program evaluation.

- Violation of the Federal law and regulations by a program is a crime. Suspected violation may be reported to appropriate authorities in accordance with Federal regulations.
- Federal law and regulations do not protect any information about a crime committed by a patient either at the program or against any person who works for the program or about any threat to commit such a crime.
- Federal laws and regulations do not protect any information about suspected child abuse or neglect from being reported under State law to appropriate State or local authorities.

Source: U.S. Department of Health & Human Services, 1987.

engender powerful countertransference reactions. These patients can be aggressive, demanding, confrontational, insistent, and defensive and they enjoy exposing the vulnerabilities, inadequacies, and lack of knowledge of a therapist. Psychoanalysts called this trait "oral insatiability." Behaviors and lifestyle that usually accompany substance abuse, especially criminality, further create conditions for the development of countertransference. In the course of an interview, the patient may reveal information and details that strain even the most objective counselor not to experience strong emotional reactions.

In the face of such presentation, counselors may (1) act the role of a good parent rescuing a bad, impulsive child, (2) become angry when the patient challenges their authority or knowledge, (3) align with the patient by identifying with antiauthority stories or by vicariously romanticizing the abuser's lifestyle, or (4) by emotionally withdrawing, becoming indifferent, or feeling bored, angry, and burned out (Imhof, Hirsh, & Terenzi, 1983).

Counselors continually need to self-monitor their emotional reactions and seek consultation and supervision to ensure that they maintain objectivity throughout their contacts with patients. Counselors can use their subjective reactions diagnostically to reveal how patients affect others.

Recommended Interview Format

The content areas that follow will provide counselors with an in-depth and comprehensive evaluation of substance abusing patients. They should not be followed sequentially, but, by time the interview has been completed, each content area should have been assessed.

Mental Status.   Drugs and alcohol affect cognitive processes; therefore patients' mental status must be evaluated. The content of a typical mental status evaluation includes areas such as speech, articulation, thought content and thought processes, sensorium, judgment, affect regulation, impulsivity, orientation to time, place, and person, appearance, perception, concentration, memory, and insight. Occasionally these areas are addressed formally and systematically, but more often this information is obtained during inquiries about other areas. Counselors need to determine whether any deficits are drug-induced or are because of underlying psychological disorders that may be unrelated to substance abuse.

Presenting Complaint.   Substance abusers rarely come for help of their own volition. Their motivation for asking for help almost always is external and precipitated by a crisis or other pressures. Threats of job loss, divorce, pending legal difficulties, lack of housing, inability to get their fix for the day, bad reactions to drugs, unexpected physical symptoms, and ultimatums by family or loved ones are some common reasons that substance abusers come for help. Counselors should find out what brought the patient in immediately. Many have hidden agendas: hiding from the police or from another drug addict, to form a record for later application for disability, and so forth, and it is important to try to identify hidden agendas early in treatment.

Because it is not uncommon for substance abusers to present with external reasons for change, counselors need not confront them at this point about such extraneous reasons for seeking help. One job of counselors is to convince patients to change for internal reasons, but in general, that is best left up to counseling interventions. Later in this chapter, motivational interviews, a type of interview that can be considered an intervention, are discussed.

Alcohol and Drug Use.   If patients primarily abuse alcohol, counselors should begin there. They should assess use of other drugs after completing the assessment for alcohol abuse and dependence. If patients primarily abuse drugs, counselors should complete the assessment on drugs and then assess for alcohol abuse and dependence.

The following content areas should be assessed for each drug used: (1) amount and frequency of use—currently and historically, (2) route of administration, (3) pattern and context of use, (4) extent of tolerance and dependence, (5) history of withdrawal.

The amount and frequency of use will help determine whether the patient is abusing substances or is physiologically dependent on them. This information has prognostic value because, usually, the longer a patient has had a substance abuse problem, the more difficult it will be to treat it. Knowing how a patient administers substances will assist in determining health risks associated with use (see Chapter 3). Understanding the pattern and context of use can suggest strategies for later counseling interventions. Almost all abusers use in certain places and in certain circumstances. Counselors can help them to concretely specify these patterns. Understanding the patient's degree of tolerance and withdrawal history will help counselors to decide if the patient needs to be referred for medical evaluation and intervention to forestall impending withdrawal.

It is also important for counselors to document this assessment, both to help the patient and to protect the assessor from subsequent legal action. If a patient left a counselor's office and went into a seizure and died, that counselor potentially would be vulnerable for lawsuits alleging failure to properly assess, misdiagnosis, failure to seek consultation, failure to refer, and so forth. Once the risk of withdrawal becomes apparent, counselors must take appropriate steps to get help for the patient and to document those steps.

This illustrates an important point. Counselors do not just collect information for some external requirement. The information collected has critical value in determining treatment needs and recommendations.

Effects and Consequences of Substance Use and Abuse.   Once the type and extent of substance use has been determined, counselors need to evaluate the consequences of this use. Substance abuse does not affect all functional domains equally. By systematically evaluating each domain affected by substance abuse, counselors can get a picture of individualized problems and individualized needs. This in turn will help in formulating and implementing individualized treatment plans.

Prior Substance Abuse Treatment.   Determine the nature and extent of any prior treatment episodes for substance abuse. Was it inpatient or outpatient? Check for overdose history. Determine the longest period of sobriety or abstinence. Do not count periods of confinement as "clean time." Hospitalization, imprisonment, and living in a therapeutic community are enforced sobriety and do not capture patients' inner capacity to remain abstinent. Determine the type of treatment: detoxification, Alcoholics Anonymous (AA) or Narcotics Anonymous (NA), methadone maintenance, antabuse, therapeutic community, drug free counseling, private psychotherapy, family counseling, and so forth, and evaluate effects. Determine reasons for relapse.

EXAMPLE TREATMENT ASSESSMENT
This is the patient's first time in treatment. She is relatively ignorant about alcoholism and recovery and needs to be educated on the disease concept and the need to attend a 12-step program.

Vocational.   Ask about job-related problems, as this is non-threatening to most patients. Alcoholics, as a rule, have trouble getting jobs (although there are many functional alcoholics), whereas many drug addicts can get jobs but have trouble keeping them. Inquire about past work history, types of employment, problems on the job—absenteeism, tardiness, theft, poor evaluations, past firings—and any involvement with Employee Assistance Programs (EAPs).

EXAMPLE VOCATIONAL ASSESSMENT

Patient has good vocational skills and may be considered a functional alcoholic. He shows no pattern of absenteeism, poor work habits, or problems at work associated with his alcoholism. His job is not in jeopardy and his employer actually was surprised to learn of the patient's alcoholism and is willing to work with program staff around issues of patient recovery.

Medical. Inquiring about medical complications, in most cases, is also nonthreatening and usually is expected by patients. Sometimes patients will minimize the extent of their substance use but report a history of medical problems that are known to be related to substance abuse. Exposing this fact to patiens later may help undercut their denial. Find out what medications patients use. Sometimes patients are unsure about their diagnoses, but are able to specify the prescribed medications with exact dose, which helps reveal the medical problem.

EXAMPLE MEDICAL ASSESSMENT

Patient shows age-related diseases of hypertension and Type II (non-insulin-dependent) diabetes. He is positive for Hepatitis C and has a history of treatment for syphilis. In his youth he used unclean needles to shoot drugs and developed cellulitis twice and endocarditis once: Both were successfully treated. Physician's medical evaluation reports all other tests normal.

Legal. Look for the presence of legal problems often associated with substance abuse. Evaluate especially and routinely for DUI or DWI charges and convictions, domestic and spousal abuse, disorderly conduct, robbery and theft, possession charges, and possession with intent to sell, as these are the most common reasons for legal troubles among substance abusers. Ask about jail or penitentiary time, legal charges pending, current parole or probation status, and for what charges and convictions in each instance: Determine if they are compliant with dictates of their parole or probation officers and the court.

EXAMPLE LEGAL ASSESSMENT

Patient has a history of drug-related crimes with total length of incarceration of 15 months on three separate occasions. All incarcerations were from charges of possession with intent to sell. He also admits to petty theft and burglaries for which he was never apprehended. He shows no history of violence. It is probable that if his narcotic hunger can be satisfied via methadone, then his criminal behaviors should cease.

Social and Familial. Inquire about marital status, and current living arrangements. Find out if patients are living with anyone who has a substance abuse problem. Get a family history of substance abuse on both sides of the family. Try and get a picture of the nature of patients' social and family relationships and the quality of these relationships. Awareness of relational patterns can form the basis of a treatment plan that involves significant others. Look especially for the presence of enabling relationships (see Chapter 8). Inquire about child-rearing practices, if the patient is a parent.

EXAMPLE SOCIAL AND FAMILY ASSESSMENT
Patient reports no family history of drugs or alcohol abuse. His older brother is alcoholic and he has a sister who regularly uses marijuana and occasionally co-caine. His wife also is a heavy drinker but he feels she does not have a problem with alcohol, though that seems doubtful to this assessor. He seems quite depen-dent on his wife, despite his self-reports that depict him as "the man of the house." Wife makes all decisions, pays the bills, arranges their social life, and runs the home. She refuses to come in for additional sessions with the counselor and is not supportive of her husband's treatment. She does not think he has a drinking problem and both seem to be in denial about the extent of their alcohol abuse, if not alcohol dependence.

Psychological and Psychiatric.   Substance abusers almost always will have co-morbid psychiatric disorders and personality disorders. The most common psychiatric disorders among substance abusers are anxiety and depression-related disorders (Khantzian & Treece, 1985; O'Brien, Woody, & McLellan, 1984; Rounsaville, Weissman, Kleber, & Wilbur, 1982). Drug addicts often abuse alco-hol and alcoholics also may abuse cocaine. The most commonly occurring per-sonality disorders in this population are antisocial, passive-aggressive, and dependent (Craig, 2000). Psychiatric diagnoses can and do affect the course of treatment for substance abuse, and dually diagnosed patients may need com-bined psychiatric and substance abuse treatment.

EXAMPLE PSYCHOLOGICAL ASSESSMENT
Patient has traits primarily associated with antisocial and narcissistic personality style. These appear to be a result of his addiction and not prodromal to it, be-cause he had no antisocial characteristics prior to the onset of his addiction. The depression that is now observed is the result of chronic drug use and therefore probably is diagnosed as a substance-induced mood disorder, rather than major depression. He has poor coping skills and is easily frustrated, impulsive, and cur-rently quite manipulative.

Recreational.   Recreational interests and pursuits can be differentiated from the social domain, as social and familial areas have more to do with relation-ships. Recreation has more to do with use of leisure time. Many abusers had recreational interests that have remained dormant since they became addicted. Knowledge of patients' recreational interest can aid in the development of a treatment plan that includes activities that compete with substance abuse.

EXAMPLE RECREATIONAL ASSESSMENT

Patient enjoyed playing basketball in his youth and enjoys watching it on TV now. However, he has given up most recreational pursuits, other than watching TV. He expresses interest in playing chess but has no one to play with and would not feel comfortable playing with someone without a history of addiction. This patient might benefit from a leisure time awareness group.

Spiritual. The drug and alcohol abuse counseling specialty differentiates religiosity from spirituality. Religiosity pertains to attendance at formal rites, whereas spirituality pertains to belief in higher powers, which may or may not involve a deity. Spirituality can be incorporated into recovery plans, when that is applicable. As an aid to spiritual assessment, counselors may ask patients if they have experienced spiritual injuries—anger, despair, disbelief, discouragement, distress, doubts, fear, grief, guilt, hopelessness, resentment, sadness, shame, worries, or lack of meaning or purpose in their lives. Counselors may ask if patients feel the need for spiritual healings—commitment, "emotional memory healing," faith, forgiveness, or reconciliation.

Spiritual assessment might also include the following questions:

Where does the patient obtain strength or hope?

Does the patient pray?

Does attendance at church, synagogue, or mosque play a role in the patient's life?

How does the patient express spirituality?

Does the patient believe in God or in a higher power?

What is the patient's religious denomination, beliefs and spiritual practices, if any?

Does the patient have any spiritual goals?

Does the patient want to integrate spirituality into a recovery plan?

EXAMPLE SPIRITUAL ASSESSMENT

Patient was raised Catholic but does not practice her faith. She is struggling with a pattern of many negative behaviors following the onset of her alcoholism that make her feel guilty and unworthy of forgiveness. She expresses little hope for a positive future in an afterlife, given her many indiscretions. She knows that the Church (God) would forgive her via the confessional, but is too uncomfortable to confess her sins to a priest.

Cultural Assessment. Counselors should ask about patients' cultural background to understand their drug use and the role the culture may play in recovery.

EXAMPLE OF CULTURAL ASSESSMENT
Patient was born in Puerto Rico but emigrated to the United States in his late teens with his parents. He was taught that women and men take different roles. Women depend on men to take care of them and the family, and women have the primary child-rearing responsibilities. Men could drink but women must abstain. Women must stay with their men, even in abusive relationships. Patient strongly identifies with his race and culture and will have difficulty attending meetings, such as AA, which are not predominantly Hispanic.

Sexual Disorders.   Substance abuse interferes with sexual performance. Cocaine may temporarily increase men's sexual performance, but over time, drugs and alcohol can result in impotence, erectile dysfunction, delayed ejaculation and loss of sexual desire. Women substance abusers may have loss of menstrual periods (amenorrhea), irregular periods (dysmenorrhea), painful intercourse (vaginismus), and loss of desire. Counselors must determine whether the patient is sexually active and engaging in sexual behaviors (not using condoms) that could put them at risk for contracting HIV or other sexually transmitted diseases. Ask if they have engaged in homosexual behavior for drugs.

SAMPLE SEXUAL ASSESSMENT
Patient is heterosexual and in a monogamous relationship with his wife of 32 years, but reports a loss of sexual desire and performance, perhaps associated with his chronic heroin abuse. He said he thinks it is not the drugs but the fact that he no longer loves his wife. He said he would much prefer watching movies on TV, but she wants to cuddle and get amorous and he finds himself making excuses about going to bed with her because he doesn't want to have sex.

Childhood Abuse.   In light of the prevalence of childhood abuse in the United States, counselors should routinely ask about any history of physical and sexual abuse. Many patients experienced childhood parental discipline that today would meet the definition of physical abuse, although a patient may not interpret it as abuse.

SAMPLE ABUSE ASSESSMENT
Patient denies history of childhood abuse or neglect. She said she was raised in a loving family, where only spanking was used, and none of the children considered this abusive. In fact, they felt they deserved it.

AIDS.   Alcohol and drugs can result in loss of inhibitions and create willingness to engage in behavior that sober people would not ordinarily do. Some users are so desperate that they will do anything to get drugs. Unprotected sexual activities and use of nonsterile needles places patients at risk for contracting AIDs. Evaluate the patient's risk for AIDS by inquiring about their sexual and needle-using practices.

Special Populations.   The recommended content of a diagnostic interview is based on adult clients from the general population. Interviews with other populations (e.g., military personnel, elderly, minorities, children and adolescents), need modifications that address the special needs and interests of each (see Chapter 8). For example, when interviewing adolescents, counselors would explore special issues in their lives, such as parental relationships, peer group network and peer pressure, school truancy, school grades, sexuality, and so forth.

Table 4.2 presents a summary of the recommended format and content of clinical diagnostic interviews with substance abusers.

SCREENING INTERVIEWS

Some programs use specific structured forms with content questions that the programs require. Program personnel may create these individualized instruments to address the specific needs of a program. Other programs rely on published structured interviews designed for use with substance abusers. Among the nearly overwhelming number of assessment devices for screening for substance abuse problems (Allen & Collumbus, 1995; Winters, 1999), the two most frequently used instruments are the Addiction Severity Index and the Comprehensive Drinker Profile.

Addiction Severity Index

The Addiction Severity Index (ASI) was developed by NIDA and researchers at Philadelphia VA Hospital and the University of Pennsylvania to provide severity levels in specific domains affected by substance abuse (McLellan, Lubosrky, Cacciola, Griffith, McGahan, & O'Brien, 1985). In its most recent edition (McLellan, Kushner, Metzger, Peters, Grissom, Pettinati, & Argeriou, 1992), the ASI is 12 pages long with a cover sheet that includes interview instructions and definitions. Aside from basic patient demographic information, the ASI provides structured questions about medical, employment, drug and alcohol use, legal, family history pertaining to substance abuse and mental health problems, family and social relationships, psychiatric status, and spirituality domains.

At the end of each interview domain, patients rate, on a scale of 0 (not at all) to 4 (extremely), how troubled or bothered they have been by that problem domain in the past 30 days. They then rate, on the same scale, how important it is now for them to receive treatment for these problems. At the end of each section, the counselor rates the patient's need for treatment in that domain on a severity scale of 0 (no problem) to 9. Ratings from 0–2 are considered not very severe, 4–6 mildly severe, and 7–9 extremely severe. At the end of the psychological and psychiatric section, the counselor responds to questions about whether the patient has misrepresented the information, whether the patient had the ability to understand, and whether the patient was having any particular symptoms (e.g., depressed, withdrawn, suicidal, anxious, hostile, etc.) at the time of the interview.

TABLE 4.2   Recommended Content for Diagnostic Interviews with Substance Abusers

GENERAL ASSESSMENTS

Do a mental status exam.
Evaluate for the presence of concurrent psychiatric disorders.

PRESENTING COMPLAINT

Assess patient's motivation for treatment.
Determine the precipitant—what brought the patient in *now*.
Determine patient goals.
Look for hidden agendas.

SUBSTANCE USE AND ABUSE

Identify drugs used.
Get data on amount and frequency of use.
Determine route of administration.
Determine amount and time of last use.
Determine pattern and context of use.
Determine tolerance, dependence, and withdrawal.

EFFECTS AND CONSEQUENCES OF SUBSTANCE ABUSE

Prior treatment history and modalities of treatment
Vocational history
Medical history
Legal history
Social and family history
Psychological and psychiatric history
Recreation and use of leisure time
Spirituality

SPECIAL ASSESSMENTS

Sexuality
Childhood abuse
AIDS risk assessment

DIAGNOSIS AND SPECIFIC PROBLEM AREAS

TREATMENT PLAN

Review plan with patient.
Reach mutually agreeable goals.

Several substance abuse programs mandate the ASI for all new patients. These patients are re-evaluated with the ASI every six months. Computer scoring programs are available and provide patient composite scores: changes in scores are used to assess patient progress in treatment.

For counselors and programs that do not have access to computer scoring of the ASI, both patients and counselors may rate the domains on a 0–9 severity scale to allow comparison of counselor and patient ratings in each domain. Ratings that essentially are identical suggest either no problem in that domain or mutual agreement about the need for treatment in that domain. Large discrepancies between counselor and patient ratings suggest the presence of denial and the need for intervention in that domain.

Figure 4.1 illustrates the way ASI severity ratings can be used as an assessment tool. In the example, counselor and patient agree in the areas of drug, medical, social/family, legal, vocational, and recreational. A discrepancy in the ratings in the domains of alcohol and psychiatric is indicated by the arrows. The counselor assessed both the alcohol and psychiatric problems as more severe than did the patient: this should then be a point of contention in further work with the patient.

Because the ASI is in the public domain, it is reproduced in the Appendix to this chapter and may be copied for individual and program use.

The ASI has been judged reliable and valid (Kosten, Rounsaville, & Kleber, 1983; McLellan, Luborsky, Cacciola, Griffith et al., 1985; McLellan, Luborsky, Woody, & O'Brien, 1980), has good predictive validity with substance abusers (Mclellan, Luborsky, Woody, O'Brien et al., 1981, 1983), and has become almost a standard assessment tool in many substance abuse programs.

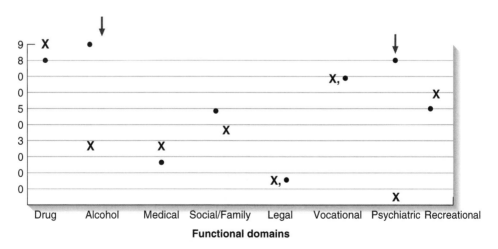

FIGURE 4.1   Sample ASI Rating Graph

Comprehensive Drinker Profile

Another frequently appearing assessment instrument is the Comprehensive Drinker Profile (CDP) (Miller & Marlatt, 1984). While the ASI can be used for alcohol and drug abusers, the CDP is specific for alcohol abusers. This structured interview presents questions in three major sections, demographic, drinking history, and motivational information. The demographic section asks questions about age, residence, family status, employment and income, and educational history. The drinking history section assesses development of the drinking problem, present drinking pattern, pattern history, alcohol-related life problems, drinking settings, associated behaviors, beverage preferences, and medical history. The motivational information section inquires about reasons for drinking, effects of drinking, other life problems, motivation for treatment, and drinker type ratings. Scoring the sections yields quantitative indices. Perhaps the CDP also has been used in research to evaluate effectiveness of alcohol treatment for this reason.

MOTIVATIONAL INTERVIEWING

Motivational interviewing (Miller, 1991) is an assessment tool and an intervention strategy.

Miller defines motivational interviewing as "a particular way to help people recognize and do something about their present or potential problems" (1991, p. 52). Motivational interviewing starts with the assumption that behavior change is not a personality trait but rather a state of readiness, which fluctuates from time to time and from situation to situation. This further implies that the behavior and actions of the counselor during the assessment interview is quite instrumental in determining whether a patient will engage in a process of change. It also implies that motivation can change as a result of the personal interaction between patient and counselor. Miller has defined six active processes that the counselor needs to engage in to maximize the possibility of behavior change in the patient. He uses the acronym FRAMES as a mnemonic aid for the counselor.

- *Feedback.* The structure of the comprehensive interview, as recommended in this chapter, can provide patients with time to reflect on their lives, their choices, and their behaviors. This reflection, itself, can be a potent motivator for change.
- *Responsibility.* This approach emphasizes that it is the patient's responsibility to change.
- *Advice.* In motivational interviewing the counselor does not assume a passive role. Rather the counselor engages in active advice giving. The nature of this advice must be clear and simple and communicated directly in a nonauthoritarian manner.

- *Menu.* Patients should be given a menu of alternative treatment choices and strategies, so they can choose the ones that best suit their needs. Having the patients select from a menu of choices creates a situation in which they take ownership of a particular goal and treatment approach and more likely will be compelled to work toward meeting this goal.
- *Empathy.* This does not mean a counselor's ability to identify with a patient. Rather, it means the ability to understand and reflect that understanding to the patient in ways that do not introduce the counselor's own judgments or attitudes into the process. A long history of psychological research has shown that accurate empathy is a powerful motivator to behavior change. Even necessary confrontation and challenge of thinking and behavior can be done in an empathic manner.
- *Self-efficacy.* This refers to patients' belief that they have the ability to succeed in meeting goals and objectives and can do this through their own instrumental behaviors. Again, a long history of social psychological research has documented the power of self-efficacy in behavior change.

To implement these processes, counselors need to be empathic, point out discrepancies, avoid argument, roll with resistance, and support self-efficacy.

- *Be empathic.* To be empathic is to express genuine warmth and use active and reflective listening techniques. Clients need to feel accepted and experience a counselor who essentially is nonjudgmental. Note that acceptance is not the same thing as agreeing with the patient. Certainly counselors can disagree with the views of their patients and still be empathic. The crucial difference, says Miller, is that the disagreement is done with respect toward the patient.
- *Point out discrepancies.* Counselors need to point out discrepancies between patients' present behavior and their longer-term goals. Miller argues that motivation to change can be created when people emotionally perceive this discrepancy.

EXAMPLE

A patient on probation for possession was told that if any subsequent urine results were positive for illicit drugs he would go to jail for three years. He was struggling with a cocaine addiction and having little success in resisting his cravings for the drug. One evening his wife asked him to go to church with her. He decided not to go, for his strategy for staying off cocaine was to stay in as much as possible, to avoid being tempted to use. Later that evening his teenage daughter asked him to drive her girl friend home. She lived in the housing projects and, when the patient took her home, he experienced a near-overwhelming desire to use cocaine because his connections lived in that area. (Fortunately, he did not give in to his temptation). I pointed out the discrepancy between his goal of avoiding incarceration and his action of driving into an area where he had used drugs in the past. I pointed out that, had he attended church with his wife, he wouldn't have put himself in such a risky situation.

While this example emanated from a counseling session, the same process can easily be used in an assessment interview.

- *Avoid argument.* Direct confrontation leads only to resistance. Argument almost always leads to a lack of listening and an increase in emotion as others stress the validity of their point of view. Confrontational approaches engender only increased resistance. It rarely instills a motivation to change behavior. A process of psychological reactance occurs when people believe their personal freedom is being reduced or threatened. Strongly directive, coercive, and confrontational techniques evoke reactance!
- *Roll with resistance.* The martial art of judo takes advantage of leverage, rather than head-on attack, to thwart opponents. This is not to convey that the relationship between counselor and client is adversarial, but to illustrate the point other means than to confront resistance can elicit behavior change. When resistance occurs, Miller argues that counselors should change strategies. Allow the clients to find their own solutions to their problems, if they resist interventions. Use whatever momentum has developed to your own advantage. Actively engage the client in the change process.

Some techniques to deal with resistance include

LISTENING REFLECTIVELY

Patient: "You think it's easy to change? I've been acting this way all my life."

Counselor: "You feel that change will be very hard for you."

SHIFT FOCUS: CHANGE THE SUBJECT

Patient: "You think it's easy to change? I've been acting this way all my life."

Counselor: "Tell me some times in your life in which you thought you couldn't do something but then learned that you were able to do it."

USE PARADOX

A paradox is a statement that is ludicrous and unexpected. By tone the person knows the speaker really doesn't mean it.

Patient: "You think it's easy to change? I've been acting this way all my life."

Counselor: "You're right. I never want you to change again. Keep on drinking and drugging—it will do you good."

EMPHASIZE PERSONAL CHOICE

Patient: "You think it's easy to change? I've been acting this way all my life."

Counselor: "Look, you could decide to change or you could keep on doing what you're doing and take the consequences. It's really up to you."

REFRAME

Reframing presents another twist or "spin" to what the patient has said. It presents ideas in a way that had not been considered.

Patient: "You think it's easy to change? I've been acting this way all my life."

Counselor: "Change is possible for anyone. When Magic Johnson, the professional basketball player, learned he was HIV positive, he engaged in a healthy diet, exercised, and changed his nightly habits. Now he is a role model for patients with AIDs and shows what can be accomplished when the person has the right motivation."

■ *Support self-efficacy.* Miller believes that self-efficacy is the key process in motivational interviewing. A critical goal is to instill in the patient the belief that they have the power to change their behavior and, if the counselor conveys this expectation as well, it can go a long way towards accomplishing that goal.

SOME SPECIFIC MOTIVATIONAL INTERVIEWING TECHNIQUES

The following suggestions should permeate assessment interviews:

■ *Ask open-ended questions.* Don't get into a question and answer routine. This blocks communication. The patient should do most of the talking in the assessment interview.

■ *Engage in reflective listening.* Counselors will communicate that they understand the patients' problems and dilemmas.

■ *Give advice.* It is appropriate to offer advice when counselors are certain of the information.

■ *Remove barriers.* Sometimes issues of cost, transportation, waiting time to entry into treatment, and so forth, are barriers that stymie even the most motivated patients. Try to remove any barriers that prevent patients from taking the next step.

■ *Provide choices.* The more that are acceptable to treatment personnel, the better.

■ *Decrease desirability.* Identify disincentives for continuing the present behavior.

■ *Actively help the patient.* Offer some concrete expression of help, support, and assistance. Conveys an attitude of caring about the person.

■ *Affirm.* Reinforce patients' statements that support therapeutic goals.

■ *Summarize.* Link material within an interview into comprehensive and holistic statements.

■ *Elicit self-motivational statements.* During an interview patients are likely to recognize a problem, express some concerns, express an intention to change, and express optimism about their ability to change. Counselors should support these types of statements because they are in the direction of change.

■ *Explore and set concrete goals.* Get clients to report what is important to them in life. Use discrepancies to illustrate how their present behaviors interfere with those goals.

LABORATORY TESTS

In substance abuse programs and in counseling substance abusers, concrete evidence that treatment has been successful is absolutely necessary. There are three ways to determine treatment success: (1) laboratory tests that provide continuing evidence of abstinence and sobriety, (2) collateral information and reports, and (3) sophisticated pretreatment and posttreatment designs with data collection strategies. The latter usually is available in research-based settings and infrequently is used in typical substance abuse treatment programs and by individual clinicians. Information from collateral sources is helpful, but some patients can avoid detection of substance abuse and even relapse, so that relying on this source of information is inadequate. That leaves laboratory tests as the most common and useful means to assess whether a patient is using substances. During initial evaluations it is strongly recommended that a blood alcohol level (BAL), Breathalyzer, or a urine toxicology screen be done.

Toxicology Urine Screens

Urine samples routinely are collected in drug treatment programs and in some alcohol treatment programs. The specimens are analyzed for the presence of illicit drugs. How reliable are these results? One study examined the performance of 13 laboratories that served a total of 262 methadone treatment facilities. Preassessed samples were sent to these laboratories as if they were being tested for the first time. Error rates on samples containing barbiturates, amphetamines, methadone, cocaine, codeine and morphine ranged from 11% to 94%, 19% to 100%, 0% to 33%, 0% to 100%, 0% to 100%, and 5% to 100%. Error rates for samples not containing these drugs ranged from 0% to 6%, 0% to 37%, 0% to 66%, 0% to 6%, 0% to 7%, and 0% to 10%. The authors concluded that greater care is taken with known evaluation samples than with routine samples, laboratories often were not able to detect the presence of drugs in urine in concentrations required by their contracts, and the reported results can threaten the treatment process (Hansen, Caudill, & Boone, 1985). It was suggested that treatment programs monitor the accuracy of laboratory test results, and not merely accept them blindly. What is responsible for these results? Before addressing this question, counselors need a rudimentary knowledge of urine collection and testing procedures.

Several concepts in diagnostic testing apply to medical tests just as they do to psychological tests. Two of the more important concepts are sensitivity and specificity. *Sensitivity* is the capability of a test to detect the presence of a substance or disorder if the patient has used substances or has the disorder. This is called a "true positive." If the test indicates the patient has used some substance or has some condition, when it is known not to be true, this is called a "false positive." *Specificity* is the ability of a test to determine that a substance has not been taken or that a patient does not have the disorder. This is called a "true negative." If it is known that the patient has used a particular substance or does not have a disorder and the test comes back as positive, this is called a "false negative."

Laboratories use the word "specificity" to report whether or not the patient has used a specific drug, such as codeine, morphine, or Demerol, rather than reporting the results as positive for opiates. They define specificity toxicologically, as the minimal concentration of a drug that can discriminate between closely related drugs or metabolites.

Four methods are commonly used to detect the presence of drugs in urine: chromotography, spectral methods, immunoassays, and spectometry. Each has unique advantages and disadvantages and laboratories need to determine which aspect is most relevant for clinician and program. Criteria used to evaluate the desirability of each method have to take into account the rapidity of attaining results, their economy and convenience, along with their sensitivity and specificity.

Chromotography.

- *Thin-Layer Chromatography* (TLC) is the most commonly-used method for the mass screening of urines. TLC requires a minimum of instrumentation, has relatively low cost, is simple to use, and obtains results in about two hours. It has reasonable sensitivity for a wide variety of drugs but the results are expressed in qualitative form only. It records the results as positive or negative. Technicians can make reading errors and test results can be adversely affected by environmental conditions. TLC is commonly used as an initial drug screen. Positive results should then be confirmed by another, more sensitive, method.

- *Gas Liquid Chromotography* (GC) is often used to verify TLC test results. GC has greater sensitivity than TLC but is more time consuming. It has a lower incidence of false positives but initial costs of equipment and supplies are higher. Although test results can be given in quantitative form, only one sample, which takes about two hours, can be run at a time. Hence, it only can accommodate low volume outputs. Also, a highly trained technician is needed to interpret the results.

Spectral Methods. *Spectrophotometric techniques* are available: spectrophoto-flurometry (SPF) is the most common. Drugs emit a fluorescent light under specific conditions and spectrophotoflurometry detects this luminescence. The technique is relatively simple and is able to accommodate to high volume operations. Initial costs are high because the equipment is expensive and the technique can produce high false positive rates. So far the technique is used mostly to confirm positive morphine results.

Immunoassays. This relatively simple method is very sensitive, attains the results rapidly, can detect the presence of drugs taken for longer periods of time than other methods, and is a good screening technique when the emphasis in on high volume. Positive results should be confirmed with another method but negative results suggest strong evidence that the findings are true. However, the method is not very specific.

Spectometry.

■ *Free Radical Assay Techniques (FRAT).* This method is extremely fast (within seconds), relatively inexpensive, very accurate, and capable of mass screening. However, it has low specificity and a high incidence of false positives. Positive results must be confirmed with another method. Equipment costs are quite high. This method is used most often by the military.

■ *Enzyme Multiplied Immuno Assay (EMIT)* has a fast turnaround time, allows for high volume testing, has good sensitivity with fair specificity, and generally is used as a mass screening technique. Positive results need to be confirmed with another method. Machine and equipment are costly.

■ *Radioimmunoassay (RIA)* is a spectometry method that is more sensitive than FRAT and EMIT. It provides a low incidence of false positives. Turnaround time is 1–2 hours and the technique is most suitable when another method is used to confirm the results. One serious disadvantage is the technique doesn't detect the full range of drugs.

■ *Hemagglutination Inhibition (HI)* provides high volume testing with uncomplicated equipment and low costs with high sensitivity. Turnaround time is about 90 minutes. The technique has not been fully evaluated and it can only detect morphine.

■ *Mass Spectrometry* is the most sensitive and specific. It is commonly used with GC but it can only accommodate to a small number of samples a day and equipment costs are high. It is often used for specific confirmation of a drug and for confirmation of an initial drug screen.

At the very least, counselors should be aware of the method used by the laboratory to detect the presence of drugs in urine and whether or not positive results have been confirmed.

What accounts for urine test results that show variability? Besides variations in the laboratory method used to test the urine, patients try to avoid the detection of drugs in their urine in a number of ways. They add various chemicals to a sample to change the Ph level or switch urine samples, substituting drug-free "clean" urine for "dirty" urine that contains evidence of illicit drug use. Persons responsible for urine collection should be trained to be aware of techniques patients use to falsify urine test results.

Technological improvements may find their way into drug treatment programs so that patients will experience less success in avoiding detection of illicit drug use. Urine collection bottles are available that will change color if the temperature of the contents in the bottle exceeds a certain range of body temperature, attesting that the urine did not come directly from the patient. Urine sample strips are available that will allow on-the-spot testing of urine samples. Sensors are in the developmental stages that detect illicit drug use in skin perspiration and send an automatic signal to a receiver at the program, giving electronic evidence that the patient has used illicit drugs.

Table 4.3 presents average detection times for illicit drugs by urinalysis.

Hair Testing

Urinalysis is the most common way to detect drugs, but illicit substances may be detected through the collection of other samples, including hair, which grows at

TABLE 4.3 Periods of Detection for Illicit Drugs by Urinalysis

DRUG OF ABUSE	PERIOD OF DETECTION
Alcohol	6–10 hours
Amphetamine	1–2 days
Barbiturates	2–10 days
Benzodiazepines	1–6 weeks
Cocaine	1–4 days
Codeine	1–2 days
Hashish	1 day–5 weeks
Heroin	1–2 days
LSD	8 hours
Marijuana	1 day–5 weeks
MDMA (Ecstasy)	1–2 days
Mescaline	2–3 days
Methadone	1 day–1 week
Methamphetamine	1–2 days
Morphine	1–2 days
Nicotine	1–2 days
Phencyclidne (PCP)	2–8 days
Tetrahydrocannabinol (THC)	1 day–5 weeks

the rate of about half an inch a month. Drugs are deposited in hair, so hair may be analyzed for the presence of drugs. To detect drugs taken during the last three months requires 40–60 strands of hair, preferably those taken closest to the scalp. There are several advantages for using hair compared to urine testing:

- Hair analysis can detect illicit drugs use for several months depending on the length of hair available. Because urinalysis detects drugs for much shorter periods, hair testing greatly expands the detection of illicit drugs.
- Brief periods of abstinence can affect urine test results but will not affect test findings from hair samples.
- Hair cannot be contaminated, whereas patients will try to adulterate or switch urine samples.
- Collection is relatively easier, as it does not require special storage and handling and also lowers the risk of disease transmission to the health agent.

There are some difficulties in using hair. Urine screens are easier to collect for patients and for the program. Patients are more willing to give up their urine than their hair. Samples of hair cannot be taken routinely over the large periods of time that often are required for program participation. Hair analysis is likely to have a limited role for the detection of drugs for most clinicians and treatment programs. However, future technology may allow easier detection by using fewer strands of hair and by using hair already loose on the body.

Blood Alcohol Levels

Blood alcohol levels (BAL) measure the concentration of alcohol in blood expressed in grams per 100 ml. Table 4.4 provides behavioral effects at various levels of BALs. These readings are affected by body weight and gender and are only rough approximations of behavior.

PSYCHOLOGICAL TESTS

Substance abuse counselors often have access to psychological reports that stipulate whether or not patients have a substance use disorder. Psychologists arrive at this conclusion by interviewing the patients, consulting with collateral sources, and by giving psychological tests that have scales that assess for substance abuse. It is important for the substance abuse counselor to know the commonly used tests administered for these purposes and to understand how they work.

There are two main kinds of psychological tests, broad band and narrow band. Broad-band tests sample an array of behaviors and problems, and narrow-band tests look only for a specific behavior or problem area.

TABLE 4.4   Blood Alcohol Levels and Expected Behavior

PERCENT BAL	BEHAVIOR
0.01	Few overt effects, slight feeling of relaxation
0.03	Relaxed with slight exhilaration decrease in visual tracking, minimal impairment in mental functions
0.05	No intoxication; feeling relaxed and warm, some release of inhibition, some impaired judgment, lowered alertness, slight decrease in fine motor skills, mild reduction in visual capability in tracking and glare recovery
0.06	Mild relaxation, slight impairment in fine motor skills, increase in reaction time, slurred speech, poor muscle control, exaggerated emotions
0.08	Legal evidence of intoxication and DUI in many states; vision impaired, increased loss of motor functions, may stagger
0.09	Judgment now clouded, lessening of inhibitions and self-restraint, reduced visual and hearing acuity, increased difficulty in performing motor skills
0.10	Legal evidence of intoxication and DUI in many states, slowed reaction times, slurred speech, drowsiness, nausea, deficits in coordination, impaired motor functioning, and difficulty in focusing, in judging moving targets, and in glare recovery
0.15	Major impairment in physical and mental functions, difficulty in standing, walking and talking; disturbed perception, blurred vision, large increases in reaction times, falling asleep, vomiting
0.20	Marked depression of sensory and motor functions, mentally confused, gross body movements can be made only with assistance, unable to maintain an upright position, incoherent speech, needs assistance to walk, decidedly intoxicated, has difficulty staying awake, vomiting
0.25	Severe motor disturbance, sensory perceptions greatly impaired, staggering, as well as behaviors seen at 0.20
0.30	Stuporous but conscious, severe mental confusion, difficulty in reacting to stimuli, general suppression of sensibility, little comprehension of what is going on, respiratory depression with severe intoxication, brain functions severely depressed, repeatedly falling down, passes out, may be in coma
0.40	Almost complete anesthesia, reflexes are depressed, breathing and heartbeat may stop, unconscious and may be dead
0.50	Completely unconscious, deep coma if not dead
0.60	Death most likely: depression of brain centers that control heart rate and breathing

The most commonly employed broad-band instruments to detect substance abuse are the *Minnesota Multiphasic Personality Inventory-2* (MMPI) (Butcher, Dahlstrom, Graham, Tellegen, & Kaemmer, 1989), and the *Millon Clinical Multiaxial Inventory–III* (MCMI-III) (Millon, 1994).

Minnesota Multiphasic Personality Inventory-2

The personality test mostly frequently given is the MMPI (Butcher & Rouse, 1996; Watkins, Campbell, Nieberding, & Halmark, 1995). The MMPI is a 567-item questionnaire that covers several clinical syndromes, including substance abuse. Three specific scales on the MMPI assess for substance abuse. The *Addictions Admission Scale* (AAS) is a 13-item scale that asks respondents if they have a specific problem with drugs and alcohol. It was designed to "detect" substance abuse among patients who are willing to admit it. The AAS alerts the psychologist to a problem that the patient endorses on the tests so that the problem is not missed in the psychologist's interpretation.

Many patients are in denial about their substance abuse and lie in responding to questions about abuse. The 39-item *Addiction Potential Scale (APS)* attempts to detect substance abuse problems by using items that are more frequently endorsed by substance abusers compared to non-substance-abusing psychiatric inpatients. Items that dealt specifically with substance abuse were dropped from the scale. The content of the scale pertains to lifestyles and personality dimensions associated with substance abuse (Craig, 1999).

The *MacAndrew Alcoholism Scale* (MAC-R), as revised, is a 49-item scale that was developed by selecting items on the MMPI that discriminated between substance abusers in a VA outpatient psychiatric clinic from psychiatric patients in the outpatient clinic who were not abusing substances. This has been one of the most well-researched scales and has excellent validity. Research shows that it can detect substance abuse with 85% degree of accuracy. The scale has good validity for both men and women and is actually a substance abuse scale, because drug addicts also score high on this scale.

There are also MMPI profile code types associated with drug and alcohol use that can also be used for assessment and detection purposes. The MMPI-2 has proved to be an extremely useful tool in assessing substance abusers.

MCMI-III

Two scales on the MCMI-III assess and detect substance abuse, the Alcohol Dependence Scale (Scale B) and the Drug Dependence Scale (T). Both of these scales have items that ask directly about alcohol and drug use and tap behaviors and lifestyles associated with substance abuse. Some patients can avoid the detection of substance abuse on the test, primarily patients whose problem severity is low or who are in the early stages of the disorder. Patients in the middle to late stages of the disorder have been unable to hide their problem on these scales, even when motivated to do so (Craig, 1999).

MICHIGAN ALCOHOLISM SCREENING TEST

The Michigan Alcoholism Screening Test (MAST) (NIAAA, 1995) is a standardized scale that assesses problematic drinking. It also frequently is used for research and as a screening tool for alcoholism. It contains 24 items about drinking habits. Scores range from 0–54: scores between 0–4 suggest no alcohol problem, between 5–6 suggest a probable alcohol problem, greater than 7 suggest alcoholism, 10–20 suggest moderate alcoholism, and greater than 20 suggest severe alcoholism.

When interpreting the MAST, it is useful to segment problematic responses into categories. Because alcohol may not affect all domains equally, this allows more targeted interventions during treatment planning.

- Questions 1, 5, pertain to psychological and attitudinal issues.
- Questions 2, 4, 7, 9, 16–18, pertain to alcoholic symptoms.
- Questions 3, 6, 10–12, pertain to interpersonal relations affected by drinking.
- Questions 8, 19–22, pertain to treatment for alcoholism.
- Questions 13–15, pertain to vocational problems.
- Questions 23, 24 pertain to legal problems.

DIAGNOSIS AND TREATMENT

Once the assessment results have been completed, a diagnosis is made by the responsible, designated clinicians. They use one of two official classification systems available to clinicians, the International Classification of Diseases (ICD) of the World Health Organization, or the Diagnostic and Statistical Manual of the American Psychiatric Association, 4th Edition (DSM-IV) (1994). Since DSM-IV is popularly used in the United States, we will focus on this system.

DSM-IV divides the substance-related disorders into two groups: Substance Use Disorders (Substance Abuse and Substance Dependence) and Substance-Induced Disorders (substance-specific intoxication and withdrawal, substance-induced delirium, amnestic disorder, psychotic disorder, mood disorder, anxiety disorder, sexual dysfunction and sleep disorder). Six course specifiers are available for the substance dependence disorders: early full remission, early partial remission, sustained full remission, sustained partial remission, on agonist therapy and in a controlled environment. The diagnosis must also specify whether there is or is not physiological dependence (evidence of tolerance or withdrawal). Specifiers for ICD substance abuse/dependence diagnosis include "continuous," "episodic," or "in remission."

DSM-IV defines Substance Dependence as "a cluster of cognitive, behavioral, and physiological symptoms indicating that the individual continues use of the substance despite significant substance-related problems (APA,

p. 176). Substance Abuse is defined as "a maladaptive pattern of substance use manifested by recurrent and significant adverse consequences related to the repeated use of substances" (APA, p. 182).

PRESENTING ASSESSMENT RESULTS

Counselors should give feedback of their assessment and ideas to the client at the end of the interview. This model emanates from medicine, where a patient reports symptoms and is examined by the doctor who may make a diagnosis. The physician tells the patient what is wrong and how it can be treated. The presenting complaint might be a manifestation of several diseases and so more tests need to be completed. Usually the physician will tell the patient what is being looked for, but if one or more of the possible diagnoses may be particularly onerous and perhaps life-threatening, the physician might not tell that to the patient until the final diagnosis is made. In mental health interviews, often patients pour their hearts out and leave the interview without knowing what the clinician thinks or how the problem can be successfully addressed. There are ways of giving feedback to clients that will maximize the likelihood that they will return for a second session. Thereafter, the counselor's skills will determine treatment retention.

1. Highlight the Patient's Problems.   *Example:* "You have been unsuccessful in trying to deal with your alcohol and cocaine problem on your own, you have had no clean time, except while in prison, people take advantage of you because you are easily influenced, you are a womanizer and, while you are not using needles, you go out with women who are using needles and you can get AIDS from them."

2. Present a Proposed Treatment Plan.   *Example:* "Because of this, you need time in a residential therapeutic community where you can deal with these problems and issues in a safe setting, away from alcohol and drugs and with supportive personnel who understand your problems."

3. Elicit Patient Feedback.   The goal here is to determine how well the patient agrees with the assessment and treatment options. Of course, another value in getting this feedback is that the clinician might be wrong. Some of the assessment may be inaccurate. This gives the client an opportunity to correct any errors and to voice an opinion about the strategy. Throughout this process check for resistance and try to reach mutually agreeable goals.

4. Implement Plan of Action.   The final part of the feedback process is the action plan. This may involve a referral elsewhere, but most often it entails working out miscellaneous details, such as fees, appointment times, and so

Addiction Severity Index 5th Edition
Clinical/Training Version

A. Thomas McLellan, Ph.D.
Deni Carise, Ph.D.
Thomas H. Coyne, MSW

Remember: This is an interview, not a test

≈*Item numbers circled are to be asked at follow-up.*≈
≈*Items with an asterisk are cumulative and should
be rephrased at follow-up.*≈

INTRODUCING THE ASI: Introduce and explain the seven potential problem areas: Medical, Employment/Support Status, Alcohol, Drug, Legal, Family/Social, and Psychiatric. All clients receive this same <u>standard</u> interview. All information gathered is <u>confidential</u>; explain what that means in your facility; who has access to the information and the process for the release of information.
There are <u>two time periods</u> we will discuss:
          1. The past 30 days
          2. Lifetime

Patient Rating Scale: Patient input is important. For each area, I will ask you to use this scale to let me know how bothered you have been by any problems in each section. I will also ask you how important treatment is for you for the area being discussed.

The scale is: 0 - Not at all
                      1 - Slightly
                      2 - Moderately
                      3 - Considerably
                      4 - Extremely
Inform the client that he/she has the right to refuse to answer any question. If the client is uncomfortable or feels it is too personal or painful to give an answer, instruct the client not to answer. Explain the benefits and advantages of answering as many questions as possible in terms of developing a comprehensive and effective treatment plan to help them.
Please try not to give inaccurate information!

INTERVIEWER INSTRUCTIONS
1. Leave no blanks.
2. Make plenty of Comments (if another person reads this ASI, they should have a relatively complete picture of the client's perceptions of his/her problems).
3. X = Question not answered.
    N = Question not applicable.
4. Terminate interview if client misrepresents two or more sections.
5. When noting comments, please write the question number.
6. Tutorial/clarification notes are preceded with "•".

HALF TIME RULE: If a question asks the number of months, round up periods of 14 days or more to 1 month. Round up 6 months or more to 1 year.

CONFIDENCE RATINGS: ⇒ Last two items in each section.
                      ⇒ Do not over-interpret.
                      ⇒ Denial does not necessarily warrant misrepresentation.
                      ⇒ Misrepresentation = overt contradiction in information.
Probe, cross-check and make plenty of comments!

HOLLINGSHEAD CATEGORIES:
1. Higher execs, major professionals, owners of large businesses.
2. Business managers if medium sized businesses, lesser professions, i.e., nurses, opticians, pharmacists, social workers, teachers.
3. Administrative personnel, managers, minor professionals, owners/proprietors of small businesses, i.e., bakery, car dealership, engraving business, plumbing business, florist, decorator, actor, reporter, travel agent.
4. Clerical and sales, technicians, small businesses (bank teller, bookkeeper, clerk, draftsperson, timekeeper, secretary).
5. Skilled manual - usually having had training (baker, barber, brakeperson, chef, electrician, fireman, machinist, mechanic, paperhanger, painter, repairperson, tailor, welder, police, plumber).
6. Semi-skilled (hospital aide, painter, bartender, bus driver, cutter, cook, drill press, garage guard, checker, waiter, spot welder, machine operator).
7. Unskilled (attendant, janitor, construction helper, unspecified labor, porter, <u>including unemployed</u>).
8. Homemaker.
9. Student, disabled, no occupation.

LIST OF COMMONLY USED DRUGS:

Alcohol:	Beer, wine, liquor
Methadone:	Dolophine, LAAM
Opiates:	Pain killers = Morphine, Diluaudid, Demerol, Percocet, Darvon, Talwin, Codeine, Tylenol 2,3,4, Robitussin, Fentanyl
Barbiturates:	Nembutal, Seconal, Tuinol, Amytal, Pentobarbital, Secobarbital, Phenobarbital, Fiorinol
Sed/Hyp/Tranq:	Benzodiazepines = Valium, Librium, Ativan, Serax Tranxene, Xanax, Miltown, Other = ChloralHydrate (Noctex), Quaaludes Dalmane, Halcion
Cocaine:	Cocaine Crystal, Free-Base Cocaine or "Crack," and "Rock Cocaine"
Amphetamines:	Monster, Crank, Benzedrine, Dexedrine, Ritalin, Preludin, Methamphetamine, Speed, Ice, Crystal
Cannabis:	Marijuana, Hashish
Hallucinogens:	LSD (Acid), Mescaline, Mushrooms (Psilocybin), Peyote, Green, PCP (Phencyclidine), Angel Dust, Ecstasy
Inhalants:	Nitrous Oxide, Amyl Nitrate (Whippits, Poppers), Glue, Solvents, Gasoline, Toluene, Etc.
Just note if these are used:	Antidepressants, Ulcer Meds = Zantac, Tagamet Asthma Meds = Ventoline Inhaler, Theodur Other Meds = Antipsychotics, Lithium

ALCOHOL/DRUG USE INSTRUCTIONS:
The following questions refer to two time periods: the past 30 days and lifetime. Lifetime refers to the time prior to the last 30 days.
    ⇒ 30 day questions only require the number of days used.
    ⇒ Lifetime use is asked to determine extended periods of use.
    ⇒ Regular use = 3 or more times per week, binges, or problematic irregular use in which normal activities are compromised.
    ⇒ Alcohol to intoxication does not necessarily mean "drunk", use the words "to feel or felt the effects", "got a buzz", "high", etc. instead of intoxication. As a rule, 3 or more drinks in one sitting, or 5 or more drinks in one day defines "intoxication".
        ⇒ How to ask these questions:
            → "How many days in the past 30 have you used....?"
            → "How many years in your life have you regulary used....?"

Addiction Severity Index, 5th Edition
GENERAL INFORMATION   (Clinical/Training Version)

G1. ID No.: ☐☐☐☐☐☐☐
G2. SS No.: ☐☐☐ – ☐☐ – ☐☐☐☐

G4. Date of Admission ☐☐ / ☐☐ / ☐☐☐☐
G5. Date of Interview: ☐☐ / ☐☐ / ☐☐☐☐
G6. Time Begun: (Hour: Minutes) ☐☐ : ☐☐
G7. Time Ended: (Hour: Minutes) ☐☐ : ☐☐

G8. Class: 1. Intake   2. Fellowship ☐
G9. Contact Code: 1. In person ☐
                   2. Telephone
                   (Intake ASI must be in person)

G10. Gender: 1. Male 2. Female ☐
G11. Interviewer Code No./Initials: ☐☐☐

_____
Name
_____
Address 1
_____
Address 2
_____( )_____
City   State   Zip Code   Telephone Number

G14. How long have you lived at this ☐☐ / ☐☐
     address?   Years Months
G15. Is this residence owned by you 0-No 1-Yes ☐
     or your family?

G16. Date of Birth: (M/D/Y) ☐☐ / ☐☐ / ☐☐☐☐
G17. Of what race do you consider yourself? ☐
     1. White (not Hisp) 5. Asian/Pacific   9. Other Hispanic
     2. Black (not Hisp) 6. Hispanic-Mexican
     3. American Indian   7. Hispanic-Puerto Rican
     4. Alaskan Native   8. Hispanic-Cuban
G18. Do you have a religious preference? ☐
     1. Protestant   3. Jewish   5. Other
     2. Catholic   4. Islamic 6. None

G19. Have you been in a controlled environment in ☐
     the past 30 days?
     1. No   4. Medical Treatment
     2. Jail   5. Psychiatric Treatment
     3. Alcohol/Drug Treat. 6. Other _____
     •A place, *theoretically*, without access to drugs/alcohol.
G20. How many days? ☐☐
     •"NN" if Question G19 is No. Refers to total
     number of days detained in the past 30 days.

ADDITIONAL TEST RESULTS

_____ ☐☐☐
_____ ☐☐☐
_____ ☐☐
_____ ☐☐
_____ ☐☐☐
_____ ☐☐
_____ ☐☐☐
_____ ☐☐☐
_____ ☐☐☐
_____ ☐☐☐

PROBLEMS	\multicolumn{10}{c}{SEVERITY PROFILE}
	0	1	2	3	4	5	6	7	8	9
MEDICAL										
EMP/SUP										
ALCOHOL										
DRUGS										
LEGAL										
FAM/SOC										
PSYCH										

GENERAL INFORMATION COMMENTS
(Include the question number with your notes)

MEDICAL STATUS

M1. How many times in your life have you been hospitalized for medical problems? ☐
- Include O.D.'s and D.T.'s. Exclude detox, alcohol/drug, psychiatric treatment and childbirth (if no complications). Enter the number of *overnight* hospitalizations for medical problems.

M2. How long ago was your last hospitalization for a physical problem? ☐☐ Yrs. ☐☐ Mos.
- If no hospitalizations in Question M1, then this is coded "NN".

M3. Do you have any chronic medical problems which continue to interfere with your life? 0-No 1-Yes ☐
- *If "Yes", specify in comments.*
- A chronic medical condition is a serious physical condition that requires regular care, (i.e., medication, dietary restriction) preventing full advantage of their abilities.

M4. Are you taking any prescribed medication on a regular basis for a physical problem? 0-No 1-Yes ☐
- *If "Yes", specify in comments.*
- Medication prescribed by a MD for medical conditions; **not psychiatric medicines**. Include medicines prescribed whether or not the patient is currently taking them. The intent is to verify chronic medical problems.

M5. Do you receive a pension for a physical disability? 0-No 1-Yes ☐
- *If "Yes", specify in comments.*
- Include Workers' compensation, exclude psychiatric disability.

M6. How many days have you experienced medical problems in the past 30 days? ☐☐
- Include flu, colds, etc. Include serious ailments related to drugs/alcohol, which would continue even if the patient were abstinent (e.g., cirrhosis of liver, abscesses from needles, etc.).

For Questions M7 & M8, ask the patient to use the Patient Rating scale.

M7. How troubled or bothered have you been by these medical problems in the past 30 days? ☐
- Restrict response to problem days of Question M6.

M8. How important to you now is treatment for these medical problems? ☐
- If client is currently receiving medical treatment, refer to the need for **additional** medical treatment by the patient.

INTERVIEWER SEVERITY RATING

M9. How would you rate the patient's need for medical treatment? ☐
- Refers to the patient's need for **additional** medical treatment.

CONFIDENCE RATINGS
Is the above information significantly distorted by:

M10. Patient's misrepresentation? 0-No 1-Yes ☐

M11. Patient's inability to understand 0-No 1-Yes ☐

MEDICAL COMMENTS
(Include the question number with your notes)

_____
_____
_____
_____
_____
_____
_____
_____
_____
_____
_____
_____
_____
_____
_____
_____
_____
_____
_____
_____
_____
_____
_____
_____
_____
_____
_____
_____
_____
_____
_____
_____
_____
_____
_____
_____
_____

EMPLOYMENT/SUPPORT STATUS

E1.* Education completed:
- GED = 12 years, note in comments.
- Include formal education only.

☐☐ ☐☐
Yrs.   Mos.

E2.* Training or Technical education completed:
- Formal/organized training only. For military training, only include training that can be used in civilian life (i.e., electronics, computers)

☐☐
Mos.

E3. Do you have a profession, trade, or skill?   0-No 1-Yes ☐
- Employable, transferable skill acquired through training.
- If "Yes" (specify) _____

E4. Do you have a valid driver's license?   0-No 1-Yes ☐
- Valid license; not suspended/revoked.

E5. Do you have an automobile available for use?
- If answer to E4 is "No", then E5 must be "No". Does not require ownership, only requires availability on a regular basis.   0-No 1-Yes ☐

E6. How long was your longest full time job?   ☐☐ ☐☐
- Full time = 35+ hours weekly; does not necessarily mean most recent job.   Yrs.   Mos.

E7.* Usual (or last) occupation?   ☐
(specify) _____
(use Hollingshead Categories Reference Sheet)

E8. Does someone contribute to your support in any way?   0-No 1-Yes ☐
- Is patient receiving any regular support (i.e., cash, food, housing) from family/friend. Include spouse's contribution; exclude support by an institution.

E9. Does this constitute the majority of your support?   0-No 1-Yes ☐
- If E8 is "No", then E9 is "No".

E10. Usual employment pattern, past three years?   ☐
1. Full time (35+ hours)   5. Service
2. Part time (regular hours)   6. Retired/Disability
3. Part time (irregular hours) 7. Unemployed
4. Student   8. In controlled environment
- Answer should represent the majority of the last 3 years, not just the most recent selection. If there are equal times for more than one category, select that which best represents the current situation.

E11) How many days were you paid for working in the past 30 days?   ☐☐
- Include "under the table" work, paid sick days and vacation.

EMPLOYMENT/SUPPORT COMMENTS
(Include the question number with your notes)

EMPLOYMENT/SUPPORT (cont.)

For questions E12-17: How much money did you receive from the following sources in the past 30 days?

(E12.) Employment?
- Net or "take home" pay, include any "under the table" money.

(E13.) Unemployment Compensation?

(E14.) Welfare?
- Include food stamps, transportation money provided by an agency to go to and from treatment.

(E15.) Pensions, benefits or Social Security?
- Include disability, pensions, retirement, veteran's benefits, SSI & workers' compensation.

(E16.) Mate, family, or friends?
- Money for personal expenses, (i.e. clothing), include unreliable sources of income. Record **cash** payments only, include windfalls (unexpected), money from loans, legal gambling, inheritance, tax returns, etc.).

(E17.) Illegal?
- **Cash** obtained from drug dealing, stealing, fencing stolen goods, illegal gambling, prostitution, etc. **Do not** attempt to convert drugs exchanged to a dollar value.

(E18) How many people depend on you for the majority of their food, shelter, etc.?
- Must be regularly depending on patient, do include alimony/child support, do not include the patient or self-supporting spouse, etc.

(E19.) How many days have you experienced employment problems in the past 30 days?
- Include inability to find work, if they are actively looking for work, or problems with present job in which that job is jeopardized.

For Questions E20 & E21, ask the patient to use the Patient Rating scale.

(E20.) How troubled or bothered have you been by these employment problems in the past 30 days?
- If the patient has been incarcerated or detained during the past 30 days, they cannot have employment problems. In that case a "No" response is indicated.

(E21.) How important to you now is counseling for these employment problems?
- Stress help in finding or preparing for a job, and not giving them a job.

INTERVIEWER SEVERITY RATING

E22. How would you rate the patient's need for employment counseling?

CONFIDENCE RATINGS

Is the above information significantly distorted by:

(E23) Patient's misrepresentation?   0-No 1-Yes

(E24) Patient's inability to understand   0-No 1-Yes

EMPLOYMENT/SUPPORT COMMENTS
(Include the question number with your notes)

ALCOHOL/DRUGS

Route of Administration Types:
1. Oral 2. Nasal 3. Smoking 4. Non-IV injection 5. IV
• *Note the usual or most recent route. For more than one route, choose the most severe. The routes are listed from least severe to most severe.*

	Past 30 Days	Lifetime (years)	Route of Admin
D1. Alcohol (any use at all, 30 days)	☐☐	☐☐	■
D2. Alcohol - to intoxication	☐☐	☐☐	■
D3. Heroin	☐☐	☐☐	☐
D4. Methadone	☐☐	☐☐	☐
D5. Other Opiates/Analgesics	☐☐	☐☐	☐
D6. Barbiturates	☐☐	☐☐	☐
D7. Sedatives/Hypnotics/ Tranquilizers	☐☐	☐☐	☐
D8. Cocaine	☐☐	☐☐	☐
D9. Amphetamines	☐☐	☐☐	☐
D10 Cannabis	☐☐	☐☐	☐
D11 Hallucinogens	☐☐	☐☐	☐
D12 Inhalants	☐☐	☐☐	☐
D13 More than 1 substance per day (including alcohol)	☐☐	☐☐	■

D14. According to the interviewer, which substance(s) is/are the major problem?   ☐☐
• Interviewer should determine the major drug or drugs of abuse. Code the number next to the drug in questions 01-12, or "00" = no problem, "15" = alcohol & one or more drugs, "16" = more than one drug but no alcohol. Ask patient when not clear.

D15. How long was your last period of voluntary abstinence from this major substance?   ☐☐ Mos.
• Last attempt of at least one month, not necessarily the longest. Periods of hospitalization/incarceration **do not count**. Periods of antabuse, methadone, or naltrexone use during abstinence **do count**.
• "00" = never abstinent

D16. How many months ago did this abstinence end?   ☐☐ Mos.
• If D15 = "00", then D16 = "NN".
• "00" = still abstinent

D17. *How many times have you had: Alcohol DT's?   ☐☐
• ***Delirium Tremens*** (DT's): Occur 24-48 hours after the last drink, or significant decrease in alcohol intake, shaking, severe disorientation, fever, hallucinations, they usually require medical attention.

D18. Overdosed on Drugs?   ☐☐
• ***Overdoses*** (OD): Requires intervention by someone to recover, not simply sleeping it off, include suicide attempts by OD.

ALCOHOL/DRUGS COMMENTS
(Include the question number with your notes)

ALCOHOL/DRUGS (cont.)

(D19)* How many times in your life have you been ⬚⬚
treated for:
  Alcohol abuse?
  • Include detoxification, halfway houses, in/outpatient
    counseling, and AA (if 3+ meetings within one month period).

(D21)* How many of these were detox only: ⬚⬚
  Alcohol?

(D23) How much would you say you spent ⬚⬚⬚⬚⬚
during the past 30 days on: Alcohol?

(D20)* How many times in your life have you been ⬚⬚
treated for: Drug abuse?
  • Include detoxification, halfway houses, in/outpatient
    counseling, and NA (if 3+ meetings within one month period).

(D22)* How many of these were detox only: ⬚⬚
  Drugs?
  • If D19 = "00", then question D21 is "NN"
    If D20 = "00", then question D22 is "NN"

(D24) How much would you say you ⬚⬚⬚⬚⬚
spent during the past 30 days on:
  Drugs?
  • Only count actual **money** spent. What is the
    financial burden caused by drugs/alcohol?

(D25.) How many days have you been treated in ⬚⬚
an outpatient setting for alcohol or drugs
in the past 30 days   • Include AA/NA

(D26.) How many days in the past 30 have you ⬚⬚
experienced:
  Alcohol problems?
  • Include: Craving, withdrawal symptoms, disturbing
    effects of use, or wanting to stop and being unable to.

**For Questions D28+D30, ask the patient to use the Patient Rating scale.
The patient is rating the need for additional substance abuse treatment.**

(D28.) How troubled or bothered have you been in ⬚
the past 30 days by these:
  Alcohol problems?
  • Include: Craving, withdrawal symptoms, disturbing
    effects of use, or wanting to stop and being unable to.

(D30.) How important to you now is treatment ⬚
for these: Alcohol problems?

(D27.) How many days in the past 30 have you ⬚⬚
experienced: Drug problems?
  • Include: Craving, withdrawal symptoms, disturbing
    effects of use, or wanting to stop and being unable to.

**For Questions D29+D31, ask the patient to use the Patient Rating scale.
The patient is rating the need for additional substance abuse treatment.**

(D29.) How troubled or bothered have you been in ⬚
the past 30 days by these:
  Drug problems?

(D31.) How important to you now is treatment ⬚
for these: Drug problems?

INTERVIEWER RATING
How would you rate the patient's need for treatment for:
D32. Alcohol problems? ⬚

D33. Drug problems? ⬚

CONFIDENCE RATINGS
Is the above information significantly distorted by:

(D34) Patient's misrepresentation?   0-No 1-Yes ⬚

(D35) Patient's inability to understand?   0-No 1-Yes ⬚

ALCOHOL/DRUGS COMMENTS
(Include the question number with your notes)

_____

_____

_____

_____

_____

_____

_____

_____

_____

_____

_____

_____

_____

_____

_____

_____

_____

_____

_____

_____

_____

_____

_____

_____

_____

_____

LEGAL STATUS

L1.   Was this admission prompted or suggested by the criminal justice system?   0-No 1-Yes ☐
   • Judge, probation/parole officer, etc.

(L2.)   Are you on parole or probation?   0-No 1-Yes ☐
   • Note duration and level in comments.

(L24.)   Are you presently awaiting charges, trial, or sentence?   0-No 1-Yes ☐

(L25.)   What for?
   • Use the number of the type of crime committed: 03-16 and 18-20. ☐☐
   • Refers to Q.L24. If more than one, choose most severe.

How many times in your life have you been arrested and charged with the following:

(L3.)* Shoplift/Vandal ☐☐   (L10)* Assault ☐☐

(L4.)* Parole/Probation Violations ☐☐   (L11)* Arson ☐☐

(L5.)* Drug Charges ☐☐   (L12)* Rape ☐☐

(L6.)* Forgery ☐☐   (L13)* Homicide/Mansl. ☐☐

(L7.)* Weapons Offense ☐☐   (L14)* Prostitution ☐☐

(L8.)* Burglary/Larceny/ B&E ☐☐   (L15)* Contempt of Court ☐☐

(L9.)* Robbery ☐☐   (L16)* Other: _____ ☐☐

   • Include total number of counts, not just convictions. Do not include juvenile (pre-age 18) crimes, unless they were charged as an adult.
   • Include formal charges only.

(L17.)* How many of these charges resulted in convictions? ☐☐
   • If L3-16 = 00, then question L17 = "NN".
   • Do not include misdemeanor offenses from questions L18-20 below.
   • Convicitons include fines, probation, incarcerations, suspended sentences, guilty pleas, and plea bargaining.

How many times in your life have you been charged with the following:

(L18.)* Disorderly conduct, vagrancy, public intoxication? ☐☐

(L19.)* Driving while intoxicated? ☐☐

(L20.)* Major driving violations? ☐☐
   • Moving violations: speeding, reckless driving, no license, etc.

(L21.)* How many months were you incarcerated in your life? ☐☐ Mos.
   • If incarcerated 2 weeks or more, round this up to 1 month. List total number of months incarcerated.

L22. How long was your last incarceration? ☐☐ Mos.
   • Of 2 weeks or more. Enter "NN" if never incarcerated.

L23. What was it for? ☐☐
   • Use code 03-16, 18-20. If multiple charges, choose most severe. Enter "NN" if never incarcerated.

LEGAL COMMENTS
(Include the question number with your notes)

_____

_____

_____

_____

_____

_____

_____

_____

_____

_____

_____

_____

_____

_____

_____

_____

_____

_____

_____

_____

_____

_____

_____

_____

_____

_____

LEGAL STATUS (cont.)

(L26.) How many days in the past 30, were you detained or incarcerated?
   • Include being arrested and released on the same day.

(L27.) How many days in the past 30 have you engaged in illegal activities for profit?
   • Exclude simple drug possession. Include drug dealing, prostitution, selling stolen goods, etc. May be cross checked with Question E17 under Employment/Family Support Section.

For Questions L28-29, ask the patient to use the Patient Rating scale.

(L28.) How serious do you feel your present legal problems are?
   • Exclude civil problems.

(L29.) How important to you now is counseling or referral for these legal problems?
   • Patient is rating a need for referral to legal counsel for defense against criminal charges.

INTERVIEWER SEVERITY RATING

L30. How would you rate the patient's need for legal services or counseling?

CONFIDENCE RATINGS

Is the above information significantly distorted by:

(L31.) Patient's misrepresentation?   0-No 1-Yes

(L32.) Patient's inability to understand?   0-No 1-Yes

LEGAL COMMENTS
(Include the question number with your notes)

FAMILY HISTORY

Have any of your blood-related relatives had what you would call a significant drinking, drug use, or psychiatric problem? Specifically, was there a problem that did or should have led to treatment?

Mother's Side	Alcohol	Drug	Psych.	Father's Side	Alcohol	Drug	Psych.	Siblings	Alcohol	Drug	Psych.
H1. Grandmother				H6. Grandmother				H11. Brother			
H2. Grandfather				H7. Grandfather							
H3. Mother				H8. Father				H12. Sister			
H4. Aunt				H9. Aunt							
H5. Uncle				H10. Uncle							

0 = Clearly No for any relatives in that category   X = Uncertain or don't know
1 = Clearly Yes for any relatives in that category   N = Never was a relative
• In cases where there is more than one person for a category, record the occurrence of problems for *any* in that group. Accept the patient's judgment on these questions.

FAMILY HISTORY COMMENTS

FAMILY/SOCIAL STATUS

F1. Marital Status: ☐
   1 - Married   3 - Widowed   5 - Divorced
   2 - Remarried 4 - Separated 6 - Never Married
   • Common-law marriage = 1. Specify in comments.

F2. How long have you been in   ☐☐ ☐☐
   this marital status (Q #F1)?   Yrs.   Mos.
   • If never married, then since age 18.

F3. Are you satisfied with   0-No 1-Indifferent 2-Yes ☐
   this situation?
   • Satisfied = generally liking the situation.
   • Refers to Questions F1 & F2.

F4. * Usual living arrangement (past 3 years): ☐
   1 - With sexual partner & children 6 - With friends
   2 - With sexual partner alone   7 - Alone
   3 - With children alone   8 - Controlled Environment
   4 - With parents   9 - No stable arrangement
   5 - With family
   • Choose arrangements most representative of the past 3 years.
   If there is an even split in time between these arrangements,
   choose the most recent arrangement.

F5. How long have you lived in   ☐☐ ☐☐
   these arrangements?   Yrs.   Mos.
   • If with parents or family, since age 18.
   • Code years and months living in arrangements from Question F4.

F6. Are you satisfied with
   these arrangements?   0-No 1-Indifferent 2-Yes ☐

Do you live with anyone who:

F7. Has a current alcohol problem?   0-No 1-Yes ☐

F8. Uses non-prescribed drugs: 0-No 1-Yes ☐
   (or abuses prescribed drugs)

F9. With whom do you spend most of your free time? ☐
   1 - Family 2 - Friends 3 - Alone
   • If a girlfriend/boyfriend is considered as family
   by patient, then they must refer to them as family
   throughout this section, not a friend.

F10 Are you satisfied with spending your
   free time this way?   0-No 1-Indifferent 2-Yes ☐
   • A satisfied response must indicate that the person
   generally likes the situation. Referring to Question F9.

F11 How many close friends do you have? ☐
   • Stress that you mean *close*. Exclude family members.
   These are "reciprocal" relationships or mutually
   supportive relationships.

Would you say you have had a close reciprocal relationship with any of the following people:

F12. Mother ☐   F15. Sexual Partner/Spouse ☐
F13. Father ☐   F16. Children ☐
F14. Brothers/Sisters ☐   F17. Friends ☐

0 = Clearly No for all in class   X = Uncertain or "I don't know"
1 = Clearly Yes for any in class   N = Never was a relative
   • By reciprocal, you mean "that you would do anything
   you could to help them out and vice versa".

FAMILY/SOCIAL COMMENTS
(Include the question number with your notes)

_____
_____
_____
_____
_____
_____
_____
_____
_____
_____
_____
_____
_____
_____
_____
_____
_____
_____
_____
_____
_____
_____
_____
_____
_____
_____
_____
_____
_____
_____

FAMILY/SOCIAL (cont.)

Have you had significant periods in which you have experienced serious problems getting along with:	0 - No Past 30 Days	1 - Yes In Your Life
(F18) Mother	☐	☐
(F19) Father	☐	☐
(F20) Brother/Sister	☐	☐
(F21) Sexual Partner/Spouse	☐	☐
(F22) Children	☐	☐
(F23) Other Significant Family (specify) _____	☐	☐
(F24) Close Friends	☐	☐
(F25) Neighbors	☐	☐
(F26) Co-workers	☐	☐

• "Serious problems" mean those that endangered the relationship.
• A "problem" requires contact of some sort, either by telephone or in person. If no contact code "N".

Has anyone ever abused you?	0 - No Past 30 Days	1 - Yes In Your Life
F27. Emotionally? • Made you feel bad through harsh words.	☐	☐
F28. Physically? • Caused you physical harm.	☐	☐
F29. Sexually? • Forced sexual advances/acts.	☐	☐

Has many days in the past 30 have you had serious conflicts:

(F30) With your family? ☐☐

For Questions F32-35, ask the patient to use the Patient Rating scale.

(F32.) How troubled or bothered have you been in the past 30 days by:
Family problems? ☐

(F34.) How important to you now is treatment or counseling for these:
Family problems
• Patient is rating his/her need for counseling for family problems, not whether they would be willing to attend.

(F31) How many days in the past 30 have you had serious conflicts:
With other people (excluding family)? ☐☐

For Questions F32-35, ask the patient to use the Patient Rating scale.

(F33.) How troubled or bothered have you been in the past 30 days by:
Social problems? ☐

(F35.) How important to you now is treatment or counseling for these:
Social problems
• Include patient's need to seek treatment for such social problems as loneliness, inability to socialize, and dissatisfaction with friends. Patient rating should refer to dissatisfaction, conflicts, or other serious problems.

INTERVIEWER SEVERITY RATING

F36. How would you rate the patient's need for family and/or social counseling? ☐

CONFIDENCE RATINGS
Is the above information significantly distorted by:

(F37.) Patient's misrepresentation? 0-No 1-Yes ☐

(F38.) Patient's inability to understand? 0-No 1-Yes ☐

FAMILY/SOCIAL COMMENTS
(Include the question number with your notes)

_____
_____
_____
_____
_____
_____
_____
_____
_____
_____
_____
_____
_____
_____
_____
_____
_____
_____
_____
_____
_____
_____
_____
_____
_____
_____
_____
_____

PSYCHIATRIC STATUS

How many times have you been treated for any psychological or emotional problems:

(P1.)* In a hospital or inpatient setting? ☐☐

(P2.)* Outpatient/private patient? ☐☐
- Do not include substance abuse, employment, or family counseling. Treatment episode = a series of more or less continuous visits or treatment days, not the number of visits or treatment days.
- Enter diagnosis in comments if known.

(P3.) Do you receive a pension for a psychiatric disability?   0-No 1-Yes ☐

Have you had a significant period of time (that was not a direct result of alcohol/drug use) in which you have: 0 - No 1 - Yes
                                                                  Past 30 Days Lifetime

(P4.) Experienced serious depression-sadness, hopelessness, loss of interest? ☐ ☐

(P5.) Experienced serious anxiety/tension-uptight, unreasonably worried, inability to feel relaxed? ☐ ☐

(P6.) Experienced hallucinations-saw things/heard voices that others didn't see/hear? ☐ ☐

(P7.) Experienced trouble understanding, concentrating, or remembering? ☐ ☐

Have you had a significant period of time (despite your alcohol and drug use) in which you have: 0 - No 1 - Yes
                                                                  Past 30 Days Lifetime

(P8.) Experienced trouble controlling violent behavior including episodes of rage, or violence? ☐ ☐
- Patient can be under the influence of alcohol/drugs.

(P9.) Experienced serious thoughts of suicide? ☐ ☐
- Patient seriously considered a plan for taking his/her life. Patient can be under the influence of alcohol/drugs.

(P10) Attempted suicide? ☐ ☐
- Include actual suicidal gestures or attempts.
- Patient can be under the influence of alcohol/drugs.

(P11) Been prescribed medication for any psychological or emotional problems? ☐ ☐
- Prescribed for the patient by a physican. Record "Yes" if a medication was prescribed even if the patient is not taking it.

(P12) How many days in the past 30 have you experienced these psychological or emotional problems? ☐☐
- This refers to problems noted in Questions P4-P10.

For Questions P13-P14, ask the patient to use the Patient Rating scale.

(P13) How much have you been troubled or bothered by these psychological or emotional problems in the past 30 days? ☐
- Patient should be rating the problem days from Question P12.

(P14) How important to you now is treatment for these psychological or emotional problems? ☐

PSYCHIATRIC STATUS COMMENTS
(Include the question number with your notes)

_____

_____

_____

_____

_____

_____

_____

_____

_____

_____

_____

_____

_____

_____

_____

_____

_____

_____

_____

_____

_____

_____

_____

_____

_____

_____

_____

PSYCHIATRIC STATUS (cont.)

The following items are to be completed by the interviewer:
At the time of the interview, the patient was: 0 - No 1 - Yes

(P15) Obviously depressed/withdrawn ☐

(P16) Obviously hostile ☐

(P17) Obviously anxious/nervous ☐

(P18) Having trouble with reality testing, thought disorders, paranoid thinking ☐

(P19) Having trouble comprehending, concentrating, remembering ☐

(P20) Having suicidal thoughts ☐

INTERVIEWER SEVERITY RATING

P21. How would you rate the patient's need for psychiatric/psychological treatment? ☐

CONFIDENCE RATING

Is the above information significantly distorted by:

(P23) Patient's misrepresentation? 0-No 1-Yes ☐

(P24) Patient's inability to understand? 0-No 1-Yes ☐

G12. Special Code ☐
1. Patient terminated by interview
2. Patient refused
3. Patient unable to respond (language or intellectual barrier, under the influence, etc.)
N. Interview completed.

PSYCHIATRIC STATUS COMMENTS
(Include the question number with your notes)

forth. If these processes are handled competently and professionally, the client will return!

CHAPTER SUMMARY

A comprehensive assessment is necessary to determine a patient's specific problems and to develop an individualized treatment plan. This chapter discussed some problems in interviewing substance abusers and then presented the major content domains to be addressed in a clinical interview with this population. Several examples (assessment models) were presented to illustrate a narrative composition that would follow specific questioning in a defined area. Laboratory tests and psychological tests also were referenced, for they often play a role in the assessment process. Motivational interviewing—a specific type of clinical interview designed for use with substance abusers—was also described.

SOURCES OF INFORMATION

Allen, J. P., & Columbus, M. (1995). *Assessing alcohol problems: A guide for clinicians and researchers*. Bethesda, MD: National Institute on Alcohol Abuse and Alcoholism.

Butcher, J. N., Dahlstrom, W. G., Graham, J. R., Tellegen, A., & Kaemmer, B. (1989). *Minnesota Multiphasic Personality Inventory-2: Manual for administration and scoring*. Minneapolis, MN: National Computer Systems.

Butcher, J. N., & Rouse, S. V. (1996). Personality: Individual differences and clinical assessment. *Annual Review of Psychology, 47*, 87–111.

Craig, R. J. (1988). Diagnostic interviewing with drug abusers. *Professional Psychology: Research and Practice, 19*, 14–20.

Craig, R. J. (1999). *Interpreting personality tests: A clinical manual for the MMPI-2, MCMI-III, CPI-R, and 16 PF*. New York: John Wiley & Sons.

Craig, R. J. (2000). Prevalence of personality disorders among cocaine and heroin addicts. *Substance Abuse, 21*, 87–94.

Craig, R. J., & Weinberg, D. (1992a). Assessing drug abusers with the Millon Clinical Multiaxial Inventory: A review. *Journal of Substance Abuse Treatment, 9*, 249–255.

Craig, R. J., & Weinberg, D. (1992b). Assessing alcoholics with the Millon Clinical Multiaxial Inventory: A review. *Psychology of Addictive Behaviors, 6*, 200–208.

Diagnostic and Statistical manual of mental disorders (4th ed.). (1994). Washington, DC: American Psychiatric Association.

Hansen, H. J., Caudill, S. P., & Boone, J. (1985). Crisis in drug testing: Results of CDC blind study. *Journal of the American Medical Association, 253*, 2382–2387.

Hawks, R., & Chiang, C. N. (1986). *Urine testing for drugs of abuse*. Rockville, MD: NIDA Research Monograph 73.

Imhof, J., Hirsh, R., & Terenzi, R. E. (1983). Countertransferential and attitudinal considerations in the treatment of drug abuse and addiction. *International Journal of the Addictions, 18*, 491–510.

Khantzian, E. J., & Treece, C. (1985). DSM-III psychiatric diagnosis of narcotic addicts. *Archives of General Psychiatry, 42*, 1067–1071.

McLellan, A. T., Kushner, H., Metzger, D., Peters, R., Grissom, G., Pettinati, H., & Argeriou, M. (1992). The fifth edition of the Addiction Severity Index. *Journal of Substance Abuse Treatment, 9*, 1–15.

McLellan, A. T., Luborsky, L., Cacciola, J., Griffith, J., Evans, F., Barr, H. L., & O'Brien, C. P. (1985). New data from the Addiction Severity Index: Reliability and validity in three centers. *Journal of Nervous and Mental Disease, 173*, 412–423.

McLellan, A. T., Luborsky, L., Cacciola, J., Griffith,

J., McGahan, P., & O'Brien, C. P. (1985). *Guide to the Addiction Severity Index: Background, administration, and field testing results.* Rockville, MD.

McLellan, A. T., Luborsky, L., Cacciola, J., Griffith, J., McGahan, P., O'Brien, C. P., & Druley, K. A. (1983). Predicting response to alcohol and drug abuse treatments: Role of psychiatric severity. *Archives of General Psychiatry, 40,* 620–625.

McLellan, A. T., Luborsky, L., Cacciola, J., Griffith, J., McGahan, P., O'Brien, C. P., & Kron, R. (1981). Are the "addiction-related" problems of substance abusers really related? *Journal of Nervous and Mental Disease, 169,* 232–239.

McLellan, A. T., Luborsky, L., Woody, G. E., & O'Brien, C. P. (1980). An improved diagnostic evaluation instrument for substance abuse patients: The Addiction Severity Index. *Journal of Nervous and Mental Disease, 168,* 26–33.

Miller, W. R. (1991). *Motivational interviewing: Preparing people to change addictive behavior.* NY: Guilford Press.

Miller, W. R., & Marlatt, G. A. (1984). *Manual for the comprehensive drinker profile.* Odessa, FL: Psychological Assessment Resources.

Millon, T. (1994). *Millon Clinical Multiaxial Inventory-III.* Minneapolis, MN: National Computer Systems.

NIAAA (1995). Michigan Alcoholism Screening Test. In J. P. Allen (Ed.), *Assessing alcohol problems: A guide for clinicians and researchers.* Bethesda, MD: National Institute on Alcoholism and Alcohol Abuse.

Nurco, D. N., Cisin, I. H., & Balter, M. B. (1981a). Addict careers I: A new typology. *International Journal of the Addictions, 16,* 1305–1325.

Nurco, D. N., Cisin, I. H., & Balter, M. B. (1981b). Addict careers II: The first ten years. *International Journal of the Addictions, 16,* 1327–1356.

Nurco, D. N., Cisin, I. H., & Balter, M. B. (1981c). Addict careers III: Trends across time. *International Journal of the Addictions, 16,* 1357–1372.

O'Brien, C. P., Woody, G. E., & McLellan, A. T. (1984). Psychiatric disorders in opiod-dependent patients. *Journal of Clinical Psychiatry, 45,* 9–13.

Rounsaville, B. J., Weissman, M. M., Kleber, H. D., & Wilbur, C. (1982). Heterogeneity of psychiatry diagnosis in treated opiate addicts. *Archives of General Psychiatry, 39,* 161–166.

U.S. Department of Health and Human Services. (1987, June 9). Confidentiality of alcohol and drug abuse patient records: Final rule. *Federal Register, 52,* No. 110, 21796–21814.

Watkins, C. E., Campbell, V. L., Nieberding, R., & Hallmark, R. (1995). Contemporary practice of psychological assessment by clinical psychologists. *Professional Psychology: Research and Practice, 26,* 54–60.

Winters, K. C. (Ed.). (1999). *Screening and assessing adolescents for substance use disorders.* Treatment Improvement Protocol (TIP) series 31. Rockville, MD: U.S. Dept. of Health and Human Services, Substance Abuse and Mental Health Administration, Center for Substance Abuse Treatment.

CHAPTER FIVE

TREATMENT PRINCIPLES AND MODALITIES

This chapter considers treatment methods that proved successful with substance abusers. Not all of the methods will be applicable to each patient, but knowledge of how each of these is implemented can be useful in treating some patients. A listing and discussion of techniques is followed by their implementations. First, however, one point is critically important.

Research studies show over and over again that (a) no specific technique has been shown to be more effective than any other technique in terms of outcome; (b) no form of treatment has been shown to be more effective than any other form of treatment; (c) patients in treatment do better than patients not in treatment; and (d) patients who satisfactorily complete treatment do better than those who drop out of treatment.

PRINCIPLES OF TREATMENT

The National Institute on Drug Abuse has published a research guide on principles of treatment. The following are highlights from that document:

- *No single treatment is appropriate for all individuals.* There is an old saying that if the only tool you have is a hammer then everything starts to look like a nail. Counselors who believe that a preferred method is the only way to treat a substance abuser, are not providing their clients with what they need to recover.
- *Treatment needs to be readily available.* Waiting lists need to be avoided. Motivation for treatment among substance abusers is ephemeral and quickly dissipates when they are blocked from receiving help. It is crucial to provide services to patients when they are ready to receive them.
- *Effective treatment attends to the multiple needs of the person, not just substance abuse.* It is only partially true that a person's life suddenly improves once they discontinue abusing substances. Although a modicum of improvement will occur in certain areas of life, others will not improve unless they

are specifically addressed in counseling. This is a critical principle in treatment that needs to be implemented in every case.

■ *The care plan needs to be reviewed periodically and adjusted to meet the person's changing needs.* Events happen in a person's life and counseling interventions may need to change accordingly. Periodic and systematic review of a patient's treatment plan will facilitate targeted interventions to maximize treatment outcome.

■ *Remaining in treatment for a sufficient length of time is critical for effective treatment outcome.* Studies repeatedly show that the longer patients remain in treatment, the more benefit they receive, and the more likely they are to remain abstinent at follow-up. Little improvement is probable for at least three months.

■ *Counseling is a critical component of effective treatment.* This applies especially to pharmacologically oriented treatment modalities, such as methadone maintenance. These patients often are unduly focused on getting this medication and consider counseling of secondary importance. While medication can control narcotic hunger, it does not necessarily rehabilitate. It is necessary for a patient to receive counseling to make lifestyle changes.

■ *Medications are an important element, especially when combined with counseling.* Some counselors believe that, if a patient takes prescribed drugs for addiction, then they are not truly off drugs. This is absolutely incorrect. Many patients need psychiatric medication and can improve by using it, especially when engaged in a therapeutic counseling relationship.

■ *Substance-abusing patients with mental disorders need both disorders treated in an integrated manner.* Heretofore, it had been a source of concern and a treatment dilemma for mental health staff, who believed that a patient's psychiatric condition could not be treated effectively as long as the substance abuse problem was not adequately treated. Conversely, substance abuse staff believed they could not effectively treat abusers with a mental disorder unless their psychiatric condition was adequately treated. After much experience with these dually afflicted patients, counselors now realize that their best method is concurrent treatment of both disorders. Treatment of the dually diagnosed patients is covered more fully in Chapter 8

■ *Detoxification is only the first step and does little to change long-term drug use.* Studies consistently report 95% failure rates after detoxification, if that is the only intervention. Detoxification must be followed with a strong aftercare plan that includes counseling and relapse prevention.

■ *Involuntary treatment can also be effective.* While many believe that a patient has to want help in order to get help, sanctions at work, in the community, and involving the criminal justice system can increase program retention rates and, therefore, the success of drug treatment interventions.

■ *Drug use during treatment must be monitored continuously.* Patients can and will test the system to see if they can get away with drug use without being detected. Others will test the resolve of the counselor by abusing. Still others have not made the final decision to stop. Only by providing procedures for detecting alcohol and drug use while in treatment will counselors know the true status of patients' success.

■ *Treatment programs should also do harm reduction.* By this we mean assessment and intervention for HIV/AIDS, Hepatitis B and C, other infectious diseases, and, in particular, sexually transmitted diseases. These diseases can affect patients' response to drug treatment intervention.

■ *Recovery from substance abuse is often a lifelong process.* Multiple episodes of treatment may be necessary before abstinence is established. Patients may relapse after years of recovery. These should not be considered failures but rather as indicators of need for another episode of care.

PROBLEMS IN COUNSELING PATIENTS WITH ACTING-OUT DISORDERS

Patients with impulse control disorders offer unique challenges to substance abuse counselors and display certain characteristics that can interfere with effective counseling. Here are some common personality manifestations displayed by substance abusers.

1. *Saying one thing in counseling and doing another thing outside of counseling.* This is why it is best periodically to get collateral information from knowledgeable sources.

2. *Maintaining an action-oriented method of handling problems.* While this sounds good, it actually interferes with effective problem solving because other possible alternatives are not considered.

Example: A 45-year-old, divorced male alcoholic was driving home from work, where he routinely drank 8–10 martinis at lunchtime without appearing intoxicated. At a stoplight, a youth waited for the light to turn green, then walked over to the patient's car and spit in his face. The patient alleged this was unprovoked. The youth jumped in a car with five friends and drove away. The patient chased them into an alley, where they stopped and jumped out of their car. The patient jumped out of his car, then realized the potential of his predicament. He got back into his car, backed out of the alley, and quickly drove away. His alcoholism had resulted in impulsive behavior and reduced his problem-solving ability.

3. *Seeking out a counselor only when there is a crisis.* Patients look to the counselor to get them out of tight spots.

Example: A 30-year-old heroin addict on methadone maintenance had been working full time and rarely coming in for counseling sessions. He received a letter from his divorced wife's attorney announcing their intention to send him to jail for non-payment of child support. The patient immediately sought out the help of his counselor, who advised him to seek legal representation and to negotiate back payments to his ex-wife. The patient was able to make those arrangements and returned to his infrequent counseling sessions.

4. *Showing poor introspection.* Many substance abusers have difficulty processing feelings, thoughts, and emotions that surround behavior. Processing is required in most kinds of counseling, which becomes far more difficult if patients have difficulty engaging in this type of recollection.

5. *Manipulating and tricking.* Counselors who believe they have never been manipulated or tricked have been. Addicts spend much their life doing this and are quite skilled at it. Counselors have little to gain by trying to convince themselves that they're smarter than their patients. Preferably, counselors will give patients the credit for this skill and admit that they can con and manipulate if they desire. This undercuts the "game" and makes it less of a challenge.

Example: A 65-year-old heroin abuser was confronted by his wife when she found a syringe in his coat pocket. He claimed that his best friend put it there and that it was not his. For "proof" he insisted that they confront his friend. The friend went along with the charade, "apologizing" for his behavior. The wife was satisfied and fooled.

6. *Taking an out-of-sight-out-of mind approach.* The patients simply do not tell the counselor relevant things that have occurred. They think not dwelling on a subject will make it go away.

Example: A male addict was having marital and vocational problems. Estranged from his wife, he was sleeping in their unheated garage. Later, when his counselor asked the status of his relationship with his wife, the patient told him that "everything was ok now" and they had made up. He was no longer sleeping in the garage, though he had lost his job and they had little income. Weeks later, the patient asked for marital counseling and suggested his wife begin to attend the sessions because she was threatening to leave him.

7. M*aintenance of self-image.* Sometimes counselors recommend patients engage in behaviors that are incongruent with their self-image.

Example: An alcoholic with two master's degrees was offered a position to manage his cousin's beef stands. The cousin, a high school dropout, had become hugely successful and needed someone trustworthy offered to manage his operations and collect the money from his several stands. He offered the patient nearly complete control for a very attractive salary—substantially more than a teacher's salary. The patient's self-image could not allow him to assume a role which he considered demeaning and not in keeping with his education.

8. *Irregular attendance.* Substance abusers are notoriously irregular in attending counseling sessions. Most do not call to cancel—they simply to do not show up. This often is part of a way addicts use to sabotage their treatment. This is more fully discussed later in this chapter.

9. *Low frustration tolerance.* Years of substance abuse, interacting with certain developmental experiences, usually result in patients having little ability to tolerate frustration. This makes counseling difficult, because counselors are often compelled to address significant and upsetting issues in a patient's life.

Example: A 55-year-old alcoholic had been in a common law relationship for twenty years. His partner complained about their sexual difficulties, but she would not come for counseling. When she left him for another woman, he was devastated and relapsed, so his counselor spent much time dealing with drug abuse counseling issues. When the counselor began to process the events of the separation, the patient did not return for several sessions. He simply had a rough time talking about this event because of his low frustration tolerance and embarrassment.

   10. *Externalization, denial, and acting out.* It is difficult to discuss patients' behavior when they constantly blame other people, when they refuse to face the truth, and when they do not control their emotions or behavior.

   11. *Premature termination.* The dropout rate from substance abuse counseling is extremely high (50%–60%) (Stark, 1992), though it can be reduced with effective intervention (Craig, 1985). Most substance abusers simply stop coming for counseling long before treatment is terminated, unless they are taking a narcotic substitution drug. This is the ultimate resistance.

PREPARING TO COUNSEL

Counseling patients can change their lives. Accordingly, counseling should not be haphazard or cursory. Preparedness may be the single most important thing counselors can offer clients initially. Here are some suggestions to aid counselor preparedness:

   1. Be on time. No one likes to be kept waiting. See clients as soon as possible.
   2. Keep the work area looking as professional as possible. It does not have to be sterile in appearance, but it should feel natural and convey an aura of knowledge.
   3. Read all possible assessment material before meeting clients. Counselors are obligated to know as much about their clients to help them. Substance abusers have the right to have helpers who are knowledgeable about their situations and problems.
   4. Orient patients to the purpose and intent of the initial interview and assessment and how the material they reveal will be used to help them.
   5. Ask questions that convey to clients the impression that the counselor is knowledgable. Use street terms. Ask questions that pertain to use and consequences of addiction in each domain affected by substance abuse.
   6. Be accepting, treat clients with courtesy and respect, try to be nonjudgmental, answer questions honestly, and ask clients if they have additional questions.

7. Orient the patients to the essential details surrounding the counseling process, such as time, place, and frequency of meetings, program and counselor rules and expectations, costs, and other administrative matters relevant to the patient.
8. Explain and reinforce *confidentiality* of the information and of the relationship with you.
9. Admit not knowing answers, but try to find them.

This list may not definitely outline all areas of counselor preparation but following it will take counselors a long way toward establishing and solidifying honest client-counselor relationships.

FORMULATING A TREATMENT PLAN

A growing consensus in the literature suggests that patients *require* formal treatment plans that contain certain common features. Accrediting agencies, such as the Joint Commission on Accreditation of Hospitals and Organizations (JACHO) and the Council on Accreditation of Rehabilitation Facilities (CARF) both mandate that formal treatment plans be developed and implemented with substance abusers in treatment. National associations, in their codes of ethics, also mandate formal treatment plans. Finally, state laws that license substance abuse counselors require the formulation of a treatment plan as a counselor competency to be demonstrated prior to licensing.

Most treatment plans require the recording of patients

- problems
- long term goals
- short term goals
- behavioral outcome criteria with which to determine whether these goals have been accomplished, stated in objective and measurable terms
- methods of intervention
- frequency of treatment
- responsible clinician
- expected date when the goal will be achieved.

Client history, case summary and case formulation, and DSM-IV diagnoses may precede treatment plans.

COUNSELING TECHNIQUES

Active Listening

Active listening is among the most important tools in counselors' overall counseling repertoire. Active listening may be defined as the ability to accurately restate the content, feeling, and meaning of what a patient has just said. It requires the counselor to *listen* to the words of the statement, to *restate* it in *reflective statements,* and then to *observe the patient's response* to the reflection. This tells the counselor whether or not the reflective statement was an accurate portrayal of what the client said. This is different from mere reflection, described later.

To actively listen, counselors position their bodies so that posture and direct eye contact communicate nonverbally that they are attending only to the client. Interruptions, such as phone calls, suggest to clients that counselors don't have time for them. Distractions interfere with counselors' ability to listen and promote the impression that they really don't care about the client. Avoid distractions and interruptions and give the patient full attention.

Even full attention to the client does not necessarily mean actively listening. This counseling technique requires practice until it becomes an automatic response.

Accurate Empathy

Empathy is another of the most important counseling tools for substance abuse intervention. A long history of psychological research has established that the communication of accurate empathy is far more important and more associated with patient changes than any other counseling intervention.

Empathy may be defined as the ability to understand people from their perspective. Patients want counselors to understand them and their situation. Accurate empathy communicates this understanding to the client and further instills a sense of confidence in the counselor's ability to help them. It does not mean feeling what the patient is feeling but it does mean understanding what the client is feeling. Many substance abusers have difficulty communicating their feelings openly or directly. In this case, the counselor may have to help clients understand what they are actually feeling, perhaps by citing how they might have felt in such situations.

EXAMPLE

Patient: I want to quit using drugs but I must admit I used the other day. My brother came over with his girl friend and baby. They both use and are living out of a car. My brother asked if they could stay with me for a while. He had some drugs, so we used, but I wouldn't let him stay with us. I knew it wouldn't work out. But I still feel guilty about it. Oh, and the other day my wife—you know, she uses too—and I went over to her sister's, who also uses. She had some and so we all used. I felt guilty over that but I couldn't help myself. Last night I knew my wife had used. She doesn't want me to know when she uses but I can tell. So we got into an argument about her using, and I felt guilty because it felt a little hypocritical, since I still am using, even though I'm trying to stop. It just seems that when I get around these people they force me to use.

Therapist: You know the one common thread in all of this is your guilt feelings over your behavior. You know you shouldn't be doing these things and when you do, you get down on yourself. Then you try to blame it on someone else!

Patient: You got that right!

EXAMPLE

Patient: My sister has cancer. She had her breasts removed and needs chemotherapy. She moved in with me 'cause we're very close and I have to take care of her. You know, take her to her appointments, talk to her so she don't get down, and so forth. I got my own problems to deal with, too. Still trying to get on disability for my problems, still can't sleep well due to my traumatic experience, can't get a straight answer from these agencies. Then I come here and have to listen to you tell me I have to stop using drugs and stop drinking. Hell, that's the only thing that keeps me going these days.

Therapist: There is so much stress in your life these days that you feel justified in using drugs and drinking. And although you love your sister and willingly take on this burden, it does add to your overall troubles.

Acceptance

Effective counseling requires that the counselor act nonjudgmentally. This is often difficult, especially when the patient may be engaging in behaviors that strain the counselor's acceptance. Only the counselor can decide if judgmental pronouncements facilitate or hinder the therapeutic process. Counselors must ask themselves if they would like to hear a professional tell them the same things if they were the client. They must ask themselves what their own reactions to this might be and then make the decision about whether or not to make the statement.

Giving Advice

Sometimes a counselor wants to give advice to patients. The danger is that clients may come to rely on the counselor and then blame the counselor if the advice turns out to be ineffective. Also, it prevents clients from making their own decisions. In general it is best to help clients reach their own conclusions, there will be times when basic advice is the appropriate counselor response:

EXAMPLE

Patient: I just met with my supervisor. I had to take a random drug test and it came back positive for methadone. I'm clean otherwise but now they say I can't get promoted until I'm off all drugs. They said my performance as a fork lift truck driver is good and that I would have gotten promoted, except for this drug test.

Counselor: They can't do that to you. That's discrimination and possibly against the Americans with Disabilities Act. I suggest you mention this to your supervisor. If they maintain the same position, you should talk to an EEO counselor.

Confrontation

This technique consists of pointing out the differences and inconsistencies between attitudes, words, and behavior. It perhaps is the most frequently used intervention tool by substance abuse counselors, who often have to deal with patient denial, manipulation, lies, and treatment resistance. They find it most natural to confront these behaviors, rather than try to understand them. It often is the only technique used by some substance abuse counselors. Substance abuse counselors surely will have to use confrontation at some point in their counseling life. It is critical to confront with an attitude of care and concern, in a friendly and understanding voice, and in such a way as not to close off communication. Confrontation must be done with sensitivity and timing and with some awareness of the client's ability to handle it.

> **EXAMPLE**
> Counselor: You say that you can handle your liquor but you go out every night and get drunk, come home late, argue with your wife, use more and more household money for your booze "allowance" and now are threatened with losing your job because of tardiness due to your drinking. Help me understand how this demonstrates your ability to "hold your liquor."

Education

Education through explanation is one technique that frequently should be used by counselors. Education is the intervention of choice when ignorance is the problem. Many patients simply do not understand addiction and recovery and need basic education and explanations of behaviors, action, and processes. In substance abuse programs this traditionally has occurred in lecture-oriented group formats, but education can be part of an individual session as well.

> **EXAMPLE**
> In taking the drug Levo–Alpha Acetylmethadol (LAAM), you accept the fact that you are addicted to heroin and therefore are addicted to LAAM. This drug takes a while to start working in your system and you cannot feel its action like you do when you take methadone. Because you think it is not working when, in fact, it is, you might get afraid that you will go into withdrawal, so there may be a tendency for you to go out and get a fix. This could result then in an accidental overdose. Do you understand?

Exploration

A rare patient will reveal to the counselor all the necessary information, and most counselors find it necessary to ask more questions and to inquire further and in more detail into a given area. Counselors must avoid the appearance of voyeurism and get that information which is necessary to help the patient, and no more.

Humor

Humor has been downplayed as a technique, yet is a basic part of human nature. Humor may have its place, especially when it has a larger purpose of advancing therapeutic goals. It can be a tension-relieving device as well.

EXAMPLE

Patient: I was walking outside and heard someone yell, "Hey, Papa G!" and. . . .

Counselor: What?

Patient: They call me "Papa G" in my neighborhood.

Counselor: Well, as least they don't call you Mother F.

Interpretation

Sometimes patients need to understand why they do certain things. Interpretation may link two or more unrelated events or behaviors to a common thread. In this way, clients may develop greater appreciation and understanding of their behavior.

EXAMPLE

Patient: You know, I've been having sex with so many women, it just amazes me. Women find me so attractive: they all want to go to bed with me. Every time I go to a bar, I pick up a girl and we go to her place to screw. It's great, but I feel something is missing. I don't know what it is. What do you think about my behavior? If you were in my shoes, would you be doing what I'm doing?

Counselor: You are still so angry at your wife for leaving you that you seem to be taking it out on every woman you meet. You get them worked up, have sex, and then drop them—just like your wife dropped you.

Paraphrasing

In paraphrasing, the counselor simply restates what the patient has already said. It is helpful with confused or disorganized clients and conveys the message that the counselor has heard and understood the client.

EXAMPLE

Patient: Yesterday my wife had surgery and I was sitting in the waiting room waiting for her to come out and I started going into withdrawal. I decided to run out and get a fix and when I got back the doctor had come and gone. I tried to have him paged but he was already in another surgery. I couldn't find out about my wife. I felt like hell. I felt guilty—but I had to get comfortable.

Counselor: You were torn between wanting to be there for your wife and the need not to get sick yourself.

Questioning

Questions may be open-end or closed-end. *Open-end* questions require comment, elaboration, and discussion (e.g., How did you feel when your wife left you for another woman?). *Closed-end* questions require a yes or no or a single word response (e.g., How old are you?). Avoid closed-end questions as much as possible, because they limit conversation and stultify the client-counselor relationship.

Exercise.   To demonstrate the effect of closed-ended questions on the client and on the counseling process, in a role-playing format, have someone be a counselor and another person be the patient. Have the counselor spend 3–5 minutes asking nothing but closed-end questions. At the end of this exercise, the patient tells how it felt to respond to this format and the counselor reports how it felt only to ask questions in this manner. They can switch roles and repeat the exercise to have both experiences.

Reassurance

Many patients are apprehensive about some aspect of their life. A simple response that assures them of an ability to handle the issue may be all that is needed. The powerful effects that valued counselors can have on patient behavior should not be minimized.

> **EXAMPLE**
>
> Patient: My wife's brother is coming in from out of town and he's a heavy drinker. He's probably alcoholic but won't admit it. Anyway, I think his presence might jeopardize my sobriety. I've only been on the wagon for six months and don't know if I can handle all the drinking that he is likely to do when he's here.
>
> Counselor: You've shown a good ability to stay off alcohol so far and there is no reason you cannot stay sober when he comes. You have your sponsor always available to you and you go to AA regularly so you have good support systems that can help you over this period of time. If you use all of your resources, I'm sure you'll be all right.

Reflection

In this technique, the counselor paraphrases what the client has just said. It allows the client to listen to what he has just said as well. If done properly, it conveys to the client that the counselor is listening and understanding. Counselors can reflect either a feeling or a thought.

Example

> Patient: I've been drinking so long, I don't think I'll ever be able to stop.
> Counselor: You feel like a hopeless drunk.

Self-Disclosure

In self-disclosure, counselors tell clients something about themselves and their background and experiences. Self-disclosure can be counter-therapeutic and always should be done only to facilitate the counseling process. Counselors should ask themselves if the disclosure will benefit the client in some way. Usually, self-disclosure is done to help the client open up with feelings, to elaborate and embellish something that has just been said, and to remove blockage and client resistance. Self-disclosure should be minimized and used selectively.

Substance abusers like to reduce and eliminate the distance between counselor and client, treating the counselor as "one of the gang." This undercuts the counselor's effectiveness, so it is important to maintain a professional distance without appearing aloof. Also, it can shift the focus of conversation from the client to the counselor. Little is to be gained from this type of non-dialogue. Self-disclosure should be used when it is relevant to the context of the here-and-now-counseling session. It should not be used for the sake of maintaining conversation.

> **EXAMPLE**
> (The patient communication under *Interpretation* elicits a different response from the counselor.)
>
> Patient: You know, I've been having sex with so many women, it just amazes me. Women find me so attractive: they all want to go to bed with me. Every time I go to a bar, I pick up a girl and we go to her place to screw. It's great, but I feel something is missing. I don't know what it is. What do you think about my behavior? If you were in my shoes, would you be doing what I'm doing?
>
> Counselor: I could only have sex with someone I love.

Silence

Sometimes the best response is no response. Silence gives clients the opportunity to think about what just has been said. It allows clients to integrate material, consolidate feelings, and to react to their own statements. Remember that counselors do not always have to say something to be effective. Sometimes, a too-immediate response can actually interrupt and interfere with counseling.

Summarizing

Briefly summarizing what the client has said or the issues under discussion sometimes is useful, particularly at the end of a session, when the counselor can recap the main content of the session and the main course of action.

GENERAL TREATMENT CATEGORIES

Social Therapies

Alcoholics Anonymous.   Bill Wilson, an alcoholic margin trader on Wall Street and Bill Smith, an alcoholic surgeon who had lost his practice, started AA as an alternative to the then-mainstream treatment approaches. AA relies on a self-help model, with alcoholics in recovery being the primary agents of change. AA developed a set of principals and traditions. It requires both the acceptance of the disorder as a disease and of a "higher power" to effect change. It requires frequent and sometimes daily attendance at AA meetings that provided a structure filled with testimonials, lectures, and focused discussion to address and redress problem drinking.

THE 12 STEPS

1. We admitted we were powerless over alcohol—that our lives had become unmanageable.
2. Came to believe that a Power higher than ourselves could restore us to sanity.
3. Made a decision to turn our will and our lives over to the care of God as we understood Him.
4. Made a searching and fearless moral inventory of ourselves.
5. Admitted to God, to ourselves, and to another human being the exact nature of our wrongs.
6. We're entirely ready to have God remove all these defects of character.
7. Humbly asked Him to remove our shortcomings.
8. Made a list of all persons we had harmed, and became willing to make amends to them all.
9. Made direct amends to such people wherever possible, except when to do so would injure them or others.
10. Continued to take personal inventory and when we were wrong promptly admitted it.
11. Sought through prayer and meditation to improve our conscious contact with God as we understood Him, praying only for knowledge of His will for us and the power to carry that out.
12. Having had a spiritual awaking as the result of these Steps, we tried to carry this message to alcoholics, and to practice these principles in all our affairs. (Alcoholics Anonymous, 1976)

THE 12 TRADITIONS

1. Our common welfare should come first; personal recovery depends on AA unity.
2. For our group purpose there is but one ultimate authority—a loving God as He may express Himself in our group conscience. Our leaders are but trusted servants; they do not govern.
3. The only requirement for AA membership is a desire to stop drinking.
4. Each group should be autonomous except in matters affecting other groups or AA as a whole.
5. Each group has but one primary purpose—to carry its message to the alcoholic who still suffers.
6. An AA group ought never endorse, finance, or lend the AA name to any related facility or outside enterprise, lest problems of money, property, and prestige divert us from our primary purpose.

7. Every AA group ought to be fully self-supporting, declining outside contributions.

8. AA should remain forever nonprofessional, but our service centers may employ special workers.

9. AA, as such, ought never be organized; but we may create service boards or committees directly responsible to those they serve.

10. AA has no opinion on outside issues; hence the AA name ought never be drawn into public controversy.

11. Our public relations policy is based on attraction rather than promotion; we need always maintain personal anonymity at the level of press, radio, and films.

12. Anonymity is the spiritual foundation of all our traditions, ever reminding us to place principles before personalities. (Alcoholics Anonymous, 1976)

Other self-help entities, such as Narcotics Anonymous and Cocaine Anonymous have adopted these principles and traditions and merely substitute the particular drug (narcotics, cocaine, etc.) that is the focus of their attention.

Rational Recovery.   For some, the invocation of God and spirituality serves as a barrier to AA attendance Although AA refers more often to a "higher power" and not necessarily to a supreme deity, many believe that the spiritual focus of AA is not for them.

To counter such objections, Jack Trimpey developed an alternative to AA, called *Rational Recovery* (Trimpey, 1992; 1995; 1996). Rational Recovery deemphasizes the disease nature of the disorder. Instead, it emphasizes personal responsibility and free choice in the process. It argues that the real problem is an inner voice that craves abusing substances and that directs your behavior. It teaches "Addictive Voice Recognition Technique," in a time-limited, self-help, group-discussion format. This technique teaches patients to be responsive to thoughts and feelings that support continued substance abuse. It argues that recovery is not a process but an *event*. Attending to and changing these automatic feelings and thoughts will result in the elimination of addiction in as little as four sessions. It tells a person to

1. Read Rational Recovery literature and "The Small Book," Trimpey's alternative to AA's the *Big Book*.

2. Never call yourself an addict or alcoholic.

3. Avoid agencies that label you an alcoholic in their records.

4. Never say your life is out of control or unmanageable.

5. Don't admit that you violated any law while under the influence of drugs or alcohol.

6. Never incriminate yourself.

7. Do not admit to alcoholic blackouts.

8. Do not reveal highly personal information at AA meetings.

As can be seen, Rational Recovery is quite the opposite of AA. Yet there may be some patients who can benefit from this thinking and approach, so counselors should not close their minds to these ideas. Counselors should not dissuade a patient from attending Rational Recovery any more than from attending AA.

Environmental Manipulation. Psychologist Abraham Maslow developed a hierarchy of needs approach and persuasively argued that physical and security needs are the basis upon which more advanced needs (e.g., ego needs and needs for personal growth and self-actualization) can be attained. A person operate primarily from a need to nurture others and assist in their development, but if the nurturer's housing is threatened, ego needs become secondary to finding a place to live.

Conceptually, counselors can intervene in the life of a substance abuser by arranging for *environmental manipulation*. A common example in the drug abusing community is arranging for a homeless patient to find food and shelter and, eventually, more stable housing.

Sometimes patients can be motivated by a desire to quit substances but the problems of someone close to them distracts them from their primary objective. Unless this problem is addressed, patients will not be able to focus enough on themselves and treatment will be ineffective:

> **EXAMPLE**
> A 35-year-old heroin addict was scheduled to initiate an inpatient detoxification program, but his wife—also a user—was a source of trouble for the patient's recovery. They were living on the street. He was too worried about how his wife would fare to enter treatment himself. The program's social worker arranged for them to receive public aid, temporary shelter, and emergency food stamps. The wife was helped to get on a methadone maintenance treatment program. Once his wife's basic physical needs were taken care of, the patient was able to enter treatment himself.

Behavioral Therapies

Behavioral therapies seek to change behaviors, without full understanding of their cause. Behavioral therapies make the following assumptions:

1. All behavior is learned.
2. Behavior is largely determined by contextual and environmental factors that reinforce the behavior and strengthen its appearance.
3. Thoughts and feelings are also "behavior" and subject to the same laws of learning.
4. The same learning processes responsible for learning the behavior can be used to change the behavior.

5. To learn a new behavior, the person must practice the behavior in the environment in which it is to occur.
6. All people are unique, and have individualized reinforcements or aversions.
7. A behavioral assessment is the first step in changing the behavior.

Behavioral therapy can be organized into techniques that (a) treat antecedent cues of drug-taking behavior, (b) treat the actual drug-taking behavior, and (c) treat the consequences of drug-taking behavior.

Drug abuse is not simply taking a drug. A behavioral chain of events precedes it. For example, a patient may begin to feel bored and lonely. He begins to recall how he felt buying drugs with his addict friends. He begins to feel anxious, nervous, excited, and agitated. He decides to get in his car, drive to his buying area, and get a fix, then drive to the dope house, where he uses. This process is referred to as a *behavioral chain*. This example will illustrate ways of interrupting this chain as an episode of treatment. Keep in mind that these interventions, as with any substance abuse therapy, require motivated patients who sincerely desire to discontinue drug use.

Treating Antecedent Cues.   The goal of this intervention is to eliminate the occurrence of the target behavior by pairing its occurrence with an incompatible response or an aversive event. To do this, the counselor must help the patient identify those internal sensations, thoughts, and behaviors that occur in a drug-taking chain. In the example, the target behaviors were feelings of boredom and loneliness, as these were the precursors to drug taking and were the initial behaviors in the behavior chain. If the patient can be taught to engage in activities that reduce boredom and loneliness, then those aspects of the chain will be broken.

Counterconditioning requires the counselor to have the patient pair desensitization procedures with the stimuli associated with the precursors to drug taking. The idea is for the patient to engage in a behavior that is incompatible with the target behavior. This cannot be specified in advance but must be identified individually for each patient. In the example, the patient needs to find a behavior which is incompatible with boredom or loneliness.

Another way to treat the antecedent cues is through *avoidance conditioning*, in which the counselor teaches the patient to avoid the antecedents, or to respond differently in the presence of the antecedents. If the patient stops in a certain bar after work and then comes home drunk four hours later, then the counselor may help the patient select alternative routes to avoid passing by this particular bar. According to behavior theory, each time the patient practices the desired response (not going into the bar), his capacity to resist increases and the old behavior (going into the bar) is extinguished. If the patient often is invited to go out for drinks after work by his buddies, then the counselor needs to teach the patient "refusal training," or to practice "assertive refusals." In either case, the idea is to avoid or reduce the antecedent cues that lead to the next step, which is treating actual substance abuse.

Treating Drug-Taking Behavior. The goal of this treatment is to change drug-taking behaviors by reinforcing prosocial, nondrug-using behaviors. Two primary techniques accomplish this: (1) contingent reinforcement, and (2) behavioral contracting.

With these interventions, the patient, with the help of the counselor, outlines specific behaviors to receive the reinforcement. In *contingent reinforcement,* the targeted behaviors receive the agreed-upon reward at the designated time. For example, perhaps the patient will set aside the money to be spent on booze that night in a jar with the eventual goal of using that money to buy something that is dearly cherished and desired by the patient. Money would only be put into the jar when the patient resists the temptation to use and when the temptation is considered serious enough by the patient so that, in prior times, he would have used. In this case, putting money into the jar is contingent on resisting temptation.

Contingent reinforcement has been successfully applied to the treatment of substance abuse. Studies have shown that patients do respond to contingent reinforcements and that such interventions can promote abstinence (Stitzer, Bickel, Bigelow, & Liebson, 1986; Stitzer, Bigelow, Lawrence, Cohen, D'Lugoff, & Hawthorne, 1977).

In *behavioral contracting,* the patient agrees to certain consequences that will occur if certain behaviors are not successfully completed. Drug treatment programs frequently use behavioral treatment contracting, usually specifying what will occur if certain treatment conditions are not met. For example, a written treatment contract drawn up and signed by staff and patient requires the patient to be abstinent from all illicit drugs and alcohol by a specific date, to have a specific number of individual sessions per month with the counselor, and to submit a specific number of urine samples or breath alcohol tests each month. If any one of these conditions is not met, then the patient will be discharged.

Behavioral contracting has been used successfully with cocaine addicts. A program in Colorado that caters to professional-level patients (i.e., physicians, lawyers, accountants, etc.), requires patients to sign a treatment contract that demands that they attend a certain number of aftercare sessions and have clean urines. Upon admission, they prepare and sign, but do not date, a letter to their professional licensing boards or to their employers that states that they are hopelessly addicted to cocaine, tried treatment but failed, and continue to abuse cocaine. Accordingly, they are no longer fit to practice, and request that their license be revoked or that they be terminated from employment. The program staff keeps the letter during treatment and aftercare. If the patient fails the treatment contract, the program dates the letter and sends it in to the state authority or to the patient's employer.

This technique is very powerful. Statistics show that it is 90% successful with patients who had good resources and who have a lot to lose. When the contingency is removed, however, success rates fall to 50% (Anker & Crowley, 1982). These types of studies demonstrate the power of reinforcements in a patient's behavior and suggest that counselors should explore where patients get their "kicks" to begin to understand what motivates a patient.

Treating the Consequences of Drug-Taking Behaviors.   The goal of these interventions is to reduce and repair the consequences of drug taking. *Aversive counterconditioning* is a series of techniques that pair drug use with anxiety-provoking stimuli—chemical, electrical, or imaginal. Chemicals such as naltrexone for opiate addicts and Antabuse for alcoholics work on this principle. Addicts who take naltrexone when there are opiates in their system, will go into withdrawal and get very sick. Alcoholics who use alcohol while taking Antabuse will also vomit and get very sick.

This type of pharmacotherapy works on the principle of aversive counterconditioning. The idea is to produce a conditioned nausea response. Similarly, mild electric shock has been tried in experimental laboratory trials in which an alcoholic may be allowed to drink but receives an electric shock when he picks up the glass. Some medications remove or block a drug's euphoria, thereby introducing an extinction paradigm, in which the patient uses drugs but gets no positive reinforcement.

Aversive counterconditioning does not require such painful experiences. *Imaginal* conditioning can accomplish the same goals: the counselor uses guided imagery by having the patient concentrate on using a preferred substance and then imagining getting sick after ingestion. Counselors can train patients in alternative ways of dealing with an aversive environment. In principle, this is also a kind of counterconditioning.

Skills training is another tool counselors can use that can be implemented at any stage of the drug-taking cycle of intervention. People learn by modeling (watching others), through *operant conditioning* (getting positive or negative reinforcement for their behavior), and through *classical conditioning*. Skills training uses both modeling and operant conditioning principles to teach substance abusers new behaviors to replace addictive behaviors.

Two types of skills can be considered within the context of drug use. *Basic skills* help the patient to stop using drugs and to deal with such issues as craving, coping with triggers, and maintaining abstinence. Patients can then build on these skills to cope with more complex issues, such as dealing with subtle cognitive or emotional states, problem solving, and so forth. *Generalized skills* are activities that will help the patient implement the basic skills and apply them to other areas of their life.

It is not easy to simply label a skill as basic or generalized and, in fact, they are quite interchangeable.

In teaching skills, several principles are worth mentioning:

1. *Use repetition.* Any new skill needs to be well rehearsed.

2. *Practice, practice, practice.* Skills are not mastered until they occur naturally. Role-playing or rehearsals are useful at this stage until "practice makes perfect."

3. *Deal with and overcome obstacles.* Few people learn how to ride a bike or to play the piano at the first session. Initially, setbacks will occur and performance will be uneven. Reward patients for behaviors that are done well and continue encouraging them to get to the next level. Remind patients that they have it in their repertoire to accomplish the task (promote self-efficacy).

4. *Explore resistance.* Use the motivational interviewing techniques (Chapter 3) to deal with resistance.

5. *Reward.* The desired behavior should be a reward in itself, but most people respond to praise. So praise patients for successes. Point out how far they have come. This is especially important in the early sessions in which the clients are learning the new skill. Cognitive behaviorists call this *rewarding successive approximations to the desired target behavior* (Carroll, 1998).

Relapse Prevention.   Relapse prevention usually is administered by clinicians in individual counseling sessions. It is designed to help addicts who have become abstinent to remain drug free, but it can also be used for addicts who are maintained (clean) on opiate substitution therapy (e.g., methadone, LAAM). It is a cognitive behavioral technique.

Many theories have been postulated to explain why patients relapse. *Genetic and biological theories* posit that relapse is part of the disease, although the exact biological mechanisms for this relapse have not been identified.

Learning theory explains relapse in terms of conditioning processes. In classical conditioning, an unconditioned stimulus paired with a response that gets rewarded increases the probability of that response the next time that stimulus appears. Applied to substance abusers, if a person imbibes (unconditioned stimulus) and then experiences pleasure (reward), the person is more likely to drink the next time that situation occurs. If the person gets a bad reaction to alcohol upon initial use, the chances of drinking again are reduced because of the nonrewarding, even punishing, experience with the drug. Over time and with repeated exposure, the stimuli associated with the now-conditioned stimulus (CS) become conditioned to the CS. The stimuli include the people and places and context of drug use and can themselves exert a powerful effect and act as an occasion to use.

A phenomenon termed *conditioned withdrawal syndrome* is well established. Addicts coming out of prison, upon seeing their old drug-using friends and upon being in the environment where they use to buy, experience an actual physiological withdrawal syndrome and seek out heroin to relieve their distress (Wikler, 1973). Internal stimuli (e.g., twinges, craving, arousal, etc.) become conditioned to the people and places and are sufficient to serve as stimuli for drug use.

To demonstrate the powerful nature of environmental stimuli, researchers addicted two random groups of rats to heroin in a particular environment. Then they gave the rats what should have been a lethal dose of heroin. One group of rats received this dose in an environment in which they had learned to experience pleasure. The other group of rats received the identical dose in a new and unfamiliar environment. All the rats in the second group died; all of the rats who got the heroin in their familiar environment survived.

The treatment implications of this phenomena are that patients should not go back to the old haunts. They should not socialize or recreate with known abusers. They should stay out of places where they had used substances before, because these situations place them at great risk for relapse because of conditioned stimuli.

Psychopathology can be a trigger to relapse. A patient using alcohol or drugs to self-medicate an underlying psychiatric condition, can relapse. Here, referral to a psychiatrist or clinical psychologist is a preferred intervention. If the psychiatric condition can be effectively managed or resolved, then drug abuse counseling may have a stronger effect. Rarely does psychiatric treatment eliminate the substance abuse, even when the psychiatric treatment is successful. The patient still needs concurrent treatment for substance abuse.

A *cognitive-behavioral* model of relapse prevention has been presented by Marlatt (Marlatt & Gordon, 1985) that has had a significant effect in mainstream treatment programs (Brownell, Marlatt, Lichtenstein, & Wilson, 1986).

Marlatt began his observations with the knowledge that relapse rates among narcotic addicts, alcoholics, and cigarette smokers seem identical. The majority of abusers relapse early (within the first 1–6 months posttreatment) and then slowly reduce their risk of relapse (from 6–12 months posttreatment) (Hunt, Barnatt, & Branch, 1971). He reasoned commonalities must cut across these substances for them to have such similar relapse rates. Marlatt applied a cognitive behavioral approach to the problem.

He argued that a lapse was different from a relapse. A lapse is a discreet event: Marlatt defined a relapse as a process requiring a series of steps. An individual's response to lapses determines when a relapse has occurred.

Marlatt initially studied the reasons substance abusers relapse by evaluating 311 responses cited for relapse among drinkers, smokers, compulsive gamblers, overeaters, and heroin addicts. He classified these reasons as *individual* or *intrapersonal* determinants, or *interpersonal* or *social* and *environmental* determinants. Marlatt noticed five different kinds of intrapersonal and three different interpersonal determinants that occasioned relapse.

Intrapersonal determinants include (1) *Negative emotional states,* such as stress, anxiety, depression, and anger abuse. (2) *Physical state,* such as withdrawal; (3) *Positive emotional states,* such as feeling good and celebrating. (4) *Testing personal control,* as when a person goes into a high risk situation believing that he can handle it without using. It may be going to a bar where the they think they can go and not drink, or to a party where they knows drugs will be but think they will go and not use, and (5) *Urges and temptations,* such as craving.

Interpersonal determinants. (1) *Interpersonal conflict* was cited as a major reason for relapse: Perhaps an argument with the spouse results in the person drinking or drugging. (2) *Social pressure*, such as a spouse who uses and tries to get the abstinent person to use with them, or peers who encourage the nonuser to try it just once, can occasion a relapse. (3) Finally, *positive emotional states* that occur in an interpersonal context were also cited as occasions for relapse.

When Marlatt looked at the percentages of situations that occasioned the highest reasons for relapse, he learned that, across all groups, *negative emotional states, interpersonal conflict,* and *social pressure* accounted for about 75% of the cited reasons. Interestingly, negative physical states, such as withdrawal, generally accounted for 3%–5% of the stated reasons for relapse.

Gender differences appear in reasons for relapse. Women cocaine addicts were more likely than men to cite negative emotions and interpersonal problems before they relapsed; men were more likely than women to report positive experiences prior to relapse (unless that was a rationalization for their behavior). This suggests that counselors should emphasize techniques that enable women to deal more effectively with interpersonal problems and unpleasant situations and techniques to enable men to cope when they feel good (McKay, Rutherford, Cacciola, Kabasakalian-McKay, & Alterman, 1996; Weiss, Martinez-Raga, Griffin, Greenfield, & Hufford, 1997).

This has clear treatment implications for counselors. Getting patients to *identify their high risk situations* is the first step in relapse prevention. To do this, the counselor reviews the circumstances in which a patient uses: *what went on immediately before the decision to use.* Often *warning signs*, feelings and behaviors, precede a decision to resume substance abuse.

Marlatt developed a cognitive behavioral model that addresses the relapse problem. After identifying their high risk situations, patients engage in either a positive or a negative *coping response.* If patients cope well and do not use, "self-efficacy" increases. That is, patients learn that they have the capacity and instrumental behavior to resist and cope in high risk situations. If patients cope poorly, self-efficacy decreases and patients come to believe that they cannot resist in such situations. This follows *initial use.* Notice that, at this point, only a lapse has occurred. When patients come to believe they have little or no capacity to cope effectively with these situations (a cognitive event), relapse has occurred.

Intermingled with this process is what Marlatt has termed "apparently irrelevant decisions" (aids). This acronym has not become popular because the word has more serious connotations as an autoimmune disease. Take, for example, the alcoholic who keeps several bottles of alcohol (an "aid") in the cabinet for his friends. In a high risk situation and with a poor coping response, this "aid" now provides the proximate occasion to drink. Another example is addicts who keep their "works." Having them immediately available allows them to use immediately.

Marlatt advises that, to maintain abstinence, individuals have to engage in three separate cognitive-behavioral processes: (1) modify their lifestyle to enhance their ability to cope in high risk situations. This will result in increased

TABLE 5.1   Example Relapse Prevention Plan

MY HIGH RISK SITUATIONS	MY WARNING SIGNS	MY ACTION PLAN
1. Drinking with my buddies	**1.** Easily angered	**2.** Attend AA 3 times a week.
2. Arguing with my mother	**2.** Feeling lonely and bored	**2.** Attend outpatient drug treatment program 1 time a week.
3. Receiving my paycheck	**3.** Feeling like I'll always be an addict	**3.** Get a sponsor as soon as possible.
4. Thinking I can hang around drug users and not use myself	**4.** Indulging in self-pity	**4.** Talk with other addicts who have significant clean time.
5. Thinking I can drink socially		**5.** Explore ways in counseling to stop arguing with my mother.
		6. Engage in positive socialization activities.

self-efficacy. (2) Identify and respond appropriately to internal and external cues that serve as their warning signs. (3) Implement self-control strategies to reduce risk of relapse. These may require home-work assignments as part of the training (NIAAA, 1989).

Counselors must help patients identify their individualized high risk situations and help them develop and practice good coping responses. A relapse prevention plan can help them identify their high risk situations and warning signs and develop an action plan that will help them avoid and cope with each high risk situation and warning sign. For patients with no coping responses, counselors may engage in behavioral rehearsing of what they will say and how they will deal with a situation the next time they encounter it (Cummings, Gordon, & Marlatt, 1980).

Table 5.1 presents an example relapse prevention plan.

Clinicians have begun to adapt this model to their individualized program needs. For example, McAuliff and Ch'ien (1986) published a relapse prevention model that incorporates systematic training based on social learning and health promotion models. The four-part program features weekly recovery training sessions, a weekly self-help group, weekend recreational and social activities, and a social support network. The 26-week sequence of didactic presentations and exercises include motivational supports and social reintegration. Modalities include group learning, role playing, personal problem sharing and problem solving, self-help, active planning, and frequent interaction with role models, along with professionally-lead presentations. Didactic presentations include such topics as

Phases of recovery

Deaddiction and loss of craving

Preparing for stressful situations

Assessing social life

Determining dangerous situations

Making new friends

Coping with pain

Handling on-the-job problems

Love and intimate relations

Planning ahead

Clinicians could easily adapt such a format to fit the needs of their particular clients.

Specific relapse prevention materials, such as the Hazelton series, are now commercially available (Daley, 1993). The Hazelton series introduces relapse and relapse prevention, lists common causes of relapse, provides space for patients to write their risk factors for relapse and their coping strategies, provides a recovery tool checklist, presents an extensive checklist of warning signs, and offers many examples of coping strategies. Homework assignments are to be reviewed with the counselor at subsequent meetings.

Treatment for Marijuana Abuse.   Several treatment protocols have been found to be effective in treating marijuana abuse.

- *Motivational enhancement therapy*. The techniques of this approach were described in Chapter 4. Treatment should be combined with cognitive-behavioral approaches and sessions should focus on factors that motivate marijuana use. Patients need to be taught marijuana refusal training skills, how to develop a social network of nonusing friends, develop and practice activities that do not include marijuana use, and relapse prevention.
- *Cognitive-behavioral training*. The techniques of this intervention have been presented in this chapter. Users are taught to develop coping skills and alternate responses to using marijuana, to practice problem-solving skills, resolve anger, as well as cope with interpersonal relationship problems.
- *Family therapy*. This technique is particularly helpful with adolescent abusers but may be helpful with any patient whose family issues are part of the difficulty or whose family is affected by marijuana abuse. Not only are the traditional techniques of family therapy employed here, but parenting classes and parental support are included. Counselors should adapt this approach to the needs of the particular family. Family counseling should be included as part of the treatment whenever family dysfunction is part of

the problem or when the marijuana abuser seriously affects the family. Treatment should include teaching parenting skills, particularly behavioral contracting and reinforcement, as well as parental support. Specific techniques must be tailored to the specific family problems.

■ *Education*. Parents and users should receive education on the effects of marijuana. Adolescents, who tend to be resistant and unmotivated to change, are accustomed to taking tests in class, so a counselor-constructed "quiz" could make the session not feel like therapy. The counselor could use the occasion to correct any misperceptions the patient has about the drug and could devise other quizzes to help them to cope in high risk situations.

Medical Therapies

Medical therapies are a loosely defined group of interventions designed to treat the consequences of substance abuse, as well as prevent relapse. While these are presented in a single format, it is important to understand that medical therapies rarely are effective unless complemented with effective counseling.

Detoxification.   Detoxification occurs naturally when an addict discontinues using alcohol or drugs. Upon cessation of use, they experience a withdrawal syndrome that ranges from mild discomfort to severe symptoms, up to and including life-threatening states, depending on length and severity of the addiction, general health of the patient, and the addictive substance.

While delirium tremens (DTs) can occur in a chronic alcoholic during unsupervised withdrawal, it occurs only in about 5% of the cases. Most alcoholics can be detoxified in social detoxification centers, where they are made comfortable, and their physiological state is monitored by medical personnel who are trained to recognize the signs and symptoms of withdrawal and to refer a patient with impending DTs to a physician. Most alcoholics who stop drinking do so without assistance.

Physicians who manage alcoholic withdrawal syndromes will often provide tranquilizers to ease the withdrawal. The medical recommendations for this intervention are a trial of tranquilizers for 6–8 weeks and then discontinue the tranquilizers. The problem is that many patients begin to become psychologically and even physically dependent on these drugs, forcing the physician to continue prescribing them. It is not uncommon for counselors to encounter alcoholics who are addicted to alcohol and to a medically prescribed tranquilizer.

Detoxification from drug addiction is a bit more complicated. True addicts will go into severe withdrawal upon discontinuing use and will seek out their preferred drug to avoid getting sick. Therefore, physicians usually prescribe methadone in decreasing doses until the patient is eventually drug free. Physicians who may not want to prescribe a narcotic drug to a narcotic addict also prescribe other drugs, including the antihypertensive drug, clonidine.

For the most part, detoxification from opiates is uncomplicated in an inpatient setting. Most addicts can be withdrawn comfortably over a few days from opiates with methadone, as long as they have group support and medical oversight. Most addicts discontinue using methadone before the detoxification schedule has been completed. Detoxification in an outpatient setting is far more complicated, because staff cannot keep the patient away from the source of drugs. Outpatient detoxification takes a longer period of time to be successful (Dorus, 1982).

In a recently initiated medical procedure, the narcotic addicts enter an inpatient unit for 24 hours. They are administered an anesthetic for up to 12 hours, during which time a narcotic antagonist is administered intravenously, detoxifying them extremely rapidly. When they awake, they are free from narcotics, not in withdrawal, and are considered drug free.

Detoxification from barbiturates can be life-threatening and can result in seizures and death, so it must be done in a medically supervised and, usually, an inpatient setting. Detoxification from cocaine is controversial, because there does not seem to be a clear-cut withdrawal syndrome upon cessation of use, although there seem to be symptoms that some call a "short-term abstinence syndrome" (Weddington, Brown, Haetrzen, Cone et al., 1990). For the most part, this syndrome is not medicated. Cocaine detoxification can also be achieved using a behavioral approach (Higgins, Budney, Bickel, & Hughes et al, 1993; Otto, Pollack, Sachs, & Reiter, 1988). Withdrawal from hallucinogens is best accomplished by keeping patients in a quiet, supportive environment without medications and by "talking down" by a trusted friend, who assures patients that they are experiencing a drug effect which will soon subside without complications.

While detoxification is an initial step in the eventual rehabilitation of substance abusers, research shows that it is uniformly unsuccessful as a single method of intervention. Up to 99% of detoxified patients relapse unless they are followed in an aftercare program that includes counseling. Detoxification should be used as part of a more comprehensive treatment plan.

Maintenance Therapies. Methadone maintenance has been considered the treatment of choice for narcotic addicts. Methadone is a synthetically derived opiate which has all the primary actions and side effects of any narcotic drug. However, whereas heroin lasts up to 4–6 hours, thereby forcing the addict to use 3–4 times a day to prevent withdrawal, methadone lasts 24 hours. This means that the patient only takes this drug once a day. Pharmacologically, methadone does not result in a drug "high." Many patients say it gives them a "buzz," but the extent to which this is a drug effect or a patient expectation effect remains unclear. Addicts, who buy methadone mostly to avoid getting sick from narcotic withdrawal, can purchase methadone on the street. Rarely do they buy it to get high.

Methadone can be used for short-term or long-term treatment. It may be prescribed as an interim tool to help patients straighten out their lives or patients may be maintained on methadone for years. Methadone has been shown to be a safe narcotic with no long-term effects.

Another long-term narcotic drug is LAAM (levo-alpha-acetylmethadol). This synthetic narcotic lasts for two days, so patients need to ingest it every other day (Tennant, Rawson, Pumphrey, & Secof, 1986). Detoxification from LAAM is reported to be easier than detoxification from methadone, but there are no long-term studies on this issue. Also, recent warnings about LAAM's effects on cardiac function are likely to see an overall reduction in LAAM use. Buprenorphine is a narcotic drug that is in the final stages of clinical trials and may receive FDA approval for use in narcotic treatment programs in the near future. It has agonistic and antagonistic effects.

Methadone and LAAM maintenance are strictly regulated by federal agencies and patients must be enrolled in narcotic treatment programs and have met certain qualifications to be enrolled in these programs.

Barbiturate addicts are sometimes maintained on barbiturates. Although some antianxiety drugs (anxiolytics), such as Xanax, are addicting (Noyes, Garvey, Cook, & Perry, 1988) some patients may be maintained on Xanax. Most physicians want patients off these drugs and try to taper the dose slowly rather than expecting to keep patients on these drugs.

Antagonist Therapies.   Disulfiram (Antabuse) has been used for many years as a prevention tool for relapse among alcoholics. Narcotic antagonists have recently been used as prevention tools for opiate addicts. Antagonist treatments work on one of two principles. First, as in the case of Antabuse, alcohol-free patients feel no effects while on this drug. If, however, they consume alcohol while on Antabuse, they become violently ill—nauseated, and vomiting. Knowing this, abstinent alcoholics are not likely to drink and hence maintain sobriety.

Second, they work by blocking opiate receptors in the brain. If a narcotic antagonist is given to narcotic addicts with opiates in their system, it precipitates an opiate withdrawal syndrome. If they are on a maintenance antagonist and use heroin, they will not feel any narcotic effects because the antagonist occupies the opiate receptors, thereby blocking the high. In learning theory terms, the patient is not reinforced by using heroin and eventually experiences extinction of the desire to use heroin at all. Narcotic antagonists are either short acting (2 minutes) or long acting (24 hours). Emergency room personnel use short-acting narcotic antagonists (e.g., Narcan) to reverse an opiate overdose, but drug treatment physicians use a long-acting antagonist (e.g., Revia [naltrexone]) as a maintenance drug to prevent relapse. NIDA continues to research drugs that might be useful to treat cocaine addiction (Kosten, 1989; 1990) but, to date, none have achieved therapeutic effects that would make them desirable for routine clinical use.

Medical therapies should be construed as adjunctive treatment in the rehabilitation process. No drug "rehabilitates." Only when patients are treated with a combination of intervention tools, which may include medication, will they be able to achieve full treatment benefits (McLellan, Arndt, Metzger, Woody et al,

1993). Recent research has demonstrated that some patients attain better results with certain substance abuse counselors than with others and these effects were independent of medication (Blaney & Craig, 1999).

TREATMENT MATCHING

Pattison (1985) has convincingly demonstrated that the substance-abusing population shows variability—not homogeneity—across a wide variety of dimensions.

There is variability in substance abusing syndromes (e.g., in consumption, patterns of abuse, dependence, addiction, etc.). There is variability in the consequences of use (e.g., vocational, legal, familial, medical, psychiatric, etc.). There is variability in personality organization (e.g., dependent, antisocial, borderline, etc.). There is variability in available treatment systems (e.g., inpatient programs, outpatient programs, therapeutic communities, halfway houses, police and court systems, mental hospitals, etc.). There is variability in treatment methods (e.g., drug therapies, behavioral therapies, social interventions, counseling techniques, etc.). And there is variability in the kinds of personnel who treat the disorder (e.g., substance abuse counselors, clergy, addictionologists, recovering addicts, AA members, mental health professionals, etc.).

Different types of programs attract different kinds of patients and different patients present with different motivations for change (Pattison, Coe, & Doerr, 1973; Pattison, Coe, & Rhodes, 1969). The research question is "What type of patient needs what type of treatment by what kind of service provider at what type of facility?" (Institute of Medicine, 1990). This is referred to as treatment matching (Craig, 1987).

Despite research that shows that substance abusers are a heterogeneous population with many subtypes and individualized problems, treatment personnel largely offer these patients a limited number of treatment options. The predominant model of intervention is attendance at AA, either as a primary or supplemental treatment intervention. Often they are treated with a shotgun approach that offers a few basic treatment components or only an AA approach.

If the only tool you have is a hammer, then everything starts to look like a nail. If counselors believe that AA and NA are the only ways to treat substance abuse successfully, then all their patients will be offered this model, whether or not other interventions may be more effective. Some research demonstrates that the advice of a respected professional simply to stop drinking was just as effective as intense treatment with multiple components for alcoholism (Edward, Orford, Egert, Guthrie, et al, 1977). The point is that patients are not all the same and should not all be treated the same.

While this sounds logical, research on the treatment-matching hypothesis has not consistently shown that treatment matching gets superior results (Skinner, 1981). The results of more than 30 empirical studies on the treatment-matching hypothesis suggests that clients who are matched to treatments will show better outcomes than clients who are unmatched, but this has not always been the case (Longabaugh, Wirtz, DiClemente, & Litt,1994; Mattson & Allen, 1991; Mattson, Allen, Longabaugh, Nickless, 1994). Most of this research was done with alcoholic populations, but the concept can be applied to drug addicts as well: there is some literature to suggest that it can be effectively applied with this population.

In one major study with heroin addicts, 476 male patients were assigned to one of six different rehabilitation programs, based on a set of previously developed hypotheses about which types of patients might get more benefit out of which type of program. For example, patients rated low in psychiatric severity were assigned to an outpatient program, unless they also had significant family and employment problems. Those patients were given inpatient treatment. The research design was prospective, that is, the researchers determined in advance what type of treatment was needed and sent the patient to that type of program. Half the patients were "matched" and half were assigned as normally would be the case. The staff in each program did not know which patients were matched and which were unmatched. All treated patients improved on average, but patients who were matched attained, on average, a 19% better outcome after six months compared to the unmatched group. However, patients rated high in psychiatric severity showed almost no improvement in any kind of treatment (McLellan, Woody, Luborsky, O'Brien, et al, 1983).

In a more recent study, researchers matched treatment with patients' problems. The outcomes of two inpatient and two outpatient matched-services programs were compared to patients who received unmatched treatment. The matched-treatment patients stayed in treatment longer, had higher treatment completion rates, and had better six-month treatment outcomes. The unmatched group improved in certain functional domains, such as reduced drug use, but the matched groups were significantly better in all functional domains (McLellan, Grissom, Zanis, Randall et al, 1997).

The major prospective research design that tested the matching thesis with alcoholics was called Project Match: it was the largest study ever conducted of different psychotherapies for the treatment of alcoholism. This multisite study, involving 1726 patients treated at 30 centers and clinics by 80 therapists, sought to determine the benefits of matching alcoholics to one of three different treatment interventions, AA, motivational interviewing and intervention, and cognitive-behavioral treatment. Patients were followed at 3-month intervals for up to a year following the completion of a 12-week treatment regimen. They were evaluated for changes in drinking patterns, treatment utilization, functional status, and quality of life. The primary variables of interest were the number of days drinking and the number of drinks per day after completion of treatment. This project has generated almost 100 research papers in professional journals. The main results were as follow: (1) Significant and sustained improvement occurred in all treatment groups; (2) There was little difference in outcome based on type of treatment; (3) Psychiatric severity did interact with treatment outcome. Patients rated low in psychiatric severity tended to do better in AA. No treatment was superior for patients rated high in psychiatric severity; (4) Aside from psychiatric severity, treatment matching on other variables had no effect on outcomes; (5) Patient characteristics, other than psychiatric severity ratings, did not predict treatment outcome; and (6) Treatment for alcoholism did improve patient status (Project Match Research Group, 1997).

Treatment matching remains a viable hypothesis. Project Match demonstrated that treatment for alcoholism is effective and need not be limited only to AA. Replication is the essence of science: it remains to be seen whether subsequent studies reach the same conclusions. Meanwhile, substance abuse counselors must make clinical decisions about type of treatment and its intensity, based on their best judgment and other rational considerations.

EXAMPLE

A substance abuse counselor had a very effective but very rigid type of intervention for assigned clients. They were required to attend various treatments at a clinic for four days a week for five hours a day. Additionally, they were required to attend program-sponsored recreational and social outings on some weekend evenings. Patients who were able to conform to these requirements did extremely well. However, not all patients need this treatment intensity and not all patients need resocialization. Two such patients were in their early 70s. One baby-sat for his grandchild and couldn't come to the clinic four days a week for five hours a day. The other had severe arthritis and couldn't sit in long sessions comfortably. The counselor asked that both of these patients be discharged for failing to comply with treatment. Instead, the supervisor interviewed both patients and determined there was legitimacy in their individual situations. In compromise, both were assigned to another counselor. Both agreed to come twice a week for group therapy for a total of 3 hours a week. They responded beautifully to this change and both eventually became clean from illicit drugs.

To implement a treatment-matching program, a clinic must (1) have a variety of treatment options available within a program or referral arrangements with those community resources that can provide the kind of treatment needed by a patient; (2) some reasonable way of matching individuals to the interventions; (3) an objective evaluation system that has no allegiances or biases to a particular approach.

While effective, 12-step programs have had much less success than traditionally is believed. Treatments that include the teaching of coping skills, use community resources, instill values towards prosocial behaviors, help abusers deal with their environment, reinforce beliefs in their own self-efficacy, deal with psychological issues in their life, and reduce confrontational approaches get better outcomes compared to therapies that are strictly AA or drug-oriented (Peele, 1990–1991).

BRIEF INTERVENTIONS AND BRIEF THERAPIES

Not all substance abusers require intensive and long-term therapy. Within the spirit of the treatment-matching hypothesis, some patients may be better served by briefer interventions. The circumstances that have compelled this way of thinking are multiple. Certainly the desire for more cost-effective treatment alternatives that are both efficacious and time-limited have been encouraged by HMO models of care. Not so coincidentally, researchers have been able to document positive outcomes in some substance abusers who have been treated with briefer forms of therapy. Interest in the treatment-matching concept has spurred new ways to think about and to approach substance abuse problems.

Brief therapeutic approaches should not be viewed as shorter versions of more typical interventions. Rather, brief therapy is construed as a different kind of treatment, with different goals, and often different behaviors required of the substance abuse counselor. These should not be in conflict with more traditional interventions or with longer-term goals for treatment.

The form and structure of brief intervention approaches are somewhat different from other types of interventions. They are characterized by:

- A highly structured form
- A focus on a single, behavioral objective that is immediately obtainable
- Focus on a problem
- Clearly defined goals
- An active and directive, yet empathic, therapeutic style
- Assumption that the client is primarily responsible for changing behavior
- Belief that change is possible and doable by the patient
- A menu of choices for the participant
- A limited number of sessions, perhaps as few as one

Brief intervention approaches can be used independently or as one intervention within the panoply of interventions in a longer-term treatment program. When considering a brief intervention approach, the counselor must (1) determine the patient's readiness for change, (2) develop a strategy of change within a working alliance between counselor and client, (3) implement the intervention, and (4) evaluate its success.

Stages of Change

An influential model of change has been proposed (Prochaska, DiClemente, & Norcross, 1986; 1992) based on cognitive processes that move slowly toward behavioral realization. This model argues that there are five phases to behavior change:

1. Precontemplation
2. Contemplation
3. Preparation
4. Action
5. Maintenance

One interesting proposal that needs further research is that treatment interventions need to be appropriate to the stage of change to produce maximal results. Patients in the precontemplation stage are ambivalent about stopping their addictive behavior. They are not yet considering change or are resisting change. Patients in the contemplation stage of change recognize a problem but have not yet made a decision to change. Ambivalence is the hallmark of patient behavior in these first two stages. Counselors should explore with the patient the pros and cons of their substance use, point out discrepancies between how the patient and others see the problem, offer factual material on the risks of continuing substance abuse, and explore why the patient is in the setting in which this session is taking place. Counselors should use a more nondirective and less confrontational technique, emphasizing clarification and reflection for patients in this stage of change.

When patients enter the preparation stage, they have committed to change in the near future but they remain unsure what to do next. Counselors should help patients clarify their goals and develop a strategy for change, offer a menu of options for change that includes a variety of treatment options, reduce barriers to change, help the patient get social support, negotiate a plan for change, and explore treatment expectancies. Counselors should encourage patients to announce to their social network that they plan to change.

In the action phase, the patient takes steps to change but has not reached stability. Here, they need to be engaged in treatment, to take small steps towards realization of their goal, to identify and reduce high-risk situations, and to get family and social support, perhaps through AA or NA.

When change has occurred, patients need to maintain it. At this point, counselors need to support these changes, review long-term goals with patients, reaffirm and reinforce patients' self-efficacy, and help patients practice strategies to avoid relapse. Note that, according to this model, patients may be in "treatment" but remain at the precontemplation or contemplation stage.

HOW PATIENTS SABOTAGE TREATMENT

Just because a patient is in treatment does not mean that they get treatment. Patients use a variety of techniques to ensure that treatment is less effective than it can be. The conscious or unconscious purpose of these techniques is to allow them to return to alcohol and drug use upon leaving treatment.

Acting Different

Some patients avoid treatment by arguing that they don't belong with the kinds of other patients that are in the program. If they are professionals, they may resent having to interact with tradesmen. If they are alcoholic, they may resent being with "criminal" drug addicts. If they are working, they feel they do not belong with those who are not working. If they are younger, they don't want to be around a bunch of older patients. If they are married, they don't want to be in treatment with streetwalkers. By getting counselors into arguments to debate whether they should or should not be mixed in with people who are so "different" from themselves, they avoid receiving effective substance abuse education and counseling.

Defocusing

The patients try to focus on everything but the concepts of addiction and recovery. Frequently, they put the majority of their attention on issues of employment, calling their job (if an inpatient) or talking about getting or keeping their job as an outpatient. Certainly economic issues and other factors impinge on patients' lives, but defocusing from treatment deprives counselors of effective intervention tools and prevents patients from actually receiving substance abuse counseling. The normal distractions in people's lives make it easy for resisting patients to use these issues to defocus from addiction treatment. Counselors need to determine when such issues are reality based and when they are conscious or unconscious manipulation.

False Compliance

Patients who have had many programmatic experiences can "talk the talk" but do not "walk the walk." They manipulate staff and counselors by seeming to go along with the program, yet have no intention to apply the tools or the concepts of addiction and recovery once they leave the scrutiny of the counselor's office. Even patients getting addiction treatment for the first time can quickly learn this technique by talking with and observing other patients. Often it is difficult to detect insincere patients: counselors should not feel bad if patients dupe them. Ultimately, the patients and their loved ones fail to benefit and reap the consequences of this resistance.

Family Rescuer

Transactional analysts have argued that it takes three roles to maintain an abusing lifestyle: (1) the user, (2) the patsy, whom the user takes advantage of, and (3) the rescuer, who comes in as a savior. Theoretically, absent any one of the last two roles and the addictive behavior subsides. It is true that family members, when present, often occupy the role of rescuer, perhaps as an overlearned habit, or perhaps for more unconscious reasons. Sometimes this is manifested by family members who contact patients and convince them to leave treatment early, maybe for financial reasons or from their own sense of loneliness. Sometimes a staff member assumes this role, perhaps without even knowing it.

I've Got a Secret

How fascinating it is and how patients can engage counselors' voyeuristic fantasies and amusements by hinting that they have some troubling event that is hard for them to talk about. Whether or not what they hint is true, counselors should advise such patients that they are ready to listen when the patients are ready to discuss these matters in counseling. Meanwhile, counselors should stay on track and provide addiction services.

Negotiating

Patients may attempt to change certain aspects of program rules, argue that certain concepts do not apply to them, provide "justification" for not needing to attend the prescribed frequency of programmatic visits, present evidence about why their family cannot participate in treatment, and so on. Some of these attempts may be legitimate; others are pure resistance and subterfuge. Negotiating can be used effectively as one of the tools of motivational interviewing discussed in Chapter 3. Too frequent negotiation can be a mechanism to avoid treatment.

Self-Pity

Some patients spend counseling sessions commiserating with themselves, engaging in self-abasement, denigrating their life decisions, assuming "poor me" roles, and providing counselors with a myriad of reasons to pity them. Much of the tenor of their moaning and whining is to convince the counselor that the situation is hopeless and that they cannot change.

Addict Games

Substance abusers also tend to play certain "games" in counseling to avoid effective counseling. Winning these games maintains their current behavior, avoids responsibility for actions, avoids behavior change, gives them a sense of power and excitement in their ability to outwit counselors, and may give them tangible rewards or idiosyncratic rewards that are unique to the individual. It may provide them with a kind of status in their deviant subgroup, because abusers then brag about such accomplishments. Here are some common types of addict games and some suggestions on how to counteract them.

Game: **Junkie versus Square.** The addicts question how counselors who have never been alcoholic or addicted can help them. Counselors may be sympathetic with this position and even believe this may be true. Research evidence, however, clearly shows no increase in differential effectiveness between counselors in recovery and counselors who have not had a history of substance abuse. The real question is whether or not counselors are good, understand the principles of addiction and recovery, and are empathic, understanding, sincere, and honest.

SUGGESTIONS

1. Counter this argument with an illogical fallacy. Suggest that, if one had to have a problem to be effective, then a physician who did not have cancer could not effectively treat someone with cancer.
2. Expose the true nature of this game. Tell patients the real issue is whether or not they are trying to avoid counseling.
3. Ultimately, patients are responsible for change—not their counselors.

Game: **Black versus White.**   In variations of this game, patients tell counselors that they cannot help because they're not of the same race, ethnicity, gender, lifestyle, religion, and so forth.

SUGGESTIONS

1. Confront this immediately.
2. Process what it means for the patient to experience himself as black, or female, or Baptist, or a skilled tradesperson, and so forth. Have a counseling session around these issues. Counselors' skill in dealing with these issues should provide the patient with an example of their skill in dealing with the substance abuse, as well.

Game: **Courthouse.**   In this game the patient tries to act as if the session were a court of law and that counselors cannot do or say certain things because of a lack of proof, improperly obtained evidence, lack of witnesses, lying witnesses, or biased judges.

SUGGESTIONS

1. Tell the patient that counseling is not a court of law. Here counselors base their decisions on the best available evidence and on their best clinical judgment.
2. Any redress can be attempted later through channels of due process that exist at the program level or through ethics boards and licensing boards at the professional level.

Counseling substance abusers is a daunting task. It requires counselors who are committed to helping people who may resist help. It requires counselors who can cope with the slow processes of change that are often part of counseling substance abusers. It requires counselors who are willing to try multiple techniques to help their clients. And it requires counselors who are willing to accept that patients are responsible for change and ultimately responsible for their own life and the consequences therein.

CHAPTER SUMMARY

This chapter presented both the principals and major modalities for treating substance abusers. The chapter began with general guidelines that tried to inculcate a general attitude among counselors regarding treatment itself. It addressed problems in counseling abusers and made suggestions on how to prepare for counseling in advance of a session. It presented basic counseling modalities that represent mainstream thinking on treating substance use disorders. It gave special emphasis to relapse prevention and introduced the concept of treatment matching. The chapter concluded with ways patients may resist treatment even when they are in a treatment program. Examples of relapse prevention and treatment plans appear at the end of this chapter.

SOURCES OF INFORMATION

Acierno, R., Donohue, B., & Kogan, E. (1994). Psychological interventions for drug abuse: A critique and summation of controlled studies. *Clinical Psychology Review, 114,* 417–442.

Alcoholics Anonymous. (1976). New York: Alcoholics Anonymous World Services, Inc.

Anker, A. L., & Crowley, T. J. (1982). Use of contingency in specialty clinics for cocaine abuse. In L. S. Harris (Ed.), *Problems of drug dependence 1981* (pp. 452–459). Rockville, MD: National Institute on Drug Abuse Research Monograph 41.

Baekeland, F., & Lundwall, L. (1975). Dropping out of treatment: A critical review. *Psychological Bulletin, 82,* 738–783.

Barry, K. L. (1999). Brief interventions and brief therapies for substance abuse. Rockville, MD: Substance Abuse and Mental Health Services Administration.

Blaney, T., & Craig, R. J. (1999). Methadone maintenance: Does dose determine differences in outcome? *Journal of Substance Abuse Treatment, 16,* 221–228.

Brownell, K. D., Marlatt, G. A., Lichtenstein, E., & Wilson, G. T. (1986). Understanding and preventing relapse. *American Psychologist, 41,* 765–782.

Carroll, K. M. (1998). Therapy manuals for drug addiction. *Manual 1: A cognitive-behavioral approach: Treating cocaine addiction.* Rockville, MD: National Institute on Drug Abuse. DHHS Pub. 98-4308

Craig, R. J. (1985). Reducing the treatment drop out rate in a drug abuse program. *Journal of Substance Abuse Treatment, 2,* 209–219.

Craig, R. J. (1987). *The clinical management of substance abuse programs.* Springfield, IL: Charles C. Thomas.

Cummins, C., Gordon, J. R., & Marlatt, G. A. (1980). Relapse: Prevention and prediction. In W. Miller (Ed.), *The addictive behaviors: Treatment of alcoholism, drug abuse, smoking, and obesity* (pp. 291–321). Elmsford, NY: Pergamon Press.

Daley, D. C. (1993). *Preventing relapse.* Center City, MN: Hazelton Educational Services.

Dorus, W. (1982) Withdrawal from opioid drugs: A review of techniques and outcomes. In R. J. Craig & S. L. Baker (Eds.), *Drug dependent patients: Treatment and research* (pp. 7–36). Springfield, IL: Charles C. Thomas.

Edward, G., Orford, J., Egert, S., Guthrie, S., Hawker, A., Hensman, C., Mitchenson, M., Oppenheimer, E., & Taylor, C. (1977). Alcoholism: A controlled trail of "treatment" and "advice." *Journal of Studies on Alcohol, 38,* 1004–1031.

Higgins, S. T., Budney, A. J., Bickel, W. K., Highes, J. R., Foerg, F., & Badger, G. (1993). Achieving cocaine abstinence with a behavioral approach. *American Journal of Psychiatry, 150,* 763–769.

Hunt, W. A., Barnatt, L. W., & Branch, L. G. (1971). Relapse rates in addiction programs. *Journal of Clinical Psychology, 27,* 455–456.

Institute of Medicine. (1990). *Broadening the base of treatment for alcohol problems* (pp. 279–302). Washington, DC: National Academy Press.

Kosten, T. R. (1989). Pharmacotherapeutic interventions for cocaine abuse: Matching patients to treatments. *Journal of Nervous and Mental Disease, 177,* 379–389.

Kosten, T. R. (1990). Neurobiology of abused drugs: Opioids and stimulants. *Journal of Nervous and Mental Disease, 178,* 217–227.

Longbaugh, R., Wirtz, P. W., DiClemente, C. C., & Litt, M. (1994). Issues in the development of client-treatment matching hypothesis. *Journal of Studies on Alcohol,* Supplement No. 12, 46–59.

Marlatt, G. A., & Gordon, J. R. (1985). *Relapse prevention: Maintenance strategies in the treatment of addictive behavior.* New York: Guildford Press.

Mattson, M. E., & Allen, J. P. (1991). Research on matching alcoholic patients to treatments: Findings, issues, and implications. *Journal of Addictive Disease, 11,* 33–49.

Mattson, M. E., Allen, J. P., Longabaugh, R., Nickless, C. J., Connors, G. J., & Kadden, R. M. (1994). A chronological review of empirical studies matching alcoholic clients to treatment. *Journal of Studies on Alcohol,* Supplement No. 12, 16–29.

McAuliffe, W. E., & Ch'ien, J. M. (1986). Recovery training and self-help: A relapse-prevention program for treated opiate addicts. *Journal of Substance Abuse Treatment, 3,* 9–20.

McKay, J. R., Rutherford, M. J., Cacciola, J. S., Kabasakalian-McKay, R., & Alterman, A. I. (1996). Gender differences in the relapse experiences of cocaine patients. *Journal of Nervous and Mental Disease, 184,* 616–622.

McLellan, A. T., Arndt, I. O., Metzger, D. S., Woody, G. E., & O'Brien, C. P. (1993). The effects of psychosocial services in substance abuse treatment. *Journal of the American Medical Association, 269,* 1953–1959.

McLellan, A. T., Grissom, G. R., Zanis, D., Randall, M., Brill, P., & O'Brien, C. P. (1997). Problem-service "matching" in addiction treatment: A prospective study in four programs. *Archives of General Psychiatry, 54,* 730–735.

McLellan, A. T., Woody, G. E., Luborsky, L., O'Brien, C. V. P., & Druly, K. A. (1983). Increased effectiveness of substance abuse treatment: A prospective study of patient-treatment "matching." *Journal of Nervous and Mental Disease, 171,* 597–605.

National Institute on Alcohol Abuse and Alcoholism (1989, October). *Relapse and craving.* No. 6, PH 277, 1–4. Rockville, MD. Department of Health and Human Services.

National Institute on Drug Abuse (1999). *Principles of drug addiction treatment: A research-based guide.* Rockville, MD: NIDA.

Noyes, R., Garvey, M. J., Cook, B. L., & Perry, P. J. (1988). Benzodiazepine withdrawal: A review of the evidence. *Journal of Clinical Psychiatry, 49,* 382–389.

Otto, M. W., Pollack, M. H., Sachs, S. R., Reiter, S. R., Meltzer-Brody, S., & Rosenbaum, J. F. (1993). Discontinuation of benzodiazepine treatment: Efficacy of cognitive-behavioral therapy for patients with panic disorder. *American Journal of Psychiatry, 150,* 1485–1490.

Pattison, E. M. (1985). The selection of treatment modalities for the alcoholic patient. In J. Mendelson, & N. Mello (Eds.), *The diagnosis and treatment of alcoholism* (pp. 189–294). New York: McGraw-Hill.

Pattison, E. M., Coe, R., & Doerr, H. O. (1973). Population variation among alcoholic treatment facilities. *International Journal of the Addictions, 8,* 199–229.

Pattison, E. M., Coe, R., & Rhodes, R. J. (1969). Evaluation of alcoholism treatment: A comparison of three facilities. *Archives of General Psychiatry, 20,* 478–488.

Peele, S. (1990-1991). What works in addiction treatment and what doesn't? Is the best therapy no therapy? *International Journal of the Addictions, 25,* 1409–1419.

Prochaska, J. O., DiClemente, C. C., & Norcross, J. C. (1986). Towards a comprehensive model of change. In W. R. Miller, & N. Heather (Eds.), *Treating addictive behaviors: Process of change* (pp. 3–27). New York: Plenum Press.

Prochaska, J. O., DiClemente, C. C., & Norcross, J. C. (1992). In search of how people change: applications to addictive behaviors. *American Psychologist, 47,* 1102–1114.

Project Match Research Group (1997). Matching alcoholism treatments to client heterogeneity: Project MATCH posttreatment drinking outcomes. *Journal of Studies on Alcohol, 60,* 7–29.

Skinner, H. A. (1981). Different strokes for different folks: Differential treatment for alcohol abuse. In R. E. Meyer, B. C. Gluek, J. E. O'Brien, T. F. Babor, J. H. Jaffe, & J. R. Strabenav (Eds.), *Evaluation of the alcoholic:*

Implications for research, theory, and treatment (pp. 349–367). NIAAA Research Monograph No. 5, Washington, DC: U.S. Government Printing Office.

Stark, M. J. (1992). Dropping out of substance abuse treatment: A clinically oriented review. *Clinical Psychology Review, 12,* 93–116.

Stitzer, M. L., Bickel, W. K., Bigelow, G. E., & Liebson, I. A. (1986). Effect of methadone dose contingencies on urinalysis test results of polydrug-abusing methadone maintenance patients. *Drug and Alcohol Dependence, 18,* 341–348.

Stitzer, M. L., Bigelow, G. E., Lawrence, C., Cohen, J., D'Lugoff, B., & Hawthorne, J. (1977). Methadone take-home as a reinforcer in a methadone maintenance program. *Addictive Behavior, 2,* 9–14.

Tennant, F. S., Rawson, R. A., Pumphrey, E., & Seecof, R. (1986). Clinical experiences with 959 opioid-dependent patients treated with levo-alpha-acetylmethadol (LAAM). *Journal of Substance Abuse Treatment, 3,* 195–202.

Trimpey, J. (1992). *The small book: A revolutionary alternative for overcoming alcohol and drug dependence.* New York: Delacorte.

Trimpey, J. (1995). *The final fix: Addictive voice recognition technique.* New York: Lotus Press.

Trimpey, J. (1996). *The new cure for substance addiction: AVRT.* New York: Simon & Schuster.

Wikler, A. (1973). Dynamics of drug dependence: Implications of a conditioning theory for research and treatment. *Archives of General Psychiatry, 28,* 611–616.

Weddington, W. W., Brown, B. S., Haertzen, C. A., Cone, E. J., Dax, E. M., Herning, R. I., & Michaelson, B. S. (1990). Changes in mood, craving, and sleep during short-term abstinence reported by male cocaine addicts. *Archives of General Psychiatry, 47,* 861–868.

Weiss, R. D., Martinez-Raga, J., Griffin, M. I., Greenfield, S. F., & Hufford, C. (1997). Gender differences in cocaine dependent patients: A 6-month follow-up study. *Drug and Alcohol Dependence, 44,* 35–40.

EXAMPLE TREATMENT PLAN FOR AN ALCOHOLIC

Problem No. 1: *Alcohol Dependence*

1. *Goals*
   a. Patient will become abstinent from alcohol.
   b. Patient will verbalize Step 1 Principle.
   c. Patient will demonstrate motivation to maintain sobriety.
2. *Outcome Measures*
   a. Patient will test negative on random breathalizers 100% of the time and collaterals will verify abstinence reports.
   b. Patient will be able to state Step 1 principle upon counselor request.
   c. Patient will attend AA and all counseling sessions as scheduled.
3. *Treatment*
   a. Patient will attend individual counseling once each week. (Counselor)
   b. Patient will attend AA, per schedule (wife to call counselor monthly to report patient status patient to attend AA daily for next 90 days; or patient to present counselor with a signed attendance sheet daily documenting AA attendance).
   c. Counselor will Breathalize patient at random at least once a month. (Counselor)
4. *Time Frame*
   a.–c. By 90 days from date of initial treatment plan

Problem No. 2: *Legal Problem (DUI)*

1. *Goals*
   a. Patient will resolve legal problem.
   b. Patient will abstain from alcohol.
   c. Patient will verbalize reasons one should not drink and drive.
   d. Patient will develop alternative travel arrangements should patient relapse.
2. *Outcome Measures*
   a. Patient will provide receipt of attendance at driving school classes mandated by the court.
   b. Patient will test negative on random Breathalizers 100% of the time.
   c. Patient will produce reasons upon request of counselor by X date.
   d. Patient will report plan that includes designated driver by X date to counselor.

3. *Treatment*
   a. Patient will attend driving education class once a week for 3 months (30 hrs.). (Patient)
   b. Patient will attend individual counseling once a week. (Counselor)
   c. Patient will attend AA daily for 90 days. (Counselor)
   d. Patient will random Breathalizers once a month. (Counselor)
4. *Time Frame*
   a.–b. by 90 days
   c.–d. within 30 days
5. *Review Date*
   90 days

EXAMPLE TREATMENT PLAN FOR NARCOTIC ADDICT

Problem No. 1: Opiate Dependence

1. *Goals*
   a. Establish and maintain abstinence
   b. Do not allow work to interfere with recovery
   c. Restore spirituality
2. *Outcome Measures*
   a. Patient will have urine free from illicit drugs 100% of the time.
   b. Patient will not miss more that 1 counseling session a month.
   c. Patient will attend church regularly, per self report.
3. *Treatment*
   a. methadone maintenance daily (Pharmacist)
   b. random urine toxicology screens twice/month (Counselor)
   c. individual counseling once/week (Counselor)
   d. group counseling twice/week (Counselor)
4. *Time Frame*
   a.–c. within 90 days

Problem No. 2: Hypertension

1. *Goal*
   a. Control blood pressure and prevent complications
2. *Outcome Measure*
   a. Blood pressure will be within normal ranges for height and weight (not over 130 and not less than 80).
   b. Patient will be able to cite three complications of high blood pressure.
3. *Treatment*
   Medication as prescribed (currently on Lotensin 10mg 1/day)
4. *Time Frame*
   within 90 days

Problem No. 3: Anxiety Reaction with Panic Attacks

1. *Goals*
    a. Reduce anxiety and panic attacks and
    b. Understand and be able to control attacks without panic.
2. *Outcome Measures*
    a. Patient will report a 20% in frequency of panic attacks.
    b. Patient will report that he no longer fears he is going to die should he have an anxiety reaction.
3. *Treatment*
    a. Buspar 1/day
    b. Cognitive-behavioral therapy by clinical psychologist 1/week
    c. Biofeedback 1/week with clinical psychologist (to include relaxation therapy).
4. *Time Frame*
    within 90 days
5. *Review Date*
    90 days

CHAPTER SIX

GROUP COUNSELING TECHNIQUES

Group therapy has long been considered the intervention of choice among and with substance abusers. Although little research validates this assumption, substantial anecdotal evidence suggests that group therapy can have salient and long-lasting effects on patient behavior. AA and NA essentially use group modalities. Almost all other treatment programs for substance abusers rely on the group therapy modality for education and treatment. It can be argued that if patients have trouble getting along with other people, then group therapy may be the treatment of choice. This is especially true if the patients are unaware of the behaviors that cause the difficulties (Flores, 1986). In group therapy, substance abusers may

- See the progression of the disorder in themselves and in others who may be at different stages. They can see clearly what may be in store for them, should they continue to abuse substances.
- Practice new behaviors and explain slips and lapses in an understanding and supportive environment.
- Discuss symptoms, problems, and dilemmas with people who can identify with and offer suggestions to deal with these issues and who can do so with credibility.
- Reduce the isolation that often results from substance abuse.
- Experience caring confrontation from other group members who can see through resistance and manipulations.
- Establish healthy recovery patterns, assuming the counselor has worked with the group to establish group norms.
- Reduce denial.
- Take advantage of positive peer pressure.
- Increase motivation to establish and maintain recovery (Barry, 1999; Nagy, 1994).

155

CURATIVE FACTORS IN GROUP THERAPY

Psychiatrist Irving Yalom (1995) wrote a classic textbook in group psychotherapy and has identified factors that he believes contribute to change in group
therapy. He calls these factors "curative" or "therapeutic." The following list
elaborates their application to substance abusers.

- *Imparting information.* This includes providing didactic instructions, and giving advice, suggestions, directions, and guidance. Explanations and information can be curative and can motivate people to change their life. Most
  commonly in substance abuse groups educational seminars impart basic information on substance abuse. Another example is patients' descriptions of
  how they handled a particular issue.

- *Instillation of hope.* Hope is necessary to keep patients coming for group
  therapy but it can be therapeutically effective because faith in a treatment
  technique is necessary for it to be fully effective. Many substance abusers
  come to treatment in a state of despair, feeling hopeless and unable to control their substance abuse. Hope is generated in a group when patients to
  see improvement in other patients. Counselors should capitalize on this
  phenomenon by focusing on patient improvement when it occurs.

- *Universality.* This factor challenges the belief that one patient is the only
  one who has these problems. Once patients learn that others have been
  through similar experiences and have similar feelings, the healing process
  may begin. Patients realize they are not alone in their struggle and that
  their situation and problems are not unique.

- *Altruism.* It seems quite natural to want to help someone in need. Substance abusers are so caught up in their own troubles that they often ignore reaching out to others. In a group format, patients receive advice,
  suggestions, insights, reassurances, and support from other patients. This
  form of help, given freely, is an act of concern that is difficult to shut out.

- *Corrective recapitulation of the primary family group.* Therapy groups resemble
  the original, nuclear family in many ways. The leader is a kind of parental
  figure. Patient feelings towards parental and authority figures are often dis-
  placed (e.g., transferred) to the therapist. Members compete to get the attention of the therapist, behavior similar to sibling rivalry. Experiences
  reported by patients in the group can evoke feelings about similar experiences other patients had earlier in life. By reexperiencing such dynamics,
  patients can work through old hang-ups. Groups thereby can provide patients with what has been termed the "corrective emotional experience."

- *Development of socializing techniques.* Socialization will occur in almost all
  therapy groups. Counselors used to instruct patients not to socialize with
  each other outside of the group, but such admonitions were rarely obeyed.
  Friendships are formed: the therapy group can provide a social experience,
  inside and outside of the group, that produces growth, providing patients

engage in appropriate social events. Patients may also learn to give up old, negative associations and to socialize with more positive people. This is especially important for drug addicts, who often feel uncomfortable around people who are "straight."

- *Imitative behaviors.* Counselors and group members can serve as role models for the behavior of other patients. Social psychologists have found, through research, that role modeling is an important element in understanding human behavior. Sometimes a patient in group counseling doesn't say too much, yet is able to realize a substantial amount of behavior change, possibly through watching and listening to others and then acting as they do.

- *Interpersonal learning.* People learn in all contexts and with all contacts. This is no less true in a therapy group. Learning will occur, even if a patient remains silent. Whether patients will implement what they learn may be another matter. Groups can be thought of as a microcosm of a larger societal group. How patients behave in the group is likely to reflect how they behave elsewhere and with other people. Patients may describe their pathology in group sessions but sooner or later will unconsciously display it for all to see. People cannot help but be themselves: this will become manifested in interpersonal transactions in group counseling. By analyzing the interpersonal relationships and transactions in the group sessions, patients can learn how they respond to others. Of course not only pathology is manifested: patients will show their strengths, abilities, talents, and so forth, as well.

- *Group cohesiveness.* Therapists often have used an analogy to describe the meaning of group cohesiveness: Cohesiveness is to group as relationship is to individual. The analogy speaks to the quality of the relationship group members have with each other and with the counselor. It is a kind of attraction that members feel toward the group—a sense of belonging. Attendance, group participation, the honest expression of feelings, and mutual respect are all signs of a cohesive group. Research shows that group members benefit more from a group when it is cohesive. They are more willing to self-disclose, report negative events, problem relationships, and failures. These processes are a necessary prelude to behavior change.

- *Catharsis.* Sometimes just talking about a problem can help patients find solutions to problems. "Getting things off the chest" usually makes people feel better. Mental health specialists call this *catharsis.* Emotional baggage carried around for years is unburdened and patients can be free, for the first time in years, to be themselves in an honest way.

- *Existential factors.* Patients need to face their basic beliefs about life and death and about themselves, and they need to take ultimate responsibility for their behavior. Groups in which conclusions and decisions can be made unencumbered from psychological distortions allow these existential issues to be played out.

Group therapy can also provide a sense of *acceptance, safety* and *support.* Many substance abusers feel a sense of anticipated rejection when they relate to "straight" people. By relating with other patients in recovery, they feel more comfortable, feel a sense of acceptance, and are more likely to invest their trust, thereby increasing self-disclosure.

TYPES OF GROUPS

Addiction treatment programs offer different types of therapeutic groups, depending on the needs of the patient and the philosophy of the program. Below we discuss various types of groups commonly used in addiction treatment but the line of demarcation between groups is porous and many groups are actually a blend of the prototype models.

- *Educational groups* probably are the most frequent type of group intervention in addiction treatment. The focus is generally on the disease concept, the need to attend AA and the need for aftercare. A specific educational content, such as AIDS or sexually transmitted diseases, may be presented in the group forum.
- *Self-help groups* probably are the next most frequent type of group experienced by substance abusers. AA and NA are self-help groups. They offer mutual support in a nonthreatening, accepting, and understanding environment. For many, the AA group is the primary treatment. Self-help groups cannot help everyone. Some people need more professional guidance and direction and have more serious problems than can be addressed by peers, but self-help groups are a valuable tool in the overall treatment intervention picture.
- *Aftercare groups* function as continued therapy and support groups. They most often follow an intense inpatient treatment for addiction. They blend education and self-help and may have a professionally directed structure.
- *Relapse prevention groups* frequently are used in addiction treatment (Wallace, 1989). The relapse prevention model (see Chapter 5) is easily employed in a group context and can provide a very economical means for conveying this approach to a large group of patients.
- *Dual diagnosis groups* are increasingly used in addiction treatment (Weiss, Najavits, & Greenfield, 1998). These groups are for patients who abuse substances and who also have a serious mental illness. Concepts from mental health and the addiction fields are blended to promote abstinence. This is more fully discussed in Chapter 8.
- *Motivational interviewing groups* are slowly finding their way into addiction treatment (Foote, DeLuca, Magura, Grauch et al, 1999). These groups employ concepts developed by William Miller (1991) (see Chapter 4) and have two purposes: (1) to help newly admitted patients develop and main-

tain a focus on recovery and (2) to help overcome resistance in patients who have not benefited from traditional methods of care.

MODELS OF GROUP COUNSELING

For the most part, models of group therapy have been based on clinical insights and on theoretical concepts derived from group work with nonaddicted patients. Such insights are not always applicable to substance abusers. Also, many substance abuse counselors use the group to identify and confront defenses—particularly denial—and to reveal characterological problems that interfere with acceptance of the disease concept. The uncovering of pathological behavior, personality disordered behavior, and other forms of psychopathology generally are not the focus of attention in substance abuse therapy groups, although these very matters may be the root cause of the difficulties.

An effective group counselor has to understand group process and group dynamics. There is no substitute for experience in leading groups and getting supervision in group counseling to acquire these skills.

Models of group counseling are important because they provide counselors with a set of theoretically-derived interventions as well as a set of goals and ways to understand the events and interactions that occur within the group. There is no uniform method of conducting group therapy. Different models have different goals and require different tasks of the counselors. The model chosen has to match the needs of the patient and the goals of treatment.

The models that will be addressed here are (1) developmental groups (the process group psychodynamic model), (2) educational groups, (3) focused change groups, (4) individually oriented growth and personal change groups, (5) interpersonally oriented groups, (6) object relations or systems groups, and (7) problem-solving groups and process groups (Brabender & Fallon, 1993; Flores, 1988).

Developmental Groups

Under this model, groups go through predictable stages of change and growth. Authors disagree on the names and number of stages, but there is consensus that stages do form in long-term groups. At each stage, different kinds and levels of tension exist that result in different sets of pressure on the group and on the counselor. Only these stages about which there is near unanimity are discussed here. This model is conducted within a psychodynamic framework, which along with systems theory, form the basis to understanding group processes (Brabender & Fallon, 1993).

Stages of Group Therapy. Many group therapy experts have tried to elucidate stages that a group goes through but have come to no real consensus, except for a very broad outline. Groups do not necessarily progress through all these stages and can become stuck at any stage, even for the life of the group, depending on the skill of the counselor to advance the group to the next stage. Furthermore, no clear line of demarcation defines the transition of one stage to the next.

■ *Stage 1: "Why am I here?"* Patients need to know why they are in the group and how it will help them. Merely telling a patient the answers will not satisfy the question. Each patient must individually determine this meaning and the answer must be experienced in the group. New patients search for this meaning by hesitating and not fully participating in the group discussion, questioning how group counseling will help, and show regressive behavior by over-dependence on the counselor. They may seek answers only from the group leader and ignore or devalue suggestions from other members. These are all signs that group norms are in the process of development and that the group members still don't know the "lay of the land."

  The Stage 1 task of group development is for the group to survive. Patients will unconsciously assume roles, goals, and develop norms that foster either survival or dissolution of the group. Group cohesion will be different at each stage of group functioning. Group members normally will identify with members who are most similar to themselves: this creates subgroups, which threaten further growth. The task of the group is to integrate these various subgroups while accomplishing the overall purpose of the group.

■ *Stage 2. Development of Cohesiveness*: After the resolution of the issues of Stage 1, Stage 2 is typified by increased participation, self-disclosure, reliable attendance, secret-sharing, and so forth. At this stage, the real reason the patient is in the groups tends to be revealed, because mutual trust has been established. At Stage 2 of group development, patients tend to be tolerant of feelings expressed toward each other and toward the counselor. The counselor's comfort in listening to members express anger and hostility can go a long way toward resolving problem emotions.

■ *Stage 3: Working through.* A working, cooperative attitude, positive feedback, and sincere expressions of help characterize this stage. Negative emotions no longer dominate the session. Interpersonal progress is identified readily. At this stage, patients tend to work on changing their behavior, attitudes, thoughts, and perceptions. They are more willing to engage in risk-taking, advance to working on the more difficult steps in AA and NA, and actively try to solve problems. They have a seriousness of purpose and a willingness to risk failure if it might result in more permanent changes in their life.

■ *Stage 4: Separation and termination.* Therapy groups are limited by time. Sooner or later, patients decide that they have gained as much benefit as the group can provide and therefore need to move on with their life. Once this decision has been reached, they may tend to regress, to report more symptoms or increased fears of relapse. Dynamically this is *separation anxiety*. Patients are having trouble letting go. When the counselor recognizes the separation anxiety and allows patients to discuss their feelings about leaving the group, these matters should subside.

Counselors operating from this developmental group model are usually nondirective, allowing the stage to develop and unfold, and trying to create an emotional climate that permits group members to resolve these processes themselves. Particularly important is for the counselor to develop an atmosphere in which group communication is accepted. This means that negative transference is appropriately dealt with and accepted. The counselor sets norms, interprets, makes observations about group functioning or individual behavior, and strives to bring the group to the next level of functioning.

This model is best used with higher functioning patients and with longer-term counseling groups. Development of the group is theorized to mirror the development of composite group members in it.

Educational Groups

The educational model probably is the most frequently used in working with substance abusers. All groups vary in the degree to which they include an educational component, but this model has, as its primary focus, the education of patients. Most often this model is designed to disseminate information about a particular disease and to help the patient cope with the illness (Brabender & Fallon, 1993). In substance abuse, the disease model of addiction is the one that this model most often addresses. Substance abuse counselors who use this model teach patients didactically, promote group discussion, questions, and interaction, and try to get patients to help one another. Brabender and Fallon (1993) argue that this model may have greater credibility to patients than other group counseling models because it appears to emphasize what patients consider important.

Focused Change Groups

There are two types of focused change groups. The first was called sensitivity training or T-group and has evolved into more concrete foci that may blend goals and techniques from other group therapy models. The second was designed for lower functioning patients. In both cases, the leader is active and supportive, and the general goal is for patients to understand how their behavior affects others and how others' behavior affects them. Sometimes the target of change is a specific kind of behavior, such as smoking cessation, or dealing with a medical problem, such as diabetes. Focused change groups can be quite confrontational. Their emphasis is on change and not on learning which factors contribute to the behavior. AA and NA embody the essence of this model.

Individually-Oriented Change Groups

The goal of this model is changing individual behavior and developing personal growth. It may be described as individual counseling within a group setting because the focus is always on the individual and never on the group. In fact, group processes and group dynamics are rarely dealt with, except to help change a particular person.

This model uses a number of techniques to accomplish its goal. Role-playing and psychodrama may be used. An individual may be put on a "hot seat" in the middle of the group circle while group members take turns telling the person their opinions or reactions of and to the person's behavior, weaknesses, or goals. Some group members may be called upon to play an alter ego or devil's advocate. The model uses many concepts and techniques from Gestalt therapy. The aim is to create in the patient an intensely encountered emotional experience that gets at the root of emotional blockages. Variations of this model frequently have been used with substance abusers.

Interpersonal or Interactional Groups

Interactional group therapy assumes that personality is formed on the basis of a person's interaction with others. Therefore, patients' behavior in groups—that is, the nature of the interpersonal relationships—will necessarily display their strengths and vulnerabilities. In interactional group therapy, members are free to talk about any issue they wish, to state any feeling they wish, and to use almost any vehicle they wish to accomplish the task. The counselor tends to be very active, maintains the group focus, promotes disclosures, strives for honesty, and ensures group interaction and inclusion of all members. The proximate goal of the therapist is to get patients to understand (a) what their behavior is like in groups, (b) how their behavior affects other people, (c) how it affects people's opinions about them, and (d) how it influences and is consistent with their sense of self (Flores, 1988). To do this, the counselor cultivates an interactive style within the group.

Usually the content of the session is unstructured and concerns here-and-now issues and concerns of patients, as well as exploring their relationships with the group members. How they relate in the group is quite likely how they relate with significant others in their life.

Object Relations or Systems Model

Brabender and Fallon (1993) describe a model in which the central tenet is that how group members relate to others in the group reflects the overall organization of their internal, mental life. Object relations refers to the total sum of how people view interactions of other people in the light of their own self-image, prior interactions with similar people, and their images of these people in "role."

Thus, how patients view a person in the group who is a father depends on their early interactions with their own father, and with people whom they have known to be fathers. These ideas and experiences form what is termed as an internal template—an object relation.

Object relations do not exist in a vacuum. General systems theory provides the theoretical foundation and additional understanding of how people relate to others. This theory defines a system as a group of elements that interact and relate in a consistent manner over time and in an emotional balance. Think of a child's mobile that floats above a crib and provides enjoyment and visual exploration for an infant: If one of the mobile elements is removed, the entire assembly becomes unbalanced and malfunctions. The same is true of people. What one person does can affect and change those closest to them. Therefore, how people behave must also be understood in terms of the relationships in which they are involved. This concept is elaborated in Chapter 7, for it forms the foundation of understanding family interactions, dynamics, and change.

The content of the group interaction usually focuses on some aspect of psychopathology or personality pathology, particularly emphasizing more negative traits, such as anger, aggression, hostility, shame, dishonesty, and so forth, as well as an exploration of their historical roots.

Implementation of this group counseling model requires a full understanding of psychodynamics, especially psychoanalytic ideas, object relations theory, general systems theory, and psychopathology. Most substance abuse counselors would not have the breadth of knowledge to conduct this kind of group, which is best left to other mental health professionals (i.e., clinical psychologists, psychiatrists, etc.).

Problem-Solving Groups

This type of group uses steps involved in problem-solving (i.e., problem identification, possible solutions, barriers to implementation, advantages and problems with proposed solutions, decision, implementation, and evaluation of effectiveness) in a straightforward and direct manner. Although many patients have deficient problem-solving skills, they can be adept at recognizing and helping others solve their problems. This group approach utilizes and capitalizes on these skills.

Process Groups

This model focuses on the here and now feelings and reactions of the group. It does not deal with childhood history except as it pertains to contemporary issues *within the group*. The counselor maintains a group focus and interprets behavior only in the light of the group experience. One assumption is that individual members regress in groups and rely on the group leader for direction, support, and change. The task of the counselor is to redirect the process of change onto the group themselves. Group processes are interpreted and individual behavior is interpreted only in the light of the group experience. The process group model is rarely used with substance abusers. In fact, this model is more often thought of as "therapy for normals."

FACTORS TO CONSIDER IN DEVELOPING A GROUP

Patient Selection

Selection of patients usually considers such factors as size of the group, its composition, and whether the grouping will be homogeneous or heterogeneous.

1. Group size depends on the purpose of the group. If the purpose is largely didactic, then the group can be quite large. Group presentations may include up to 50 people. If the purpose is interactional, most experts recommend that the group include around eight people.
2. Composition of the group also is dependent on the purpose of the group. At one point a group might consist of substance abusers in recovery for more than a year, and another group might consist of abusers with no clean time after six months of treatment.
3. Groups are either homogeneous or heterogeneous. A homogeneous group consist of members selected for some commonality (e.g., people in recovery, victims of spousal abuse by alcoholic partners, teenage marijuana abusers, and so forth), whereas a heterogeneous group consists of a variety of patients who may be dissimilar in personal characteristics. For all practical purposes, even a homogeneous group, while similar in terms of the initial selection criteria, is heterogeneous in other characteristics.
4. Patients may also be selected based on level of functioning. In general, low functioning patients are best served in groups that provide a low level of stress, modest self-disclosure, strong therapeutic support, and a didactic focus (Brabender & Fallon, 1993).

Inclusion and Exclusion Criteria

Not every patient is amenable to participation in groups. Counselors would do well to consider, *in advance*, what kinds of patients will be included and which will be excluded from group attendance. There is a general consensus on which kinds of patients are not amenable to group counseling interventions and are served better through individual modalities. Common exclusion criteria are

- Active mental illness (hallucinations, delusions, lack of contact with reality, etc.)
- Organic brain damage that reduces attention, concentration, memory, and decision-making capability

- Severely narcissistic persons who cannot attend to anyone but themselves
- Monopolizing patients, who dominates the group discussion and cannot defocus
- Acutely suicidal patients

Psychopathic or sociopathic patients often have been cited as those to exclude from most group therapies that are heterogeneous in diagnosis. These patients tend to manipulate and get other patients in the group to act out their anger, while they sit back and avoid the consequences of such behavior. The most common personality disorder diagnosis among substance abusers is antisocial personality disorder (Craig, 2000), so, practically speaking, most substance abuse groups will be replete with this kind of personality pathology.

Selection Procedures

Two procedures are commonly used to select patients for group counseling. In a *clinical interview,* the counselor tries to determine if the patient can tolerate group counseling and will be able to benefit from it. In selection by *clinical policy,* a program's rule might be that all patients newly admitted to a substance abuse program must participate in 10 consecutive sessions of didactic group therapy. These sessions often are highly structured with planned content dimensions (e.g., disease concept, the progression concept, aftercare attendance, etc.) for each session. In this case, exclusion criteria are predetermined, and, once the criteria are ruled out, all other patients are referred automatically to this group.

Group Structure

Patients need to be informed about such administrative issues as the time, place, and duration of the group. Most groups do not go beyond two hours. The minimum amount of time required for good interaction is 45 minutes and one to one-and-a-half hours is the most common group therapy time.

Limit Setting

Group counselors will find themselves setting limits about group behaviors within the group but it is also a good idea to set limits with individual patients before they attend the first session. Counselors must tell their patients what they do and do not expect from them in the sessions.

Open or Closed Groups

One type of limit setting in advance is whether to allow new members to enter the group at any time in the life of the group (e.g., *open group*), or not to accept new members until the "natural life" of the group has been realized (e.g., *closed group*). An example of a closed group might be the requirement that new patients attend 10 sessions of didactic group therapy in which the content of the last session builds on and is the basis of content for the next session. In this case, it would not be appropriate for patients to come in at different points in the life of this group: all patients should start and end together.

Physical Setting

It is important to conduct the group in an aura of professionalism. This means that the place where the group is conducted must maintain patient privacy and confidentiality and be devoid of distractions and interruptions. Counselors should silence pagers, avoid phone calls, place a "do not disturb" sign outside the door, and take other precautions that convey to the patients that they value this intervention and are serious about it. Avoid barriers, such as tables, and arrange patients in a circle, except for an essentially didactic presentation in which patients could be seated classroom style. Counselors should position patients to allow them to see full body language during the session.

GROUP INTERVENTIONS

Counselors may intervene at several different levels. First they may interpret the *group process,* the particular set of circumstances or behaviors in the group that led to the group's reactions at a particular moment.

EXAMPLE
Background. A patient with a histrionic personality disorder came late to group therapy. He immediately became dramatic in citing the reasons for his lateness, drawing attention to himself and focusing only on his own needs.

Group Reaction. The group became quiet, sullen, and nonreactive, although immediately prior to his entrance they had been mutually involved and interactive.

Therapist Response. Why has this group suddenly become so quiet?

Second, counselors can focus on the *interpersonal processes that occur between two group members.*

Background. Bill, a patient in long-time recovery, was becoming impatient with another group member, Steve, who continually professed his resolve to stop using drugs yet repeatedly gave excuses for why he has to use.

Interpersonal Process. Bill confronted Steve with his rationalizations, saying that if he really wanted to stop using, he would just stop. Steve got angry, saying that Bill doesn't know his circumstances and doesn't "walk in his shoes." Bill countered that he's been there and stopped using when he made up his mind to stop. Steve became more irate at not being believed.

Therapist Response. Bill, why is it that you get irritated when Steve talks about his triggers and Steve, why is it that you get angry when Bill confronts your excuses that we've heard over and over again. Aren't you both correct?

Third, counselors can intervene at the level of *interpersonal processes occurring with the group as a whole.*

Background. A patient came irregularly to group but, when there, would object whenever the counselor or another group member asked him anything about his personal situation. The patient was HIV+ and was afraid this would be discovered. He steadfastly objected to such questions and said he was only there to listen.

Interpersonal Process. The group stopped asking him any questions and never asked for his comments.

Therapist Response. This group seems to be avoiding Willie and seems to be reluctant to interact with him.

Fourth, counselors can choose to *interpret group behavior at the psychological level,* either individually or collectively.

Background. All patients in the group came from families that were matriarchally dominated, and in which the father essentially was absent during their childhood. These men were either divorced or in relationships in which there was no fidelity. Adultery was the norm and they "allowed" the female in the relationship to raise their children. They would periodically stop in and see their "partner" and children, but without warning. They were unpredictable and unreliable.

(Female) Therapist Response. You know, it seems to me that you are all treating me like you treated your spouses. You come and go to and from this group as you please, you rarely get involved with each other, and you tend to give orders to group members. This is just the way you acted at home.

SPECIFIC PROBLEMS

Dropouts, Absences, and Tardiness

Dropout from substance abuse programs seems to be the norm (Baekeland & Lundwall, 1975), and although various efforts have been proposed to reduce the dropout rate in substance abuse programs (Craig, 1985), substance abusers more often than not simply stop coming to the group. Also, irregular attendance is a common problem with substance abusers. The best way to deal with this is through group norms, in which the members strive to get each other to attend on a more regular basis.

Confidentiality

Material discussed in the context of a professional relationship in group therapy is usually protected from discovery in evidentiary procedures by ethics and law. Even common sense would dictate that disclosures to a therapist would remain private, except under the most unusual circumstances (e.g., child or elder abuse or neglect, imminent danger to self or others, etc.). Despite these strictures, and despite the good intentions of substance abuse professionals, who tell patients that material discussed in group is confidential and will not be discussed outside of group, counselors cannot guarantee the confidentiality of such material. Substance abuse counselors are in control of the material they divulge to others and can assure their clients that they will not discuss it, except with those who need to know (e.g., members of the treatment team), but patients in group do not keep such material private. They often tell other patients about it—especially if it's "juicy" or sensational. The confidential nature of group counseling should periodically be discussed in group, but patients will have to weigh the risk of disclosing the material and the possibility that someone outside this group eventually will hear about it.

The Intoxicated or High Patient in Group

Freud said insight was soluble in alcohol. Common sense, rationality, effective decision-making, and other ego resources dissolve under the effects of drugs and alcohol. Most substance abuse therapists suggest that, under such circumstances, the patient be politely told to leave and to return when sober.

Suspected Illicit Use without Acknowledging It

Although counselors cannot always know when someone has been using, there are times when such use is obvious. It is best to gently confront the behavior, promote honesty, explore for relapse, or use triggers to help the patient understand the circumstances of their use, including proximal and distal variables related to such use. It is also important to discuss reasons for not disclosing this information in group and reasons for continued denial of this use. Group members should be particularly valuable here, as they most likely to be able to pick up clues to use that many counselors who have no history of substance abuse may miss.

Continued Use with No Intention to Stop

There is little consensus on how to deal with this situation. Counselors vary philosophically on the issue. Some believe that continued use ultimately destroys the group and hence such patients should be excluded during active use phase. Others believe they might be able to eventually influence such patients, as long as they continue to attend the group. If a patient is talking about meaningful issues in their life and is gaining some benefit from doing so, continued group attendance should be encouraged. The fact that patients come regularly suggests they are getting something from the group experience. Some research suggests that counseling may not be immediately effective but, following an incubation period, which could last for several months, counseling eventually "takes hold" (Carroll, Rounsaville, Nich, Gordon, et al., 1994).

CHAPTER SUMMARY

Chapter 6 emphasized group counseling, the mainstream treatment modality in most addiction treatment programs. (The tools and techniques discussed in Chapter 5 may also be used in group contexts.) It discussed factors that are responsible for change in group counseling, referred to as curative factors. It addressed the types of groups most often used with addictive disorders together with different models of group counseling. It discussed methods for selecting members for group counseling and concluded with a discussion of special problems extant in group counseling with patients with substance use disorders.

SOURCES OF INFORMATION

Baekeland, F., & Lundwall, L. (1975). Dropping out of treatment: A critical review. *Psychological Bulletin, 82,* 738–783.

Barry, K. L. (1999). *Brief interventions and brief therapies for substance abuse.* Rockville, MD: Substance Abuse and Mental Health Services Administration.

Brabender, V., & Fallon, A. (1993). *Models of inpatient group psychotherapy.* Washington, DC: American Psychological Association.

Carroll, K. M., Rounsaville, B. J., Nich, C., Gordon, L. T., Wirtz, P. W., & Gawin, F. (1994). One-year follow-up of psychotherapy and pharmacotherapy for cocaine dependence. *Archives of General Psychiatry, 51,* 989–997.

Craig, R. J. (2000). Prevalence of personality disorders among cocaine and heroin addicts. *Substance Abuse, 21,* 87–94.

Craig, R. J. (1985). Reducing the treatment dropout rate in drug abuse programs. *Journal of Substance Abuse Treatment, 2,* 209–219.

Flores, P. J. (1988). *Group psychotherapy with addicted populations.* New York: Haworth Press.

Foote, J., DeLuca, A., Magura, S., Warner, A., Grauch, A., Rosenblum, A., & Stahl, S. (1999). A group motivational treatment for chemical dependency. *Journal of Substance Abuse Treatment, 17,* 181–192.

Nagy, P. D. (1994). *Intensive outpatient treatment for alcohol and other drug abuse.* Rockville, MD: Substance Abuse and Mental Health Services Administration.

Wallace, B. C. (1989). Relapse prevention in psychoeducational groups for compulsive crack cocaine smokers. *Journal of Substance Abuse Treatment, 6,* 229–240.

Weiss, R. D., Najavits, C. M., & Greenfield, S. F. (1998). A relapse prevention group for patients with bipolar and substance use disorders. *Journal of Substance Abuse Treatment, 16,* 47–54.

Yalom, I. D. (1995). *The theory and practice of group psychotherapy,* 4th ed. New York: Basic Books.

CHAPTER SEVEN

COUNSELING FAMILIES OF SUBSTANCE ABUSERS

Many view substance abuse as a family disease. Even without accepting the notion that substance abuse is a disease, counselors must accept the fact that substance abuse affects the entire family. Families can influence the etiology of substance abuse through genetics and through family environment. Family researchers have used separate methodologies in studying families of substance abusers. Those employing psychiatric epidemiology methods emphasize genetics using twin studies, adoption studies, and biological marker studies. Those emphasizing family processes have relied upon family interviews, clinical observations, ratings of family functioning, and self-report questionnaires (Ripple & Luthar, 1996).

This chapter addresses four salient concepts that help in understanding addictive behavior and its effects on the family, as well as their treatment implications. Specifically, it discusses (a) *families of substance abusers,* (b) *enabling behaviors,* (c) *codependence,* and (d) *children of alcoholics* and *adult children of alcoholics.*

An early theory was that an alcoholic had a wife who needed to have a husband that she could baby, nurture, and keep in a dependent position to satisfy her own needs. This wife would make very few sexual demands on the husband, and continued to dominate him in other ways (Taylor, Wilbur, & Osnos, 1966). The corollary to this was that the "successful" treatment of alcoholism required therapy of the wife. It is interesting that this theory actually found a way to blame the wife for the alcoholic's behavior. Today therapists recognize that much of a wife's behavior toward an alcoholic husband is related to the stress of living with substance abuse in the family (Janzen, 1977).

The situation can become more complicated. Relationship patterns and family dynamics can feed and perpetuate substance-abusing behavior. Understanding these relationships can improve treatment responsiveness in the patient and can have direct implications for treating the family. Furthermore, evidence from demographic, clinical, and family pedigree research demonstrates that a significant proportion of relatives of patients have psychiatric diagnoses that are highly similar to psychiatric diagnoses among their substance-abusing relatives (Mirin, Weiss, Griffin, & Michael, 1991). Most of these relationships would be described as "enmeshed" (Cervantes, Sorensen, Wermuth, Fernandez, & Menicucci, 1988). Many of these patients and their relatives have boundary inadequacy characterized by an overly rigid boundary that prevents intimacy or have dysfunctional intimacy patterns, characterized by marital disharmony, family violence, and incest (Coleman & Colgan, 1986). The patients perceived the marital and family environment as providing little preparation for social roles, but with the expectation of high achievement, but their wives and mothers perceived the same environment in substantially different ways (Kosten, Novak, & Kleber, 1984).

Still, families can have important positive influences on addict recovery. For example, addicts who admitted their drug use to their family were able to stay clean for longer periods of time than addicts who denied it to their family (Kosten, Jalali, Hogan, & Kleber, 1983). Thus, it appears that families can have either positive or negative influence on the development, maintenance, and recovery of substance abusers.

FAMILY SYSTEMS THEORY

General systems theory has been credited with influencing thought about psychopathology. In *linear* thinking, factor A causes factor B, but general systems theory posits *open systems* that interact with an environment, in which each has the capacity to influence the others. The system itself has *subsystems* that interact with the larger whole in predictable ways. People do not act in isolation. Rather, they are part of another system. People receive feedback—called communication loops—which apprise them if they are straying too far from acceptable behavior. This is called *homeostasis*. The system requires that all elements within the system function at a certain level and in a certain way to maintain the emotional equilibrium of the system. *Tension* results in either the individual or within parts or the whole of the system whenever these "family rules" deviate from a norm. In this model, cause and effect is not linear but rather *circular*. Furthermore, each subsystem within the whole operates at the same microlevel to achieve emotional balance and homeostasis within the subsystem.

Consider the following example. A 26-year-old female marries a 28-year-old male alcoholic. She knows about his drinking problem but loves him and believes she can change him. She nags him to stop drinking, and he increases his episodes of drinking. A linear model would explain that her nagging causes him to drink more. But here is more information: Her father also was an alcoholic and her mother told her never to confront him about his drinking because he was "sick." The daughter grew up hating her father but could never vent her disgust at his behavior, so she married a man like her father so she could express her true feelings. In the circular model, her "system" consists of her parents, her husband, and herself. It is a closed system, of which she and her father are a subsystem, she and her mother are a subsystem, and she and her husband are a subsystem. Her need to express her feelings towards her father's alcoholism influences her choice of mates and influences her need to harass her husband. The entire system needs treatment.

The system can change if one or more elements within the system change. If the husband decides to stop drinking and maintain recovery, it changes the system. It no longer provides a reason for the wife to nag him. Closed systems do not want change and resist change. The system would act in ways to maintain the original homeostasis, creating conditions for relapse. Perhaps the wife nags her husband about something else, again threatening her husband's sobriety. Perhaps her father tells his son-in-law that he need not attend AA because he has stopped drinking, thereby creating another condition for relapse. Perhaps the husband is not serious about stopping but is testing his wife to prove to her that if she didn't nag him about drinking then she would nag him about something else.

Notice, however, that if the husband is able to stop drinking and if the wife is able to discontinue her nagging, then the entire system has been changed. Systems can be changed through family counseling, but even changes that occur as a result of counseling can have the effect of changing the larger system—an example of circular cause and effect.

Whether or not substance abusers live with their parents, they are closely allied with them or with significant family members through direct communication or through communication with siblings, other relatives, and spouses. Family rules, communication patterns, subsystems, and emotional responses to family issues do not change simply because people no longer live with their parents. Circular causative models continue to have their effect, long after people move out and become "independent."

FAMILIES OF SUBSTANCE ABUSERS

The necessity of counseling families of substance abusers stems from four factors: (1) substance abuse affects everyone in the life space of the substance abuses; (2) family stress can cause of individuals begin to use; (3) family history can put individuals at risk for developing a substance abuse problem; and (4) certain behaviors within a family can have the effect of perpetuating or enabling the substance abusing behavior.

Families of substance abusers have been studied extensively. The following list summarizes the main findings. Although any individual conclusion may not appear in every individual family, these characteristics are likely to appear in most of the families of substance abusers:

- Alcohol and drug abuse appear in higher frequency in addict families. This history provides modeling behavior for the children, however inadvertent it may be.
- Substance abusing families have more conflict. In particular, parental support for developing adult responsibilities is absent.

- Alliances within and among substance abusers' family subsystems often are explicit. This may appear as nurturing behavior but actually is more akin to infantalizing behavior. Mothers are often indulgent and overprotective. Fathers are weak and ineffectual.
- Caregivers of substance abuser, usually their mothers, show a great degree of attachment and symbiosis with them. This extreme relatedness makes it difficult for substance abusers to separate and individuate, because caregivers treat them as younger than they really are.
- Substance abusing families have more episodes of premature, untimely, unexpected and tragic deaths than nonaddict families. Some believe this high mortality is a kind of suicidal phenomenon with a family base. The "death wish" is exhibited by substance abuse, which puts users at risk for death and provides a kind of noble suffering for the family pain (Stanton, 1977).
- Substance abusing families are exposed to more trauma, including divorce, separation, accidents, deaths, and sexual trauma than other families (Alexander & Dibb, 1975; 1977; Harbin & Maziar, 1975).

These characteristics are thought to maintain addictive behavior, but also maintain the stability of the family or of the family relationships.

Family Structure

The family of the substance abuser usually is characterized by an absent, dependent, or very passive-aggressive, emotionally distant father. The mother is described as dominant and aggressive. Two themes that pervade discussion of the family dynamics of substance abusers are the nature of parental relationships and the nature and quality of parental discipline and control (Ripple & Luthar, 1996).

The *interpersonal boundaries* in families of substance abusers have been found to be dysfunctional. Specifically, these families are described as *enmeshed* or *disengaged*. In enmeshed families, one parent is overinvolved with the identified patient (e.g., the user), while the other is described as uninvolved, underinvolved, disengaged, or absent from the nuclear parenting triad. Enmeshed families are further characterized by a low tolerance for independence and autonomy and they resist the substance abuser's efforts to individuate and form an identity apart from the family. Family crises provide the context for keeping the substance abuser within the sphere of family influence. Poor marital relationships form the basis of this overinvolvement, which is most typically between the male patient and his mother. This pattern continues in adult life, *whether or not the substance abuser is living at home.*

Disengaged relationships have also been found in family histories of substance abuse. These are characterized by a sense of estrangement from the home, a lack of feeling loyal to or supportive of parents, and a desire to maintain a disengagement from early parental control that the substance abuser felt were too authoritarian and overly concerned with discipline and control. Parental control exists along a continuum and has a curvilinear relationship with psychological health. That is, too much control or too little control is considered uniformly to result in problem children and problem adults. Extremes of parent control have been observed in substance abusing families. An extreme level of parental control and excessive demands will perpetuate a child's sense of dependence and interfere with the development of life skills that would foster independent behaviors. Parents who take a "laissez faire" approach to child rearing (e.g., "boys will be boys") risk having their children engage in negative behaviors, such as substance abuse, so the parents will pay attention to them. Evidence from family studies indicates that the parent who is disengaged from the family, whether or not present in the house, is hostile toward the identified patient; the enmeshed parent overcompensates for this hostility with overindulgence (Ripple & Luthar, 1996).

Abusive Relationship Patterns

Many possible types of relationships can characterize substance abusers' relationships with significant others. Those that follow have been brought to the attention of substance-abuse professionals:

- *"Easy rider."* One pattern in a dyadic relationship has been termed the "easy rider" syndrome. In this dyad, the female partner cares for the male substance abuser. The female adopts the role of the substance abuser's mother, who had to contend with an abusive and alcoholic husband. The female partner, mother, often was confined in a role of taking care of her husband and family and sacrificing her own needs to accommodate the needs of others. Thus the partner of the substance abuser takes in a male who appears passive-aggressive in dealing with maternal objects but inwardly feels guilty for the behavior that sustains his habit. The female is also highly dependent, but not on substances: she is dependent on maintaining a relationship with the male that requires her to keep him in a dominant-appearing position within their relationship, when, in actuality, she, like the substance abuser's mother, is the controlling person.
- *Pseudoassertive substance abusers.* Sometimes drugs and alcohol appear to release suppressed aggression. In a clinical context, substance abusers may appear passive and dependent but in moments of conflict, they become belligerent and assertive toward family members. When not under the influence of substances, users maintain a deferential attitude to that same relationship. Such users may be using drugs to express long-standing conflicts within that relationship. Often their mothers, who stifled aggressive behavior, controlled oppositional behavior and prohibited attempts at autonomy, have overprotected them.
- *Dominant-adaptive relationships.* An overly dominant partner and an overly adaptive or dependent partner characterize many substance abuse rela-

tionships. Usually the dependent partner is the substance abuser. Many substance abusers in marital or committed relationships marry or live with nurses or others, such as flight attendants in nurturing roles. The choice of these roles provides good content for counseling sessions.

Family Rules

1. The alcoholic's use of alcohol is the most important thing in the life of the family.
2. Alcohol is not the cause of the family problems.
3. The alcoholic is not responsible for the alcohol dependency; that was caused by someone else or something else.
4. The status quo of the family functioning must be maintained at all costs.
5. Everyone in the house must be an "enabler."
6. The family is self-sufficient and does not need anyone's help.
7. The family may not discuss what is going on in the house, either with one another or with outsiders.
8. The family may not say what they are feeling.

ENABLING BEHAVIORS

Enabling behaviors have the effect of (1) perpetuating the substance abuse and (2) helping users avoid the consequences of their negative behavior.

Substance abusers live in a world characterized by havoc: those in their environment bear the brunt of the drunkenness, verbal and physical abuse, family arguments, and self-destruction. Substance abuse is not a victimless crime. It affects all those around them. Substance abusers are only part of the dynamics of use: those in users' life space also contribute to the problem.

A heroin addict's mother gives her son money to get a fix on his promise that this the last time he will use. Some clinicians might argue that, psychodynamically, the mother unconsciously is maintaining her son in a dependent position so she can continue her motherly instincts well into his adult life. The mother says her motivation is that she doesn't want to see her son get sick (in withdrawal). Whatever the true motivation, the effect of her behavior is to allow the son to continue using heroin and to avoid the negative consequences of using heroin.

A wife calls for her husband, telling his boss that he has the "flu" and is vomiting and unable to come to the phone, when, in fact, he is passed out from his drunk from the night before. Whether she unconsciously wants to keep her husband in a dependent position or whether she is fearful of a loss of income and economic deterioration should her husband be fired, the effect of her behavior remains the same. She is allowing her husband to continue drinking and helping him to avoid the negative consequences of his behavior.

Physicians give substance abusers medications that really do not help and also create yet another form of dependence—all in the guise of trying to "treat" the substance abuse: that is a form of enabling too.

Types of Enablers

Some enablers act in the role of a *messiah*, trying to change their loved ones by helping them secure drugs, paying bills for the substance abusers, and ignoring verbal and physical abuse because "that's the alcohol talking." Enablers' behavior insulates substance abusers from predictable consequences of continued substance abuse and perpetuates the abuse in the process.

Some enablers do not try to change their substance abusers, nor do they rescue them. Instead, they assume the role of *silent sufferer*. They do not confront the behavior—they just act as if nothing is wrong. They do not mention all the problems that are resulting from the use of drugs or alcohol. Instead they adopt the suffering. They ignore the insults, the loss of friends, the problems in paying bills, the unreliability and undependability of the user. In some ways they may have given up, feeling that past attempts to change the situation have been useless. The silent sufferers' enabling behavior helps substance abusers avoid the natural negative consequences of their own behavior.

A third type of enablers *accepts* the behavior. They neither act as messiahs nor as silent sufferers. These enablers appear unaffected by the substance abuse. They may complain but do little to change the situation. They accommodate and adapt. They appear to have reached a happy union and, as a result, the substance abusers get the idea that the abuse is acceptable to their enabler because they get no hassles for doing it.

The detection of enabling behaviors and the type of enabling is easy. When family members discuss the difficulties they are having with a substance abuser, they tell how they have reacted to the problem and the things they have done to try to resolve it. In so doing, they reveal their enabling behaviors.

Enabling behaviors do not cause the addiction and enablers are not responsible for changing substance abusers. Because enablers play a role in the overall process of substance abuse does not imply that they control the behavior of the addict. Their behavior is one small cog in a very big wheel of addiction. However, the stress of engaging in enabling behaviors can have a negative effect on their own psychological adjustment and can result in symptoms and disorders in enablers. Furthermore, cessation of enabling behaviors will change the overall dynamic field within the life-space of substance abusers and have a potentially positive effect on them. Think systemically: changing one role in a system disrupts the system.

Counseling the Enablers

In working with enablers, counselors take an *educational* approach to teaching enablers about their enabling behavior and its consequences. Counselors may attempt and achieve several associated goals with this poulation.

■ First, to help enablers identify situations in which they have enabled the substance abuser through their own behavior. The purpose is to illustrate that enabling behaviors have changed neither the problem nor the substance abuser, but have encouraged both.

■ Second, to help enablers understand that discontinuing enabling behaviors may make matters worse in the short run. If enabling stops the addict from experiencing the natural negative consequences of addiction and if the enabler stops enabling, then the substance abuser will begin to suffer those consequences. Home life could deteriorate.

■ Third, to help enablers understand that the addict may continue to abuse substances after the enabling has stopped. Substance abusers have many enablers to help them maintain their addiction, but discontinuing enabling at home *ends the support* of the addiction in that environment.

■ Fourth, to help enablers understand that ending their enabling will result in beneficial psychological changes in themselves. They will no longer feeling responsible for the addict's behavior and they will stop trying to control the behavior. Their anxiety levels should diminish, and they will move to the next level of counseling.

Once the enabling has stopped, the counselor can help the former enablers focus on the rewards they get from an unsatisfying relationship. Perhaps they need help developing self-assertion, problem-solving skills, negotiating skills, or control of emotions. When enabling stops, the relational dynamic within the dyad is changed and the former enabler has to negotiate a different kind of relationship with the substance abuser to continue in the relationship. Counselors should not advise clients to leave a relationship, but should help them learn the benefits and negative consequences of remaining in it.

CODEPENDENCE

Substance abuse affects everyone in the life space of substance abusers, especially their family. The concept of codependence connotes the idea that living with a substance abuser results in a set of predictable behaviors, feelings, and thoughts that accrue from being involved with someone who is chemically dependent. Codependence implies that family members have something of their own from which to recover (Timmons, 1986).

Origins of Codependence

Codependence originates from one of two sources: First, living in a household characterized by alcoholism or drug dependence in the family often results in codependent behaviors typical of the adult child of the alcoholic, discussed later in the chapter. Second, emotional and frequent involvement with a substance abuser develops codependence. A parent or spouse of a substance abuser represents the most common example. A childhood history of familial substance abuse and marriage to an active user compound the codependent traits. People are forever changed by these experiences. They develop a powerful adaptational restrictive response to cope with the stress.

Codependent Traits

Currently, no list of traits acceptably defines the concept of codependence, but some commonly associated ones frequently are referenced. Issues of *self-esteem, boundaries, relational dependence, responsibility, and control* often are included in any discussion of the codependence concept. Problems associated with codependence can affect individuals long after the original relationship with the substance abuser has gone.

The following list elaborates on the traits that have been most frequently mentioned as characteristics of codependents.

- *Self-esteem.* Codependents' self-esteem is mercurially tied to their substance abuser's success or failure in not using substances. Codependents believe that when the substance abuser fails, they have failed. This often continuous self-blaming leads to lowered self-esteem.
- *Control.* Codependents believe they can or should control the behavior of the substance abuser. They do not fully understand the nature of addiction and believe that willpower should be enough to end the problem. They readily adopt such notions as "just say no!" and berate themselves when the substance abuser uses or relapses.
- *Responsibility.* Codependents feel overly responsible for meeting the needs of others, and do so at the expense of failing to meet their own needs. They may believe they caused or should solve the problem. Because codependents fear being abandoned, they do everything possible to solve the problem. They feel bored, empty, and worthless without a problem to solve or people to help. Gradually they lose the ability to distinguish their needs from the needs of others.
- *Boundaries.* Boundary distortion is common in codependents. Role reversals and role blurring occur, as when the child of an alcoholic assumes parental responsibilities, or a family member acts in a quasi-spousal role.
- *Denial.* Addiction is a disease of denial. Users believe they can quit whenever they want to and therefore deny the seriousness of the problem. Codependents use excessive denial as well, believing that (a) the problem is really too serious, or (b) it is a passing phase that will go away, or (c) they use denial to ward off conflicting emotions, such as anger, shame, embarrassment, and resentment. Usually, they are not aware of denial.
- *Depression.* Emotional constriction inevitably leads to sadness and depression. Codependents experience helplessness and hopelessness repeated failures that they dare not express. Focused on satisfying the needs of others rather than addressing their own needs, codependents believe they can

never do enough and feel guilty for their sensed inadequacy. Depression is anger turned inward—they cannot feel the anger towards the substance abuser, which leads to a downward spiral of negative emotionality.

■ *Emotional constriction.* Codependents squelch negative emotions, fearing that expressing these will result in chaos and a loss of the valued relationship. They become emotionally numb.

■ *External focus.* Codependents center their attention on other people rather than on themselves. They tend to get involved in addictive relationships or with people who themselves are selfish and uncaring. They tend to stay in relationships long after others would have left and when such loyalty is not deserved. This extreme loyalty is a hallmark trait of the codependent. They sacrifice their own identity to please other people.

■ *Impression management.* Codependents are very concerned about what others will think and take extreme actions to gain approval. They feel intense guilt when they say no.

■ *Rigid and compulsive.* Codependents have difficulty in adjusting to change, get stuck in relationships, and are overly serious and have problems having fun. They demonstrate compulsive behaviors, such as smoking, orderliness, a hard-working ethic, and stay extremely busy to occupy their time and block off feelings.

■ *Recurrent physical or sexual abuse.* Such abuse may have happened in childhood and may be manifested in the current relationship. Sometimes the responsible abuser has no memory of the event because it occurred in a blackout. At other times the abuser is conscious and aware. Codependents minimize the extent of violence in their life or explain it away through denial. The codependent relationship prevents them from seeing the situation realistically. The dynamics of abusive relationships come into play, as well. The abused are embarrassed and ashamed to tell other family members what is happening, because that is a betrayal and results in excessive guilt. The communication ethics of addictive families—don't trust—do not permit the abused to trust others about what really is going on in the home.

■ *Stress-related medical problems.* The human body is not totally resilient nor is it immune to living under conditions of chronic stress without breaking down. Codependents tend to get disorders that are associated with chronic stress: headaches, ulcers, gastritis, sexual dysfunction, hypertension, spastic colon, and so forth.

Given these characteristics, it is not unusual that codependents often find themselves abusing substances themselves. Table 7.1 summarizes the salient characteristics of many people who are codependent. It is important to recognize that not all codependents have these traits and, in fact, that most appear to function well.

CASE EXAMPLE
The patient is a 35-year-old, single white female. She was referred for professional help by a friend for problems related to her current boyfriend. They met

TABLE 7.1 Codependent Characteristics

Boundary Disturbance

Compulsive Behaviors

Denial

Depression and Anxiety

Emotional Constriction

External Focus

Impression Management

Low Self-Esteem

Overly Responsible

Physically or Sexually Abused

Rigid

Stress-Related Medical Problems

about three months ago and he moved in with her about one month later. She has been employed full time in a steady job for about 15 years. The manifest problem is that her boyfriend, a cocaine abuser, has relapsed and she has to decide what to do about their relationship.

She describes him as pleasant and helpful, with a good personality: she enjoys being with him. She knew he was a cocaine addict prior to his moving in with her but she was certain it could work out. He has used cocaine for 7 years, has been through rehab twice, attended an aftercare program, sporadically attended NA but relapsed several months ago. She wonders if she might have caused his relapse.

He is unemployed, has a divorce pending, has children in foster care, and always seems to be depressed. His mother supports him financially: his parents are wealthy. The patient has caught him in lies, which he denies, on several occasions. She also found female articles in his room: women's deodorant, earrings, a bra, a bag of women's clothing, and a teddy bear. He claimed they were his ex-wife's possessions, but were not the ex-wife's size. She never has seen him cross-dressing and he does not do anything unusual during sex. He has been spending a lot of time in strip joints. He won't let her inside his car and she wonders if he's been stealing these items to support his cocaine use.

She denied using drugs herself. However, she shows many signs of codependence. She was going to school but quit because she no longer could concentrate or focus on her studies. He stole her credit cards, causing her to cancel them and then get new cards, which she is forced to hide so he won't steal them. She attributes his relapse to her behavior: she is showing increased anxiety as she learns more about him. She finds a degree of elevated self-esteem when she's with him, because of his loving attitude, but also a sense of depression over her situation. She feels she can change his behavior and that she remains with him long after most other women would have dropped him.

At a recent counseling session, she reported that he asked her if she had renter's insurance. She seems at a loss to explain why he wanted to know this.

When the counselor suggested that he was planning to steal more of her things and then get her to claim it as an insurance loss via a burglary, she seemed quite naïve and reluctant to believe he would do this.

Codependent Roles

These problems can be construed as a kind of personality disorder or can be viewed as a relationship deficit. In either case, codependents adopt certain types of roles in their relationship with the substance abuser. The "definitive" roles of codependents have not been officially codified. Some roles that have been more commonly observed in clinical situations follow:

■ *Apathetics.* Some codependents simply stop caring. They are so demoralized that apathy rules their life. Apathy brings a certain amount of peaceful resignation, but it is accompanied by depression.

■ *Approval-seekers.* Codependents measure their self-worth by seeking and receiving approval from others. Because their self-esteem is so low, they need this approval for emotional sustenance.

■ *Caretakers.* Probably the most frequent role seen among codependents, caretakers manage their life by taking care of the addict, putting their needs on the back burner. They become enablers by taking over responsibilities from their substance abusers, lying for them, making sure everything gets done, thereby reducing the chance that something will go wrong. This takes away attention from the partner, who is unable to function well. They often are in occupations characterized by taking care of other people: nurses, mental health therapists, flight attendants, and so forth.

■ *Coconspirator.* Some codependents continually undermine the abuser's efforts to achieve and maintain sobriety. They are complete enablers, use denial to the maximum, and maintain an identity based on chemical dependence in the family system. They try to hide the problem by nondisclosure of feelings, they stop having visitors, and they make excuses for the addict.

■ *Controllers.* These codependents use manipulation to control events and the lives of other people. They learn manipulation in dealing with the out-of-control behavior of the addict and the response generalizes to other relationships in their life.

■ *Martyrs.* Self-destructive traits may result from dealing with the day-to-day behavior of the substance abuser. The codependent martyr takes great pleasure at having to deal with so much aggravation. They act in a long-suffering manner. Martyr codependents believe they have no choice, because changing their behavior could result in abandonment. Not only do they remain in these bad relationships, but they also tend to sabotage good relationships.

■ *Persecutor.* The opposite of martyrs, persecutors express the rage and bitterness that martyrs are unable to express. They blame everyone else for their troubles and for their unhappiness. They express their anger and guilt, externalizing the responsibility for their own experience.

■ *Substance abuse*. Given that codependents have these traits, it is no wonder that many of them abuse substances themselves.

Many of these traits and behaviors are outside the awareness of codependents. They become accustomed to reacting in certain ways in the process of living with an addict.

Counseling the Codependent

Treatment of codependence may be related to age of onset. If onset is in childhood (primary), then counseling or psychotherapy may be the treatment of choice. If onset is in adulthood (secondary), then support groups and bibliotherapy, or the use of relevant reading material on codependence, may be all that is required.

Whatever the intervention, recovery takes time. The urge to control may never go away and its quiescence is an individual matter. The aim, however, is to get the codependent to stop focusing on others and to begin focusing on themselves, to stop fulfilling the needs of others and to fulfill their own needs. They can do this through a variety of treatment modalities, including attending individual or group counseling, support groups and self-help groups, and codependent workshops, and by reading the many books that have been published about this relational disorder.

Counseling may need to operate at three levels. First, counseling at the emotional level, in which squashed feelings and emotions are released in therapy, but not necessarily outside of therapy. Sharing personal experiences is particularly helpful to such emotional catharsis. Another technique is for codependents to write a letter to the addict, reporting all they have felt about the substance abuser's behavior. The letter is never sent, but is processed in counseling.

Second, counseling at the cognitive level can help codependents develop a certain detachment and an understanding that worrying doesn't help. Detachment does not mean becoming indifferent or uncaring, nor does it mean avoiding legitimate responsibilities. It does mean finding a balance in satisfying codependents' needs with the needs of others. The codependent learns to set boundaries and to set limits. They must accept the fact that substance abusers are responsible for their own behavior. One technique is to write a personal "bill of rights" and to develop the attitude that they are entitled to pursue these rights.

Third, counseling at the behavioral level can help the codependent put into practice the new behaviors developed in the emotional and cognitive levels. The patients should expect resistance. They are changing the family system. As noted earlier in this chapter, people will take action to restore the previous level of family homeostasis. The new behaviors should be practiced in moderation: A starting point is for patients to tell others what they want. The best way to effect change is to select one task and practice it in small steps.

To overcome codependence requires dealing with at least three processes (George, 1990). First, recognition, acknowledgement, and discussion of past abuses must occur. Certainly there will be a litany of examples to illustrate the pain. Second, expression of the hurt, pain, anger, and resentment that has been suppressed for so many years must occur. This catharsis is part of the healing process. Most patients will not improve as long as they hold on to their anger. Third, abandoning the "victim" lifestyle must occur. Whether or not they forgive the substance abuser is a matter of individual choice but they must move on and forge a new relationship with or without the substance abuser.

Codependents have to learn to say no, have to stop controlling others, and have to accept that others are responsible for change.

CHILDREN OF ALCOHOLICS

Living in a household in which there is substance abuse results in thoughts and behaviors that affect the lives of all in this house. Surrounded by family turmoil, children of alcoholics (COAs) live in an atmosphere of anxiety, guilt, and denial that can last a lifetime. Although they may appear to be like everyone else, COAs actually have special needs. In fact, COAs are more at risk for becoming alcoholic themselves, often marry alcoholics, and, as adults, have problems related to their childhood exposure to alcoholism in the family. However, the literature has focused primarily on the effects of alcoholism on the subsequent development of the child who is a product of an alcoholic home, but there is every reason to believe that the material discussed below also applies to children living in a household in which there is drug abuse.

Clinicians believe that, while COAs appear to be well adjusted, they adopt defenses that do not work very well as adults. As a result they become dysfunctional (Burk & Sher, 1988). Research has determined that COAs tend to have low self-esteem, are distrustful, live behind a defensive façade, have unfulfilled dependency needs, are emotionally distant, are prone toward behavior and conduct disorders, and often have authority conflicts (Brown, 1986). They tend to keep problems to themselves, try to make others in the house feel better, may assume many responsibilities that should belong to a parent, stop trusting others, and adapt to bad situations (often through self-isolation). Researchers suspect that the reason for the development of these traits has to do with the alcoholic family "rules," which are (1) don't think, (2) don't trust, and (3) don't feel.

COAs are taught not to think about the alcoholism in the house. This is like having an elephant in the living room that everyone must pretend does not exist. COAs are taught not to trust anyone outside the family. They must never reveal that one of the parents is an alcoholic. This finally requires that COAs not express any feelings about the situation, and they develop a defensive barrier to outsiders and live in denial.

Adults COAs may have a variety of negative outcomes as a result of exposure to familial alcoholism. These include reversal of parent and child roles within the family, alternating feelings of love and hate towards parents, infidelity, physical abuse of children, and substance abuse.

Roles

Role theory has been invoked to provide a theoretical explanation of the behavior of COAs. The roles that COAs play help elucidate their coping and ways of adjusting to a dysfunctional family. Claudia Black (1981) and Wegscheider-Cruise (1977; 1990) have been the most influential clinicians in delineating the roles that COAs play. The role structure of COAs can be described in six categories: (1) role, (2) visible characteristics, (3) true feelings, (4) value to the family, (5) functioning with help, and (6) functioning without help. A closer look at the more common roles played by COAs follows:

- *Family hero* presents as a happy, achievement oriented, "good" child. Outwardly they feel special and often overachieve. They act like "little princes," and tend to take over parental responsibilities. They are "little enablers" and act confidently. They seem "all together." Family heros take the focus off the alcoholism and provides a source of pride for other family members. Inwardly, COAs feel like failures, have low self-esteem, often feel inadequate and humiliated, and have much guilt. Without help as adults, they tend to become workaholics, have problems with intimacy, are emotionally blocked, and tend to seek ways to escape from feelings. With help they make good executives, are more willing to accept failure, can open up, and can work at a somewhat slower pace.
- *Scapegoat.* These COAs are angry, defiant, rebellious, and act out. They underachieve and value their peers more than their family. They are sullen, self-destructive, act up to get negative attention, and are "problem children." Their behavior takes the family focus off the alcoholism, and COAs assume the role of the identified patient. Inwardly these children feel like failures, feel hurt, have low self-esteem, have guilt (which is rarely displayed) and feel rage (which is expressed through their behavior). Without help, they experience legal problems, have alcohol and drug abuse problems, and continue to defy authority. With help, they have a sensitivity that provides them with the potential to be good substance abuse counselors, once they abandon their rage.
- *Lost child.* These COAs become withdrawn, isolated, quiet, silent, and independent. This provides the family with relief, since they are not causing any problems. Inwardly they feel powerless and unemotional and they often feel ignored. Without help, they remain emotionally shallow,

withdrawn, passive, and may develop a substance abuse problem and have problems with intimacy. With help, they seem to become assertive and creative.

■ *Mascots.* These COAs clown and seem to be the "life of the party." They exude humor and are a delight to be around. They act as a family pet, seem "special" to the nonalcoholic parent, and may even be babied. This comic relief provides relief from the family stress and also a kind of entertainment, but inwardly, these COAs feel terrified and fragile and that their world will erupt around them. Without help they remain emotionally fragile with poor tolerance for stress, act compulsively, and continue their clownish ways in adult settings. They may develop substance abuse problems. With help they improve their ability to handle stress and show a good sense of humor.

Much of this information has been derived from the clinical study of COAs, but some research corroborates the clinical findings. Stoval and Craig (1990) gave the *Thematic Apperception Test,* a projective test consisting of pictures to which the children would make up stories, to children of alcoholics with a history of physical abuse and a history of sexual abuse, and to children without evidence of physical or sexual abuse but who were being seen by mental health counselors for conduct problems. In analyzing these stories, the researchers found that COAs had the feeling that a parent's constant concern and attention were absent. Rather than perceiving parental figures as bountiful and nurturing, they were viewed as hostile, destructive, and abandoning. Their stories often depicted the need for a child to assume the responsibility of caring for their incompetent parents. At the same time, the COAs felt helpless, frightened, and confused. They perceived life as unsafe and unpredictable. Drugs and alcohol, along with its devastating effects on the family, permeated their stories. Berkowitz & Perkins (1988) found that COAs were more self-depreciating than their peers.

Children of substance abusers have not received the same amount of attention from researchers as COAs. Researchers have concentrated on examining the effects of maternal substance abuse on the neonate. This research demonstrates that babies born to addicted mothers tend to have low birth weight and many are addicted at birth because drugs cross the placental barrier. These infants are irritable, cry frequently, and are difficult to cuddle. The parents seem inadequate to parent them responsibly, resulting in inadequate parent-child bonding. This results in attachment and intimacy problems later in life.

As these infants mature, sleep and feeding problems continue, along with hyperactivity and colic. Growth problems may exist and they are at risk of developmental disorders. In their teens they tend to have behavior and school adjustment problems. These children also tend to score lower on measures of cognitive ability. They show greater anxiety, more insecurity, and shorter attention spans (Deren, 1986; Herjanic, Barredo, Herjanic, & Tomelleri, 1979).

Treatment

The treatment of COAs must include a functional parent and should begin by helping the COA accept that one or both parents are alcoholic. They need to learn to express their needs and emotions by asking for help and by letting others know how they feel. They need to understand that they are not responsible for the behavior of their parents and must not carry blame. Counselors need to help them explore key issues in their life, particularly around issues of self-esteem, relaxing, trusting others, and handling emotions appropriately. Self-help programs also may be part of their treatment. Alateen is a self-help group for young people, 12–19 years old, to address the problem of substance abuse in their homes. School and religious personnel may also provide sympathetic understanding and direction.

ADULT CHILDREN OF ALCOHOLICS

It is argued that adult children of alcoholics have experienced emotional deprivation, role confusion, and social maladjustment. They were reared with a sense of profound frustration and prolonged stress and developed a behavior pattern of a compelling need for approval and a tendency to ignore the feelings of others and to cater to the needs of others. They often have difficulty with intimate relationships, constantly seek approval and affirmation from other people, are either superresponsible or superirresponsible, and extremely loyal despite evidence that this loyalty is undeserved. They overcompensate by seeking positions of high visibility. Cermak (1986) has argued that they show symptoms of post-traumatic stress disorder, including hypervigilance, psychic numbness, and survivor guilt.

Table 7.2 presents traits that have often been ascribed to ACOAs. These traits may not appear in every ACOA, but an individual ACOA may have one or more of them. In fact, research shows that ACOAs are a heterogeneous population with respect to personality traits (D'Andrea, Fisher, & Harrison, 1994). These traits developed under conditions of prolonged stress and frustration characterized by emotional deprivation, role confusion, and possible social maladjustment. Their object relations, or the way they perceive people in certain roles, and their perceived quality of maternal caregiving seems to be different from adult children from normal families (Hardwick, Hansen, & Bairnsfather, 1995). The counselor may use these traits as a rough screening and counseling tool to begin an assessment and intervention with ACOAs.

The majority of ACOAs function adequately and successfully and do not experience any particular problem (NIAAA, 1990). It has not yet been established that the traits and problems discussed in this chapter are specific to a substance abuse household or whether they are also seen in households in which there is a chronic illness.

TABLE 7.2 Characteristics of Adult Children of Alcoholics

If you grew up with substance abuse in your immediate family, then you may have some of the characteristics described below. These traits may be causing problems in your adult life. Not all of these traits appear in all adults who were raised in substance-abusing homes, but you probably have some of them. Check the ones that pertain to you and discuss how they affect you in your present life with your counselor.

CHARACTER TRAIT	YES	NO
Difficulty in determining what is normal behavior		
Tendency to put things off		
Frequent lying and covering up		
Harsh expectations of yourself		
Difficulty in having fun		
Taking yourself very (too) seriously		
Difficulty in dealing with intimacy		
Overreacting to changes beyond your control		
Constant approval-seeking		
Feeling different and isolated		
Being superresponsible or superirresponsible		
Showing extreme loyalty, even though it is undeserved		
Impulsivity		
Fear of personal criticism		
Focusing on the needs of others to the exclusion of your own		
Frightened by angry people or by authority figures		
Fear of abandonment		
Exaggerated need to control others		
Exaggerated need for excitement		
Strong guilt feelings		
Problems in trusting people		
Low self-esteem		
Finding it easier to give in		
"Stuff" your feelings		

Treatment

Approaches to the treatment of ACOA traits and behavior include education (such as bibliotherapy), group support, and validation (such as attending ACOA workshops and seminars), and cognitive reframing (Wanck, 1985). Issues that the counselor must address in therapy with ACOAs include (1) issues of mistrust, (2) trying to control their own environment, as well as that of others, (3) ignoring their personal needs, (4) denying feelings, and (5) problems in limiting their responsibility, especially with regard to the alcoholic parent or partner.

CHAPTER SUMMARY

This chapter concludes the treatment section of this book by focusing on issues of the family of substance abusers. The principles and ideas discussed in Chapters 5 and 6 also can be applied to the families of substance abusers. The chapter includes sections on research on the families of substance abusers, enabling behaviors, origins of codependence, traits, and treatment, and sections on Children of Alcoholics and Adult Children of Alcoholics. Principles of Family Systems Theory preceded and should also permeate these special topics and populations.

SOURCES OF INFORMATION

Alexander, B. K., & Dibb, G. S. (1975). Opiate addicts and their parents. *Family Process, 14,* 499–514.

Alexander, B. K., & Dibb, G. S. (1977). Interpersonal perception in addict families. *Family Process, 16,* 17–28.

Ben-Yehuda, N., & Schindell, B. J. (1981). The addict's family of origin: An empirical survey analysis. *International Journal of the Addictions, 16,* 505–525.

Berkowitz, A., & Perkins, H. W. (1988). Personality characteristics of children of alcoholics. *Journal of Consulting and Clinical Psychology, 56,* 206–209.

Black, C. (1981). *It will never happen to me.* Denver, CO: M. A. C.

Brown, S. (1986). Children with an alcoholic parent. In N. Estes & M. Heinemann (Eds.), *Alcoholism: Development, consequences and interventions* (pp. 207–220). St. Louis: Mosby.

Burk, J. P., & Sher, K. J. (1988). The "forgotten children" revisited: Neglected areas of COA research. *Clinical Psychology Review, 8,* 285–302.

Cermak, T. L. (1986a). Diagnostic criteria for codependency. *Journal of Psychoactive Drugs, 18,* 15–20.

Cermak, T. L. (1986b). *Diagnosing and treating codependence.* Minneapolis, MN: Johnson Institute Books.

Cervantes, O. F., Sorensen, J. L., Wermuth, L., Fernandez, L., & Menicurri, L. (1988). Family ties of drug abusers. *Psychology of Addictive Behaviors, 2,* 34–39.

Children of alcoholics: Are they different? (1990). *Alcohol Alert, 9,* 1–4.

Cleveland, M. (1981). Families and adolescent drug abuse: Structural analysis of children's roles. *Family Process, 20,* 295–304.

Coleman, E., & Colgan, P. (1986). Boundary inadequacy ion drug dependent families. *Journal of Psychoactive Drugs, 18,* 21–30.

D'Andrea, L. M., Fisher, L., & Harrson, T. C. (1994). Cluster analysis of adult children of alcoholics. *International Journal of the Addictions, 29,* 565–582.

Deren, S. (1986). Children of substance abusers: A review of the literature. *Journal of Substance Abuse Treatment, 3,* 77–94.

Ellis, B. G. (Ed.). (1980). *Drug abuse from the family*

perspective: Coping is a family affair. Rockville, MD: National Institute on Drug Abuse.

Ganger, R., & Shugart, G. (1966, December). The heroin addict's pseudoassertive behavior and family dynamics. *Social Casework*, 643–649.

George, R. L. (1990). *Counseling the chemically dependent: Theory and practice.* Boston, MA: Allyn & Bacon.

Gierymski, T., & Williams, T. (1986). Codependency. *Journal of Psychoactive Drugs, 18*, 7–13.

Harbin, H. T., & Maziar, H. M. (1975). The families of drug abusers: A literature review. *Family Process, 14*, 411–431.

Hardwick, C. J., Hansen, N. D., & Barirnsfather, L. (1995). Are adult children of alcoholics unique? A study of object relations and reality testing. *International Journal of the Addictions, 30*, 525–540.

Herjanic, B. M., Barredo, V. H., Herjanic, M., & Tomelleri, C. J. (1979). Children of heroin addicts. *International Journal of the Addictions, 14*, 919–931.

Janzen, C. (1977). Families in the treatment of alcoholism. *Journal of Studies on Alcohol, 28*, 114–130.

Kaufman, E. (1980). Myth and reality in the family patterns and treatment of substance abusers. *American Journal of Drug and Alcohol Abuse, 7*, 257–279.

Kaufman, E. (1981). Family structures of narcotic addicts. *International Journal of the Addictions, 16*, 273–282.

Kosten, T. R., Jalali, B., Hogan, I., & Kleber, H. (1983). Family denial as a prognostic factors in opiate addict treatment outcome. *Journal of Nervous and Mental Disease, 171*, 611–616.

Kosten, T. R., Jalali, B., & Kleber, H. (1983). Complementary marital roles of male heroin addicts: Evolution and intervention tactics. *American Journal of Drug and Alcohol Abuse, 9*, 155–169.

Kosten, T. R., Novak, P., & Kleber, H. D. (1984). Perceived marital and family environment of opiate addicts. *American Journal of Drug and Alcohol Abuse, 10*, 4912–501.

Madanes, C., Lic, J. D., & Harbin, H. (1980). Family ties of heroin addicts. *Archives of General Psychiatry, 37*, 889–894.

Maddux, J. F., & Desmond, D. P. (1984). Heroin addicts and their non-addicted brothers. *American Journal of Drug and Alcohol Abuse, 10*, 237–248.

Mirin, S. M., Weiss, R. D., Griffin, M. L., & Michael, J. L. (1991). Psychopathology in drug abusers and their families. *Comprehensive Psychiatry, 32*, 36–51.

NIAAA. (1990, July). Children of alcoholics: Are they different? *Alcohol Alert*, No. 9. Rockville, MD: National Institute on Alcohol Abuse and Alcoholism.

Ripple, C. H., & Luthar, S. S. (1996). Familial factors in illicit drug abuse: An Interdisciplinary perspective. *American Journal of Drug and Alcohol Abuse, 22*, 147–172.

Schwartzman, J., Bokos, P. J., & Lipscomb, S. (1982). Westend, a methadone clinic: Structural aspects of addiction. *International Journal of the Addictions, 17*, 271–281.

Stoval, G., & Craig, R. J. ((1990). Mental representations of physically and sexually abused latency-aged females. *Child Abuse and Neglect, 14*, 233–242.

Stanton, M. D. (1977). The addict as savior: Heroin, death, and the family. *Family Process, 16*, 191–197.

Stanton, M. D. (1979). Family treatment approaches to drug abuse problems: A review. *Family Process, 18*, 251–280.

Stanton, M. D. (1997a). The role of the family and significant others in the engagement and retention of drug-dependent individuals. In L. S. Onken, J. D. Blaine, & J. J. Boren (Eds.), *Beyond the therapeutic alliance: Keeping the drug-dependent individual in treatment* (NIDA Research Monograph No. 165, pp. 157–180). Rockville, MD: National Institute on Drug Abuse.

Stanton, M. D., & Shadish, W. R. (1997). Outcome, attrition, and family-couples treatment for drug abuse: A meta-analysis and review of the controlled, comparative studies. *Psychological Bulletin, 122*, 170–191.

Stanton, M. D., & Todd, T. C. (1981a). Engaging "resistant" families in treatment. *Family Process, 20*, 261–291.

Stanton, M. D., & Todd, T. C. (1981b). Engaging "resistant" families in treatment. *Family Process, 20*, 261–293.

Stanton, M. D., Todd, T. C., Heard, D. B., Kirschner, S., Kleiman, J. I., Mowatt, D. T., Riley, P., Scott, S. M., & Van Deuse, J. M. (1978). Heroin addiction as a family phenomenon: A new conceptual model. *International Journal of the Addictions, 5*, 125–150.

Taylor, S. D., Wilbur, M., & Osnos, R. (1966). The

wives of drug addicts. *American Journal of Psychiatry, 123*, 585–591.

Van Deusen, J. M., Scott, S. M., & Stanton, M. D. (1980). *International Journal of the Addictions, 15,* 1069–1089.

Wanck, B. (1985). *Treatment of adult children of alcoholics*. Belle Mead, NJ: Carrier Foundation.

Wegscheider, D. (1977). *Families in crisis*. Crystal, MN: Nurturing Networks.

Wegscheider-Cruse, D., & Cruse, J. R. (1990). *Understanding codependency*. Deerfield Beach, FL: Health Communications.

Wellish, D. K., Gay, G. R., & McEntee, R. (1970). The easy rider syndrome: A pattern of hetero- and homosexual relationships in a heroin addict population. *Family Process, 9,* 425–430.

Wermuth, L., & Scheidt, S. (1986). Enlisting family support in drug treatment. *Family Process, 25,* 25–33.

CHAPTER EIGHT

WORKING WITH SPECIAL POPULATIONS

The assessment and intervention techniques discussed in the previous chapters are not fundamentally different when counseling special substance abusing populations, each special population presents with issues unique to their minority status. These matters must be considered and evaluated in assessing and treating members of these populations. There is considerable variation in patterns of alcohol and drug use and abuse among distinctive racial and ethnic subgroups. These groups are exposed to special influences and have to contend with issues in their life over and above those of the dominant culture. Groups that have been labeled as "special populations" in the area of substance abuse are adolescents, women, minorities—especially African Americans, Latinos, and Native Americans, geriatric, gay or lesbian patients, military personnel, and patients with dual diagnoses. This chapter presents the unique issues that have appeared in the professional literature for each of these groups.

ADOLESCENTS

Chapter 1 discussed how teen-age drug and alcohol use continues at unacceptably high levels. School-based prevalence surveys are likely to be an underrepresentation of the problem, because of teenagers' skepticism about the confidential nature of the survey. A substantial percentage of teens will go on to abuse drugs of sufficient intensity to require treatment. They will be brought to counselors' attention by concerned parents, school authorities, or representatives of the legal system and almost never will be self-motivated for help. This results in a real challenge for the substance abuse counselor.

One rule of treatment is that it is almost always necessary to involve parents in the treatment of adolescents. Parents of these teens most probably had used drugs themselves during youth and may take a tolerant view of their children's drug use, believing that they'll "grow out of it." Even when they see their children getting into more and more difficulty, they may not take this drug use as seriously as it should be taken. Parents will need education on the seriousness of the drug abuse problem in their child.

Stages of Adolescent Drug Use

The data presented in Chapter 1 make it clear that many adolescents will experiment with illicit drugs and alcohol. Such use should in and of itself not be considered deviant. It should be construed as part of a developmental experience characterized by rebellion, testing the limits of parental and institutional authority, and trying new behaviors. Thus Stage 1 of adolescent drug use is *experimental use*.

Stage 2 might be called *social use,* in which youths use alcohol and drugs in social situations and have as their motivation to be an accepted part of a valued group. Although this may be thought of as part of their life situation, some unknown percent of users will advance to *continued use* (Stage 3). In this stage, youths are preoccupied with using substances, not only in social situations but for their effects independent of circumstances. The focus is on getting high and looking forward to the next high. Periods of abstinence may wax and wane, giving the illusion that young users are not addicted but alcohol and drugs are now rarely absent from their life.

Stage 4 is *dependence.* This stage is characterized by regular drug-seeking and drug-using behavior. Drug use is now out of control and negative and deleterious effects of this problem use now begin to appear. They feel desperate when they do not use daily. They have major problems with their parents and local authorities.

Problems with Diagnostic Criteria

No validated criteria exist that are specific to adolescent substance abuse and the current official diagnostic classifications do not include a diagnosis specific to adolescent drug or alcohol abuse. *The disorder of substance abuse may manifest itself differently in adolescents than in adults.* Adolescents, as a rule, do not develop the more severe and progressive symptoms of alcoholism, which takes years to develop. Most adolescents are insulated from adult roles and responsibilities, such as the need to maintain a job and care for a family. These areas of life are particularly vulnerable to the effects of drugs and alcohol in adults but may not apply to the adolescent. They get drunk faster than adults after consuming amounts of alcohol that may seem small by adult standards, but which can be quite disruptive and result in pronounced negative consequences in the adolescent. Teenagers are more sensitive to the effects of alcohol than adults and are affected differently by a given amount of the drug. They also have less practice and less ability in effectively managing themselves when using. The psychology of adolescent drinking has changed: At one point in our cultural history, teens got drunk inadvertently, because they had not yet learned when to quit. Today, teens set out to get drunk intentionally. Adolescence is a period of acquiring and developing physical social and cognitive skills, goals, and personal values, and these are vulnerable to and adversely affected by drugs and alcohol.

Although many of the physical signs of alcoholism and drug abuse may not be manifested in adolescents, signs of physical withdrawal and brain malfunctioning are seen in this population. These facts add up to the following conclusion: *Adolescent substance abuse should be evaluated in terms of the negative effects it has on important areas of function specific to this age period.* This includes social relationships, conflicts with friends, impaired performance at school, difficulties with teachers, traffic problems, trouble with law enforcement personnel, and relationship with parents. Another factor to evaluate is whether the problem behavior is a sign of substance abuse or part of adolescent development. Such behaviors as adolescent rebellion, irresponsibility, poor initiative, and lack of goals could be consequent to substance use but they may also be developmental issues unrelated to substance use. Adolescence is a period in which teenagers are adapting to rapid physical and hormonal changes, beginning to separate from their parents and consolidate a new identity, continuing to develop social and cognitive skills, postponing immediate gratification, and preparing for educational and vocational goals that will occupy their adult life. Part of this exploration and adaptation could be to experiment with alcohol and drugs.

Adolescents' peers may have more influence on their behavior than their parents, and adolescent substance abusers are likely to socialize with peers who are also abusers. Peers approve more of alcohol use, parents are likely to be less disapproving of alcohol use than of drug use, and adolescent substance abusers are likely to come from families that are either dysfunctional or that have little sway in managing adolescent behavior. Research shows that adolescents who abuse drugs show interpersonal alienation, poor impulse control, and much emotional distress. This maladjustment predated initial drug use. These problems have been shown to be related to the quality of parenting in the earliest childhood years (Shedler & Block, 1990). Thus early psychological factors are central to understanding current drug use.

Finally, *adolescent alcoholism and drug abuse will result in arrested psychological and emotional development.* When youths go into recovery, they resume that delayed period of development and begin to deal with the issues appropriate to that stage of life. This occurs no matter what age the person eventually reaches recovery.

Parents of teenage substance abusers should be interviewed and evaluated, although they are unlikely to be able to provide much information on the extent of drinking and drugging. They can give testimony to such behaviors as tantrums, mood swings, violence, and oppositional behaviors. They can provide data on prior treatment history, problems at home and in school, and perhaps information on their own substance abuse history. There is little direct relationship between youth problem drinking and the subsequent development of alcoholism. Alcohol consumption rates decline with age and many middle-aged alcoholics report abstinence or moderate drinking during their teen years. For many teens, problem drinking is self-limiting (Lex, 1985).

Interviewing Adolescents

Adolescents are particularly difficult to interview because they are reluctant patients. They are strongly in denial and minimize the problem. They consider talking to counselors and mental health professionals to be stigmatic. Some techniques for interviewing youths follow:

1. *Establish rapport.* This may not be easy. Counselors may start by asking them the reason they think they are seeing you today. A particularly useful strategy is to try to help the patient to see that their parents are the problem by asking them what their parents think is wrong.
2. *Emphasize confidentiality.* Adolescents are especially concerned with issues of privacy. Stressing the confidential nature of the counseling relationship could help build rapport. Counselors must tell the young patients that, from time to time, they will report general progress to the parents. Counselors should encourage these patients to tell the parents any significant information themselves.
3. *Structure the interview.* Systematically obtain responses about significant content areas. Seek information about the parents before beginning to explore significant areas in the patient. Procedures for systematically assessing adolescent substance abusers are available (Harrison & Hoffman, 1985; Kaminer, Bukstein, & Tarter, 1991; Tarter, 1990) and are worth considering. A structured assessment tool that is completed by parents can save counselors and patients some time.
4. *Focus on the family system.* Chapter 4 details the domains to be assessed and should be referenced for the specific areas needing comprehensive assessment. In assessing adolescents, focus on parents and family as well as the patient could deflect the emotional aspects of the questions and the treatment. Young patients may conceal a significant amount of clinical issues and material from the counselor and the parents and may not tell the truth.
5. *Keep the assessment process as brief as possible.* Counselors should seek information on use patterns, and frequency, context, and severity of use, as well as information on family, legal, educational, and social problems and functioning.
6. *Get information from other sources, including parents and school officials.* Parents may minimize or may not even be aware of the extent of their child's difficulties associated with problem substance use, so counselors should obtain information from school officials.

Problems in Treating Adolescents

Lack of motivation and commitment to change. Adolescents often present in massive denial. They see nothing wrong with their behavior, feel they can "handle it," have a peer network that uses drugs, and see no reason to change their behavior.

Counselors and staff are likely to be viewed as authority figures. They are rebelling from parental authority and they see counselors as authority figures who try to put unreasonable limits on them. They will have problems choosing between alcohol and drugs and a new way of life; between their peer group and the need to develop new friends. This attitude is a barrier and an impediment to recovery.

Reluctance to accept the idea that they can never use again typifies adolescent users. When counselors tell them they are alcoholics or drug addicts and that they have to remain sober and abstinent for the rest of their lives, most adolescents will not accept or believe them. Promoting the idea of maintaining abstinence until they reach certain life milestones, such as high school or college graduation and looking then at the question of moderate use is one approach. By then, they will have developed greater maturity and will be in a position to make better choices about total abstinence.

TREATMENT

1. *Use an educational model.* Explain facts and encourage patients to respond with their own attitudes toward these ideas to help assess and identify resistance.
2. *Set clear limits.* Don't be fooled and don't allow them to get away with things that they shouldn't. Adolescents ask for help through their behavior, so counselors may expect anger and not expressions of gratitude from the patient.
3. *Include the parents in the treatment plan.* Confront their enabling behaviors. Include sessions with patient alone, parents alone, and parents in session with the patient. Parents must be taught effective child-rearing techniques as part of the treatment.
4. *Set clear and reachable goals* on which the patient and parents can agree.
5. *Promote contact with nonusing peers.*
6. *Promote a stronger bond* between parents and patient by encouraging activities in which both can participate.
7. *Use client treatment and behavioral contracts* that spell out parental expectations of specific behavior changes and the rewards to be earned when the goals have been attained.
8. *Include conflict resolution* as a specific part of the treatment (Winters, 1999b). Adolescents will require this skill to negotiate with parents and to deal with the peer group.
9. *Address adolescent risk-taking behaviors,* especially in the area of sexuality.

Three types of age-specific treatment options have been proposed for youthful substance abusers: (1) special programs for adolescents, (2) special therapies for adolescents within a traditional substance abuse treatment program, and (3) AA or NA groups that are primarily for adolescents and young adults (Bennett, 1986). Counselors will need to determine which of these is best suited for a particular client.

Monitoring Use

Adolescents treated in the context of a program will probably be monitored occasionally for alcohol and drug use with breathalyzers or urine assays. Some programs do not do such testing and most practitioners in private practice rarely engage in such testing. Usually they relay on parental information and continuing collaboration with the school to assess progress in treatment. Practitioners who do not do such testing cannot be absolutely certain that the patient is clean and sober.

Legal Issues

Material discussed in assessment and treatment sessions with substance abuse counselors may be protected from discovery in legal proceedings by laws and codes of ethics. These laws generally do not allow release of any information without written consent. Parents of minors may provide written consent, although adolescents may authorize the release, depending on age and state law. Counselors should be acquainted with the federal law on confidentiality and with such laws in the state in which they practice. Counselors should discuss confidentiality with patient and parent during the initial phases of treatment. In general, unless required by law, counselors should not release any information without written consent from patient or parent.

WOMEN

Much knowledge about substance abuse comes from studies of males. Researchers have been reluctant to study women alcoholics because hormonal influences may skew research results and because of potential teratological effects of medication trials, should the women be in the early stages of pregnancy and not know it. Researchers also debate whether the criteria for a diagnosis of alcoholism should be the same for women as for men, because the effects of alcohol and the symptoms of alcoholism are not precisely the same for women as for men (Gomberg, 1986).

The setting in which the surveys are obtained influences epidemiological data on the extent of female drinking. The data will be different between community survey data and clinical reports, because women tend to use health care facilities more than men do, and there is a general reluctance to diagnose them as alcoholic. Studies in general suggest that fewer women drink than do men. Women who drink socially drink less than male social drinkers. Female heavy drinkers consume as much as male heavy drinkers but experience more health consequences associated with drinking. Drinking problems are lowest among widows and most frequent among never married, separated, or divorced women (NIAAA, 1990).

Compared to male alcoholics, female alcoholics

tend to become alcoholic at a later age;

tend to have a more serious form of alcoholism that progresses more rapidly ("telescoped drinking"), despite late onset;

become intoxicated after drinking less alcohol;

are more likely to report divorce, death, abandonment, health problems or other disruption in their social ties, that precipitates their problem drinking;

have more disruptive early life experiences, such as more deprivation and childhood emotional traumas;

are more likely to have a depressive disorder prior to the onset of drinking;

get involved with heavy drinking through the influence of males;

more often drink alone and at home;

drink large amounts of alcohol less frequently, report less binge drinking and early morning drinking, and have shorter bouts of drinking;

enter treatment programs for alcoholism earlier after the onset of problem drinking, but may go to a general physician or to a psychiatrist instead of to an alcohol treatment program;

experience more stigma (Lex, 1985).

The 1996 National Household Survey reported that

about 30% had used an illicit drug at least once in their life;

4.7 million had used an illicit drug at least once in the month preceding the survey;

26 million had smoked cigarettes and 48 million had drunk alcohol;

30.5 million had used marijuana at least once;

more than 600,000 had used cocaine in the preceding month;

56,000 used needles to inject drugs on a regular basis.

The National Drug Control Strategy Annual Report (2000) found that

82% of high school women reported using marijuana at least once in their life;

47% of high school women said they used marijuana currently;

33% reported lifetime use of cocaine;

13% used cocaine currently;

60% said they smoke cigarettes;

43% reported periodic heavy drinking.

Compared to male drug abusers, female drug abusers

are initiated into drug abuse by males;

have lower rates of drug abuse;

are more likely to abuse prescription drugs;

may engage in sex for drugs;

report significant histories of physical and sexual abuse;

report parental history of alcohol and drug abuse;

may become more quickly addicted than men.

Etiology

The development of alcoholism is a complex process that is even more complex among women than among men. Many sources of influence have been speculated. Excessive needs for dependency, attainment of power, conflicts in gender identity or role conflicts, family background factors, and social status have been suggested as possible reasons for female alcoholism. They remain untested. As with male alcoholics, genetic, physiological, hormonal, environmental, psychological, and social factors also have been proposed as possible influences in the development of female substance abuse. Like male substance abusers, female substance abusers are a heterogeneous group, and different etiologies may result in the same diagnosis.

Treatment

Many women addicts are reluctant to enter treatment because of multiple fears. They fear reprisals from spouses or boyfriends, that they will not be able to properly care for their children, or that authorities will take their children away from them. Like men, women addicts have particular difficulty with abstinence if their partner also is using drugs. Treatment of women substance abusers needs to take into account their occupational and economic position as well as their family and child care responsibilities. Their needs may be as basic as food, clothing, shelter, transportation, child care, family planning services, and other social services—parenting training, arranging for medical care, legal assistance, and job counseling. Programs may not be able to provide these services, so substance abuse counselors need a panoply of referral agencies for adjunctive treatment. Many women feel more comfortable when treated individually or in a women's group and several AA groups have been developed for women only.

MINORITIES

Minority substance abuse may differ in pattern or frequency from mainstream abuse in the majority culture. Even if it does not, the motivation and reasons for use may differ in minority populations. The next paragraphs treat substance abuse among African Americans, Hispanic, and gay and lesbian populations.

African Americans

Although Black people have higher rates of abstinence from alcohol than White people, those who drink have higher rates of medical problems associated with drinking. The incidence of fetal alcohol syndrome among African Americans is about seven times higher. Access to treatment has sometimes been a problem for minorities, the rate of treatment success among African Americans is comparable to that of Caucasian Americans (NIAAA, 1994). Rates of abstinence may be increasing among them, while rates of heavy drinking may have stabilized (Caebano & Clark, 1998). However, compared to White drinkers, Black drinkers

> begin drinking at an earlier age;
>
> drink more often on weekends;
>
> are involved in manual labors and more often go to bars after work;
>
> tend to be younger alcoholics;
>
> experience more severe substance abuse;
>
> are at higher risk for alcohol-related morbidity and mortality;
>
> have more severe psychiatric consequences associated with substance abuse;
>
> often lack or are ignorant of factual information about alcoholism;
>
> are less likely to seek treatment (Lex, 1985).

Various factors have been proposed to explain differential patterns and consequences of substance abuse among African Americans. These include the effects of poverty, prejudice and discrimination, inferior education, segregation, unemployment, and unstable family life often characterized by an absent father. However, matching the ethnic background to client ethnicity appears to have no relationship to treatment outcome on a number of variables (Maddux & Desmond, 1996).

Hispanics

The Hispanic American minority populations (e.g., Mexican American, Puerto Rican American, Cuban American, Central American, and other Spanish-speaking groups) often are grouped for presentation and discussion, but there may be large differences between these subgroups, but the somewhat sweeping conclusions from the literature in this area usually do not make such distinctions. In fact, most information about substance abuse among Hispanics comes from studies with Mexican Americans.

In general, Hispanic males tend to use heroin, PCP, inhalants, marijuana, and cocaine as their primary drugs of abuse. Drug abuse seems to be more serious for Mexican Americans than for their counterparts living in Mexico. Puerto Rican Americans have the highest prevalence of using illegal drugs except for inhalants, which are more often used by Mexican Americans. Although Hispanic drug use varies according to type and level of drug used, Hispanic subgroup, age, gender, and degree of acculturation, Mexican American, and Puerto Rican American males are the most at risk group. They have high rates of gang involvement, criminal activity, and school dropout. Hispanics utilize drug treatment programs to a lesser degree than other minorities, perhaps because they perceive these programs to be culturally insensitive and more oriented to meeting the need of White and Black people. This results in a high dropout rate among this group (De La Rosa, Khalsa, & Rouse, 1990). Alcohol and drug use and misuse among Latinas is infrequent and abstinence rates are high (Chavez & Mora, 1994).

Among the reasons cited to explain Hispanic drug abuse are poverty, limited opportunities, discrimination, acculturation stress, and the lessening of family ties, especially with the extended family systems (De La Rosa, Khalsa, & Rouse, 1990), as well as the machismo ethic, which requires manly behavior characterized by autonomy, strength, dignity, honor, an absence of shame, and a demand for respect (Lex, 1985). Reasons cited for explaining the low prevalence of substance abuse among Latinas include cultural mores that prescribe strong social disapproval of substance abuse by women: a culturally influenced protective factor. Also, the almost angelic role imposed on females by the traditional Latin culture is a further protective factor.

Mexican Americans represent the largest ethnic minority group in the United States after African Americans. Reviews of their substance abuse warrant the following conclusions: Among Mexican Americans, the onset of daily opiate use occurs at an early age, but voluntary admission to a substance abuse treatment program occurs at a later age compared to other ethnic groups. They tend to be arrested more frequently and spend longer time in correctional institutions. Legal infractions, especially motor vehicle accidents and drunkenness, are the major adverse factors associated with Hispanic substance abuse (Lex, 1985). They tend to prefer individual and group counseling and do not respond well to therapeutic community interventions. They have higher dropout rates from all types of treatment (De La Rosa, Khalsa, & Rouse, 1990; Desmond & Maddux, 1984).

Gays and Lesbians

Historically it had been taught and assumed that gays and lesbians were at disproportionately high risk for substance abuse, particularly alcohol. Recent research sheds new light on substance abuse among these groups. Both gays and lesbians are less likely to abstain from alcohol than are heterosexuals. Recent data demonstrate that gay men are at no higher risk for heavy drinking or for developing problem drinking than are heterosexual men. Among lesbian women, heavy drinking does occur at slightly higher rates than among heterosexual women, but not at the high rates reported in earlier studies (Bux, 1996).

One reason for the historical inaccuracy of epidemiological data was methodological problems, particularly with sampling errors. Rather than select representative samples, researchers tended to study gays and lesbians in urban areas, which have higher rates of alcohol consumption and use of other drugs, and also studied bar patrons, where the likelihood of problem drinking is increased. When these sampling errors were corrected, the previous conclusions remain warranted.

The remaining issues are (1) what are the specific risk factors with this population, (2) what theoretical factors account for the development of a substance abuse problem, and (3) are the rates high enough to suggest specialized treatment for this population?

Risk Factors.   Three factors seem to exist that heighten the risk of substance abuse in the gay and lesbian population that may not apply to others: (1) The degree of stress and tension that the culture imposes on someone who is gay or lesbian, (2) the culture's attitude toward substance use by gays and lesbians, and (3) the degree to which the culture offers an alternative means of satisfaction and coping with anxiety.

Culturally the gay community seems to support heavy drinking. Gay bars are one of the few places that gays and lesbians can mingle and socialize free from the restraints and taboos of the larger culture. This openness provides a seductive quality to the experience. Furthermore, society offers only limited alternative opportunities for stress reduction to an openly gay or lesbian user. The growth of coffeehouses, musical events, and bookstores that allow socializing without the use of alcohol and illicit substances may change this. However, although the stigma associated with being gay or lesbian is declining in the larger society, much discrimination toward them exists and they continue to face isolation and alienation.

Gays and lesbians face a great deal of stress and tension associated with sexual identity, over and above the level of stress emanating from other sources. Being a member of a stigmatized group results in negative affectivity (i.e., depression, lowered self-esteem, alienation, resentment, etc.), continued fears of exposure for those who are not "out," and fears of contracting AIDS. Add to this other forms of social discrimination and victimization, such as hate crimes, in which people are singled out for abuse because of their sexual identity, and it is easy to understand why alcohol provides a means of coping for this population.

Theories of Substance Abuse among Gays and Lesbians.   Bux (1996) has detailed the various theoretical notions to explain the relationship between substance abuse and sexual orientation. These theories have relied on intrapsychic but mostly on sociocultural factors as explanatory variables.

- *Internalized Homophobia.* This theory argues that gays grow up in a culture that denigrates homosexuals: this idea is introjected during childhood and adolescent development to the point that they develop self-hatred. Gays and lesbians turn to alcohol and drugs to cope with the psychological and social pressures inherent in the developmental task of consolidating a homosexual sexual identity.
- *Gender Role Conflict.* According to this theory, gays and lesbians use substances to relieve doubts about their adequacy as men and women, or to facilitate expression of femininity or masculinity. From this perspective, gays and lesbians have some discomfort with or actually reject their traditional gender role.
- *Social Stress.* This social theory argues that discrimination and prejudice from a stigmatizing society result in stress, tension, and anxiety that are so severe that affected individuals resort to alcohol and drug use to reduce the discomfort.
- *Aspects of the Subculture.* Certain aspects of the gay and lesbian subculture might put them at greater risk for developing a substance abuse problem compared to heterosexuals. For example, much of gay and lesbian lifestyles is oriented toward frequent attendance at gay bars. The community seems focused on youth and attractiveness, and this idealized self-image of youth and beauty will eventually give way to reality. To cope with this stress, they turn to alcohol and drugs. Various writers have argued that a certain level of hedonism is associated with the gay and lesbian lifestyle. Drugs and alcohol might fit in with this pursuit.
- *Differences in Social Roles.* While the main culture proceeds through normal social roles of marriage and parenthood, gays and lesbians rarely have opportunity to participate in these roles. Substance abusers in the general population may mature out of their youthful abuse as they develop into the expected social roles of adulthood, but gays and lesbians are less likely to experience such factors. This could account for continued substance use and abuse throughout the lifecycle in this population.

Treatment.   Sensitivity to these issues would seem to be important to counselors providing substance abuse services to gays or lesbians. However, discrimination by staff and patients is prevalent in nongay treatment programs. Clients fear harassment from staff and patients about their sexual orientation. Some staff may believe that discussion of sexual identity is not a part of patient care and avoid the topic. Treatment staff may have as many homophobic attitudes as the general population. Gay addicts may be forced out from the larger patient community by other patients who do not accept this sexual orientation. Patients handle this by dropping out of treatment.

It appears that specialized treatment programs for gay and lesbian substance abusers are warranted until mainstream substance abuse programs and the larger society begin to appreciate and understand the special problems associated with the gay identity. The treatment atmosphere must include an accepting and receptive tone for discussion and for treating issues specific to gay and lesbian substance abusers.

Finally, family therapy rarely is offered to gay and lesbian substance abusers because most have negligible relationships with their family of origin. They are most often offered individual or group counseling. The treatment community must develop a larger perspective on "family therapy" that would include the people in the psychological and emotional life space of the client. The tenets and techniques of marital therapy could be applied to the gay or lesbian couple. Partner therapy easily could be included in the overall treatment regimen for this population.

Geriatric Populations

More information is available about geriatric alcoholism than about drug abuse in the elderly, so much of this section will focus on alcoholism. In general, drug use and alcohol consumption patterns decline with age. Winick (1962) provided evidence that many drug addicts mature out of their addiction. No such phenomenon occurs with alcoholics: many continue to drink at rates and patterns similar to those seen in earlier age ranges. A precipitous drop off in alcohol use rates seems to appear after the mid-70s. New cases also emerge, but for reasons that differ from early-onset alcoholics. Generation differences also affect prevalence rates. This cohort was much more at risk for alcoholism than for drug addiction and may have had a different sense of morality that would not condone drug use: Combined with cognitive impairments, increasing dysphoria produced by continued drug use, and reduced income, this may limit the extent of drug use in old age.

Epidemiological studies report that about 10% of the geriatric population meet DSM criteria for alcohol dependence and 2%–4% (ranging up to 10% in community samples in some studies) meet the criteria for alcohol abuse or dependence. Another 10% are heavy drinkers. Different definition of alcoholism in various studies affect reported prevalence rates. Older men outnumber women by five to one in problem drinking. Medical manifestations associated with problematic drinking among older people include increased incidence of hypertension, cardiomyopathy, alcohol dementia, malnutrition, impairment of the immune system, and increased incidence of cancer, especially esophageal cancer, and alcohol-related fractures. Additionally, older people develop problems associated with the interaction between alcohol and other drugs, including prescribed medication. These problems include altered blood levels of medications, liver toxicity, oversedation and delirium, and gastrointestinal inflammation and bleeding. They are also likely to misuse medications by forgetting to take them or by taking too much, or by otherwise not taking them as prescribed

(Gurnack, 1995; Hoffman & Heinemann, 1986). It is difficult to differentiate the effects of alcohol on the body from those attributed to the normal aging process. Aging does modify the body's responsiveness to alcohol and other drugs, including the rate of absorption, distribution, and excretion.

Older alcoholics fall into three groups. First, those who drink before the age of 40 and continue to do so into old age are likely to have medical problems associated with chronic drinking. Second, those who have late-onset alcoholism, with no prior history of alcohol problems, may drink because of social stresses associated with their current life stresses. Third, intermittent alcoholics who drink episodically and continue this pattern into later life may drink because of life stresses.

Manifestations of substance abuse among the older population are less related to quantity and frequency of use than among younger age cohorts. Older people are more sensitive to the effects of alcohol and therefore are likely to have high rates of physical and psychological disorders associated with problem drinking. Alcohol is distributed to a smaller volume of blood in older people and results in higher blood alcohol concentration, so reports based on such criteria as the amount and frequency of alcohol consumption in a given period could be misleading and result in faulty conclusions. The frequency of general medical problems among older people makes them likely to be on prescribed medication: up to 50% of all drugs interact with alcohol.

Alcoholism often is misdiagnosed or overlooked among older people. Identifying alcoholism in older people poses special problems, because many of the criteria that define the disorder are not applicable to them. For example, DUIs, public intoxication, absences from work, and so forth are infrequent in this population. Older people generally do not fit the alcoholic stereotype and are not brought to the attention of society's gatekeepers. Many fail to attract any attention, resulting in reporting of lower than actual prevalence rates. Denial is as strong among older alcoholics as in younger ones. Family members, ashamed to admit the problem, are in denial. Denial by the older alcoholic may be associated with memory loss, complicating the assessment picture. Interviewing collaterals could be useful in evaluation. Effects of alcohol, not merely the amount consumed, should be the prime consideration in evaluating older people for alcoholism.

The predisposing factors for the development of substance abuse in a geriatric population are the same as for patients of other ages.

Treatment.   Older alcoholics respond as well to treatment as any other population of alcoholics. Counselors must address the specific issues that are affecting the person's life, as with people of any other age. Special concerns of older people include loneliness, declining health, loss of friends, changing social roles, loss of independence, hearing decrements, reduced physical movements, and increased social restrictions. Together, these concerns could develop into anomie and lack of meaning in their lives. General treatment strategies include attention to medical, social, and psychological aspects of their lives.

Treatment of older alcoholics addresses changing their daily habits, including family in the treatment plan, and improving life conditions to replace alcohol with more positive forms of coping. An encouraging aspect of treating older people is that they tend to be more compliant than younger alcoholics. Grouping older patients homogeneously could be beneficial. Treatment should be supportive and nonconfrontational and counselors need to maintain linkages with a variety of social agencies. Nutritional assessments and social casework may be appropriate.

Native Americans

Drinking patterns of Native Americans may vary according to tribes. Extremely high rates of drinking and alcoholism are associated with male Native Americans, among whom cirrhosis is a leading cause of death. This prevalence may be caused by prejudice, discrimination, poverty, lack of upward mobility, loss of traditional culture, substandard housing, social isolation, poor diet and health, low income, poor adjustment to urban life, and a higher tolerance for overall deviance (Lex, 1985; Westernmeyer & Baker, 1986). Biological susceptibility in the way their bodies respond to alcohol may be another factor.

Native Americans are caught in a double bind. On the reservation, they face few opportunities for personal advancement, limited employment, and inadequate education. In urban settings they face discrimination and social rejection. Any of these problems may increase the likelihood of substance abuse among this population.

Among tribal members who drink, drinking is a group activity whose goal is intoxication, often in public. Group norms place little stigma on public drunkenness.

Heavy alcohol consumption among Native Americans results in higher rates of fetal alcohol syndrome, higher arrest rates for drunk driving, and reduced life expectancies (Westermeyer & Baker, 1986).

Native Americans have been reluctant to enter treatment programs that were predominantly non-Native American. The cultural and social values of Native Americans seem quite different from mainstream society. Treatment for this population has been ineffectual.

Effective substance abuse treatment programs for Native Americans must include counselors who understand their culture, values, beliefs, traditions, mores, and especially religious ceremonial rites (which may include the use of hallucinogens, such as peyote), chanting, and symbolism.

MILITARY PERSONNEL

Studies repeatedly report considerable substance abuse—especially alcohol abuse—among land-based military personnel. Military women have lower rates of heavy drinking than military men but report similar rates of illicit substance use and cigarette smoking. Many men and women find the military lifestyle more stressful than their family and personal civilian lives. Many military—especially soldiers—have little opportunity to socialize other than in bars. Men drink to excess to demonstrate that they can "hold their liquor," which further reinforces heavy drinking (Bray, Fairbank, & Marsden, 1999). Military personnel usually are treated in military hospitals and rarely are treated by the private sector while they are in the military.

PEOPLE WITH DUAL DIAGNOSES

Dual diagnosis indicates *a major psychiatric disorder in tandem with addiction.* Common major psychiatric diagnoses are major thought disorder (the schizophrenias) or major affective disorder (DSM IV Bipolar: Manic with or without psychotic features or Major Depression).

Mental health staff believed psychiatric problems could not be successfully treated until addiction was under control. Addiction staff believed addiction could not be successfully treated until the psychiatric problem was under control. Accordingly, many patients with dual diagnoses fell through the cracks in the system and did not receive treatment in either venue.

Related Dual Diagnoses

Specific combinations of psychiatric disorders and addiction disorders seem to occur. Dual diagnoses can be

- *Possible risk factors* Axis I (Clinical disorders) or Axis II (Personality disorders) disorders. People with Bipolar: Manic Disorder are at increased risk for developing alcoholism. People with an antisocial personality disorder are at increased risk for developing a substance abuse problem.
- *Modifiers of Axis I or Axis II disorders.* Substance abusers with an antisocial personality disorder have poor likelihood of successful treatment. People with a coexisting depression disorder have increased rates of improvement.
- *Acquired during the course of intoxication.* Psychological symptoms that suggest a dual condition may occur in this way.
- *Results of chronic use.* Loss of abstraction, short-term memory deficits, and visual spatial processing deficits often occur with chronic alcoholism.
- *Linked.* Patients may use illicit substances to self-medicate an underlying psychiatric disorder.
- *Independent disorders* may coexist.

Assessment

Tests that might tap dual diagnoses have been developed. Psychological tests include the *Minnesota Multiphasic Personality Inventory-2 (MMPI-2)*, the *Millon Clinical*

Multiaxial Inventory-III (MCMI-III), and the *Personality Assessment Inventory (PAI)*. All have scales that assess psychiatric and addictive disorders. The *Addiction Severity Index* (ASI) has composite ratings that would identify these disorders. However, *dual diagnoses are identified most often in clinical interview.*

Treatment

Dual disorders can be treated (a) separately, (b) concurrently, (c) or though a hybrid approach in which the treatment is mixed and matched depending on individual needs. Psychiatry has reached a consensus that, in general, dually diagnosed patients require concurrent treatment. If a treatment facility does not have the capability to treat both conditions at the same time, the patient should be referred to a facility that could treat the condition for which the original program lacks resources.

Goals

For many dually diagnosed conditions, counselors need to (1) redefine "recovery." Because many of these patients do not do well in treatment, total abstinence may not be a reasonable goal—reduced frequency of use may be the more likely outcome with these patients; (2) offer support and nurturing: Confrontation is the worst intervention with these fragile patients who do not have the ego resources to respond to such challenges and whose psychiatric symptoms and substance abuse may increase when they are confronted; and (3) respect patients' space and boundaries and try to understand their defenses.

CHAPTER SUMMARY

This chapter discusses principles of assessment and treatment with special populations that include adolescent drug users, women, substance abusers (African Americans, Hispanic Americans, gays and lesbians, older people, Native Americans, and military personnel), and concludes with a section about dually diagnosed substance abusers.

SOURCES OF INFORMATION

Bennett, G. (1986). Alcohol problems among the young. In N. Estes & M. Heinemann (Eds.), *Alcoholism: Development, consequences and interventions* (pp. 221–240). St. Louis: Mosby.

Bovan, J. (1995). *Substance abuse treatment issues for gay and lesbian clients*. Unpublished paper. Chicago, IL: Illinois School of Professional Psychology.

Bray, R. M., Fairbank, J. A., & Marsden, M E. (1999). Stress and substance abuse among military women and men. *American Journal of Drug and Alcohol Abuse, 25,* 239–256.

Bux, D. A. (1996). The epidemiology of problem drinking in gay men and lesbians: A critical review. *Clinical Psychology Review, 16,* 277–298.

Caebano, R., & Clark, C. L. (1998). Trends in alcohol consumption among Whites, Blacks and Hispanics: 1984 and 1995. *Journal of Studies on Alcohol, 59,* 659–668.

Chavez, E. L., & Mora, J. (Eds.). (1994). Special issue on substance use patterns of Latinas. *International Journal of the Addictions, 29,* 1079–1204.

Council on Scientic Affairs, American Medical Association. (1996). Alcoholism in the elderly. *Journal of the American Medical Association, 275,* 797–801.

De La Rosa, M. R., Khalsa, J. H., & Rouse, B. (1990). Hispanics and illicit drug use: A review of recent findings. *International Journal of the Addictions, 25,* 665–691.

Desmond, D. P., & Maddux, J. F. (1984). Mexican American heroin addicts. *American Journal of Drug and Alcohol Abuse, 10,* 317–346.

Gomberg, E. S. (1986). Women with alcohol problems. In N. Estes & M. Heinemann (Eds.), *Alcoholism: Development, consequences and interventions* (pp. 241–256). St. Louis: Mosby.

Grisham, K. J., & Estes, N. J. (1986). Dynamics of alcoholic families. In N. Estes & M. Heinemann (Eds.), *Alcoholism: Development, consequences and interventions* (pp. 303–314). St. Louis: Mosby.

Gurnack, A. M. (Ed). (1995). Social issue on drugs and the elderly: Use and misuse of drugs, medicines, alcohol and tobacco. *International Journal of the Addictions, 30,* 1685–2027.

Harrison, P. A., & Hoffman, N. G. (1985). *Substance use disorder diagnostic schedule manual.* St. Paul, MN: Ramsey Clinic.

Hoffman, A. L., & Heinemann, M. E. (1986). Alcohol problems in the elderly. In N. Estes & M. Heinemann (Eds.), *Alcoholism: Development, consequences and interventions* (pp. 257–272). St. Louis: Mosby.

Kaminer, Y. (1991). Adolescent substance abuse. In R. J. Frances & S. I. Miller (Eds.), *Clinical textbook of addictive disorders* (pp. 320–346). New York: Guilford Press.

Kaminer, Y., Bukstein, O. G., & Tarter, R. E. (1991). The teen addiction severity index: Rationale and reliability. *International Journal of the Addictions, 26,* 9–46.

Lex, B. W. (1985). Alcohol problems in special populations. In J. Mendelson & N. Mello (Eds.), *The diagnosis and treatment of alcoholism* (2nd ed.). New York: McGraw-Hill.

Maddux, J. F., & Desmond, D. P. (1996). Ethnic matching of caseworker and patient in methadone maintenance. *Journal of Substance Abuse Treatment, 13,* 233–239.

Minkoff, K. (2001). Developing standards of care for individuals with co-occurring psychiatric and substance use disorders. *Psychiatric Services, 51,* 597–599.

National Institute on Alcohol Abuse and Alcoholism. *Alcohol Alert,* No. 10, PH290, October, 1990. Washington, DC: U.S. Department of Health and Human Services.

National Institute on Alcohol Abuse and Alcoholism. *Alcohol Alert,* No. 23, PH 347, January, 1994. Washington, DC: U.S. Department of Health and Human Services.

Shedler, J., & Block, J. (1990). Adolescent drug use and psychological health: A longitudinal inquiry. *American Psychologist, 45,* 612–630.

Tarter, R. E. (1990). Evaluation and treatment of adolescent substance abuse: A decision-tree method. *American Journal of Drug and Alcohol Abuse, 16,* 1–46.

Westermeyer, J., & Baker, J. M. (1986). Alcoholism and the American Indian. In N. Estes & M. Heinemann (Eds.), *Alcoholism: Development, consequences and interventions* (pp. 273–282). St. Louis: Mosby.

Winick, C. (1962). Maturing out of narcotic addiction. *Bulletin on Narcotics, 14,* 1–7.

Winters, K. C. (1999a). Screening and assessing adolescents for substance use disorders. *Treatment improvement protocol (TIP) Series 31.* Rockville, MD: Substance Abuse and Mental Health Services Administration. Center for Substance Abuse Treatment.

Winters, K. C. (1999b). Treatment of adolescents with substance use disorders. *Treatment improvement protocol (TIP) Series 32.* Rockville, MD: Substance Abuse and Mental Health Services Administration. Center for Substance Abuse Treatment.

Winters, K. C., & Henley, G. (1988). Assessing adolescents who abuse chemicals. In *The chemical dependency adolescent assessment project in adolescent drug abuse—Analysis of treatment research,* (Monograph Series 77, pp. 4–18). Kensington, MD: National Institute on Drug Abuse.

CHAPTER NINE

PUBLIC POLICY

This chapter highlights policy issues in substance abuse. This list is not comprehensive but offers topics to stimulate critical thinking for debate. These issues are not elucidated in depth, but may be classroom or seminar activities or topics for term papers or theses.

The issues are contained in five main topic areas, *national policy, international policy, social intervention, law enforcement,* and *government intervention.* Each section follows a pattern: It details a *learning* objective, summarizes basic issues, and offers *suggested activities.*

NATIONAL POLICY

The national policy activities may be addressed separately or as a group learning module.

Learning Objectives.
1. To understand how U.S. drug and alcohol policies affect contemporary life.
2. To consider ways to address the nation's substance abuse problem.
3. To suggest new laws that might be enacted to help solve the problem.
4. To understand how current laws can affect contemporary life.

Background.   Drug-sniffing dogs and x-ray machines inspect luggage of international travelers entering or returning to the United States for contraband. People who buy a six-pack of beer pay a liquor tax. People who cross a state line during a holiday may encounter a police roadblock checking for drunk drivers. The government tries to balance the need for social control with the right of privacy. This principle increasingly is challenged with the development of new technologies and government policies are challenged by much litigation.

Suggested Activities.
1. Write or discuss how substance abuse has affected their own life.

2. Research the Constitution and the Supreme Court about basic civil liberties, especially rights of privacy and protection from unlawful search and seizure.
3. In small groups, discuss how to reduce the problems of substance abuse in the United States and present these ideas to the class. The teacher or facilitator guides the discussion of the proposed solutions.
4. In small groups, propose new laws and argue and defend them with the class. The teacher acts as a discussant.
5. Discuss the rights students might be willing to give up to "win the war on drugs."

INTERNATIONAL POLICY

Learning Objective.   To understand the forces that result in foreign nations producing illicit drugs.

Background.   The National Drug Control Strategy has a two-pronged approach to prevention: (1) supply reduction and (2) demand reduction. To reduce the supply of drugs entering the United States, various strategies, from crop-eradication programs to interdiction, have been implemented. Interdiction means that the government attempts to find, confiscate and destroy drugs about to enter U.S. territory. Crop eradication means that the government works with foreign governments to help them destroy crops destined for the illicit market to persuade farmers, through crop substitution programs, to grow legal crops.

Suggested Activities.
1. Research and report on the nations that are major exporters of illicit drugs.
2. List of reasons that individual growers would produce an illegal crop.
3. Suggest ways that growing illicit crops might be useful to a nation.
4. Discuss the merits of U.S. policy that might focus on reducing the supply of illicit drugs in the United States.
5. Discuss the effect legalization of certain drugs might have on the illicit market and the effect this would have on profit margins.

SOCIAL INTERVENTION

Urine Testing

Learning Objectives.
1. To understand the issues and consequences in drug testing programs.
2. To appreciate the feelings of a person submitting a urine test for analysis for illicit drugs.
3. To evaluate how far society is prepared to go to control illicit drugs.

Background. Should schools require athletes to produce urine for drug testing under monitored conditions to participate in extracurricular activities? Should students in general, municipal workers, and hospital workers be required to submit to mandatory drug tests?

In Euclid, Ohio, an apartment complex requires prospective tenants to submit to drug testing. Residents there are enthusiastic about the program, feeling that it helps to maintain a safe place to live. Should this practice be expanded, and, if so, with what consequences?

The Supreme Court has already ruled that that mandatory drug testing of railroad workers, custom agents, police, and pilots (e.g. those involved in public safety) is constitutional. Some argue that such requirements violate privacy rights and protection against unreasonable searches and also question the rightful role of public schools in drug testing.

Suggested Activities.
1. Poll the school, neighborhood, or community to determine how much drug testing and of whom people are willing to accept.
2. Sample attitudes of students not involved in extracurricular activities about their willingness to undergo drug testing.
3. Discuss how far schools should go to prevent drug abuse in a school.
4. Discuss and critique the school or institution's policy on alcohol and drugs.

Over-the-Counter Drug Testing

Learning Objectives.
1. To understand the motives of parents and teens to discover and to hide use of illicit substances.
2. To discuss how and if parent-child relations might change if parents insist on testing their child for drugs.
3. To understand the science and limitations of drug testing kits.

Background. The Food and Drug Administration has approved a nonprescription urine drug test that can be used at home. Test results may be "negative," "inconclusive" (need laboratory analysis), or "positive" for one of five drugs. Test kits usually come with a urine collection cup and a test strip containing antibodies against specific drugs. The test strip is placed in the urine cup immediately after urination. In about 10 minutes, color bands become visible on the test strip. The different colors suggest different results.

Another kit is available that allows drug testing without the knowledge of the suspected user. A moist pad is wiped over clothing, skin, or furniture of the person being tested. The manufacturer contends that the product can detect as little as a single molecule if the person has been using drugs. The tester mails the pad in a special envelope with an ID number and calls the company in a few days with the ID number to get the results.

Over-the-counter hair testing for drugs is also available. Hair testing, alleg-edly, can detect drug use within a 90-day period. Parents send a sample of the child's hair to the manufacturer of the test kit and calls a toll-free number five days later for get the results. These products are marketed mostly to parents of teens. Some raise concerns about issues of privacy, parents spying on their chil-dren, and the reliability of such tests.

Suggested Activities.
1. Research the science behind typical drug testing kits for home use. Report on the accuracy and reliability of these tests.
2. Discuss how parent-child relationships might change if children discover that parents are testing them without their knowledge.

Media Representation of Substance Abusers

Learning Objectives.
1. To determine if the media accurately portray the extent of substance abuse in the United States by race, gender, and ethnicity.

Background.   Research on smoking cessation has found that modeling is a particularly strong motivator in getting people to start smoking. If desirable characters are seen smoking or using alcohol or drugs in publications, movies, or television, then people of a similar age are apt to emulate them. Such conse-quences may be unintended by the producers of these media, who may be try-ing to portray "real life."

Suggested Activities.
1. Watch a TV program and record the age, race, gender, and ethnicity of characters and how they are portrayed in the program (e.g., a middle-aged white female takes a drink when she learns that her husband is having an affair).
2. Research demographic patterns across different drugs of focus and report findings.
3. Determine obvious trends.
4. Determine if minorities are portrayed in a biased or unbiased manner.
5. Discuss whether the environment portrayed in the movie is an accurate portrayal of students' experience.

Medicinal Use of Marijuana

Learning Objectives.
1. To understand the social forces that prevent more marijuana research.
2. To understand the possible medical benefits of marijuana.

Background.   The federal government lists marijuana as a drug with no medi-cal benefits. It is on the same DEA schedule of drugs as heroin. Nevertheless, anecdotal evidence and some research shows that marijuana may have some benefits as a prescribed medication for certain diseases. Debate continues on the extent to which the government should allow marijuana to be used in clinical research trials.

Suggested Activities.
1. List diseases in which marijuana has shown possible effectiveness; cite some of the disadvantages of using marijuana in this way.
2. List arguments for and against marijuana use as medicine.
3. Determine the policy stand on medical marijuana use by the following organizations: Office of National Drug Control, Drug Enforcement Administration, Food and Drug Administration, Federal Bureau of Investigation, American Medical Association, and any other interested group that may have a stake in this policy.

Eliminating Happy Hours

Learning Objectives.
1. Understand the arguments for and against use of happy hours.

Background. "Happy hours" are times when bars offer drinks at a reduced price. Some argue that happy hours contribute to increased alcohol consumption by encouraging people to drink when they would not normally use alcohol. Civil libertarians argue that alcohol is legal and that nothing in a free market economy should prohibit retailers from selling their product.

Suggested Activities.
1. List reasons for and against happy hours.
2. Interview bartenders to determine whether happy hours increase business.
3. Interview bar patrons to determine whether happy hours influence their use of alcohol.

End "Ladies' Nights"

Learning Objectives.
1. Understand social influences that encourage drinking.

Background. "Ladies' nights" are periods when bars offer alcohol at reduced prices. Arguments in favor of ladies' nights are similar to those for happy hours. Some argue that they discriminate because bars do not offer men the same privilege. Statistics show that men drink more than women, and critics of this approach argue that the alcohol industry is trying to increase alcohol consumption among women to increase profits.

Suggested Activities.
1. Research why men drink more than women.

2. Discuss pros and cons of having and advertising "ladies' nights" at bars.
3. Interview bartenders and bar patrons and record their attitudes towards this idea.

Ban the Sale of Alcohol at Sporting Events

Learning Objectives.
1. Understand social attitudes and social forces that pressure the use or banning of alcohol at sporting events.
2. Understand the economic impact of serving alcohol at these events.

Background.   Prohibitionists no longer try to ban alcohol throughout society. Instead, they try to limit or prohibit the use of alcohol in specific situations. More men than women drink and sporting events tend to be more frequented by men. Eliminating alcohol from sporting events would reduce arguments and possible violence at these events, reduce DUIs that occur after games, and model to youth that society frowns on the widespread use of alcohol in our social institutions.

Suggested Activities.
1. Identify elements in society who would not want alcohol banned at sporting events. Discuss counter-measures they would attempt to maintain the status quo.
2. Identify the kind of alcohol that typically is served at local sporting events. Sample community opinion about eliminating alcohol at these events.
3. Determine the economic effect of serving alcohol at a particular sporting event.
4. List events in society that should ban alcohol and discuss why.

Ban Colleges from Operating Bars or Selling Liquor

Learning Objectives.
1. To understand the association between age and drinking prevalence.
2. To discover how colleges cope with drinking on campus.

Background.   College campuses typically have high rates of alcohol consumption, particularly among males. To curb this problem, it has been proposed to ban campuses from operating bars or selling liquor.

Suggested Activities.
1. Survey nearby colleges and find out how many serve liquor on campus.
2. Survey college students on their attitudes toward selling liquor on campus.
3. Obtain a college plan to curtail or curb drinking on campus.

Ban Smoking by Actors in Movies and Television

Learning Objectives.
1. To understand the role of movies and television in stimulating certain behavior.
2. To see the subtle kinds of reinforcement movies and television provide.

Background. Because movie and television stars influence youth, some have suggested that these stars should not be seen smoking in their roles. The counter-argument is that tobacco is legal and the media try to portray life realistically.

Suggested Activities.
1. Record scenes on television or in a movie in which the actors smoke. Record the circumstances surrounding the scene, and what the director is trying to demonstrate by having the actor smoke.
2. Compare the results in a large group discussion.
3. Discuss how much the group believes that movies and television affect viewers' behavior.
4. Examine the research of social psychologists on the effects of television on violence, smoking, and drinking.

Do Not Insure Tobacco-Related Illnesses

Learning Objectives.
1. Understand the link between disease and tobacco use.
2. Understand how insurance companies work.
3. Develop an attitude or a position on the question of insuring diseases which are contracted through "voluntary" means.

Background. Tobacco use over a long time often results in specific diseases. It can be argued that such use is voluntary and that diseases associated with its use should not be paid for by insurance companies. Insurance carriers have to pass on all such costs to their subscribers, so why should the majority pay for diseases that only a relative few have and that could be avoided. If people know that they must pay such expenses themselves, they won't smoke.

Suggested Activities.
1. Develop a list of health problems associated with smoking.
2. Find out how much tobacco is grown in the United States in any given year.
3. Discuss the pros and cons of banning the growth and production of tobacco products in the United States.
4. Discuss the possible effects of such a policy on the U.S. economy, taking into account the savings in health care.
5. List other diseases that are caused by voluntary behavior.

Fire Workers Caught Using Drugs

Learning Objectives.
1. Determine societal community attitudes toward this proposal.

Background.   Many suggestions have been offered to eliminate drug abuse in the workplace. Statistics show that preemployment drug screens and random drug testing in the workplace have sharply reduced drug abuse by employees. Drug treatment statistics have shown that those with the most to lose (e.g., professionals such as physicians, lawyers, accountants, etc.), have higher treatment success rates compared to other work groups. This information lead to the idea that workers would not use illicit drugs if they knew that they could lose their jobs if they test positive.

Suggested Activities.
1. Poll workers about their position on firing employees who test positive; poll managers and supervisors separately. List the reasons they cite for their positions.
2. Discuss whether drug abuse is a disease and whether people who have the disease should lose their job.
3. List pros and cons of this proposal.

Eliminate Public Pay Phones

Learning Objectives.
1. Understand how this proposal is but one of several drastic measures suggested to control the drug abuse problem in the United States.
2. Learn whether a particular community or neighborhood favor this proposal.

Background.   Drug dealers and abusers use pay phones to conduct drug deals or other illegal activities. In an experiment, pay phones in a Chicago neighborhood no longer accepted coins between 6 p.m. and 6 a.m. Customers can use calling cards, call collect, or bill to a third party, but when they do they leave a trail. The American Civil Liberties Union (ACLU) argues that this restriction disproportionately affects poor people and is discriminatory, and that drug action will move to another telephone location. The experiment has received no opposition from business or community residents.

Suggested Activities.
1. List the efforts the United States has used or considered to stop drug abuse nationally.
2. Poll the community to determine attitudes toward eliminating public telephones, if it can be proved that they are being used for drug deals.
3. Discuss the pros and cons of making this proposal a public policy.
4. List the social forces that surround this proposal.

Pay Addicts Not to Get Pregnant

Learning Objectives.
1. Discover the social costs of addicted babies.
2. Consider the consequences on patient rights if this proposal were to become law.

Background. Anaheim, California offers cash to drug-addicted women who are sterilized or use long-term contraception. The idea was the brainchild of a California mother who had drug addicted children and wanted to stop such births. Anaheim gives women $200 upon verification: Generally the government pays for the sterilization or contraception. Other cities are considering the idea. The American Civil Liberties Union (ACLU) and Planned Parenthood have labeled this "drastic."

This program is consistent with a larger issue that seeks to prevent women from harming their unborn children. Some states have charged pregnant, drug-addicted women with child abuse or neglect if they are arrested on drug-related charges. Some argue that parental rights should be terminated after a drug-related conviction.

Suggested Activities.
1. Research the statistics on mothers giving birth to addicted babies in the local state or community.
2. Research the effects of babies born to addicted mothers.
3. Invite an expert physician to discuss this problem.
4. Poll community members to determine whether they would support the use of public money to pay women to be sterilized.
5. Discuss whether a woman's parental rights should be terminated if she delivers an addicted baby.

LAW ENFORCEMENT

Legalization and Decriminalization

Learning Objectives.
1. To develop a position on the legalization and decriminalization of drugs.
2. To understand the social forces shaping this debate.

Background. Under *decriminalization*, a drug would remain illegal, but the penalties for personal possession, without the intent to sell, would be reduced or eliminated. Possession would be treated like a traffic violation. With *legalization*, the possession and sale of a drug would be treated like the possession and sale of alcohol. The debate has generally centered on marijuana, but some have argued to make cocaine and heroin legal, as well. The debate centers on public order and social control versus personal liberty and paternalism versus permissiveness (MacCoun, 1993).

Supporters of legalization argue that drug laws have created problems that are far worse than the drugs themselves—corruption, violence, street crime, and disrespect for the law. They argue that previously passed legislation to control drugs has failed to reduce demand. And they argue that legalization would result in falling prices, reduced crime, corruption, and stigma, and allow the police to concentrate on more serious crimes. Those opposed to such legislation fear that free access to drugs would increase the health, social, behavioral, and moral consequences of their use, and would have little effect on the illegal market (which would add inducements such as better quality to use their products).

Twelve states already have decriminalized marijuana and the available evidence suggests that such decriminalization has had negligible effects on the prevalence of use of this drug in those states. Generally, the use of the drug increases slightly immediately following legalization and gradually decreases to initial baseline rates.

Suggested Activities.
1. Research states that have legalized marijuana and determine the effects on the consumption of marijuana and of illicit drugs before and after legalization.
2. Discuss the effects and possible consequences to society: if cocaine were legalized; if heroin were legalized; if club drugs were legalized.
3. Discuss how the black market might respond to drug legalization so that consumers would prefer their products to those obtained through legal channels.
4. List the social forces behind suggestions to legalize drugs.

Videotape Suspected DUIs

Learning Objectives.
1. Understand society's need to curtail drunk driving.
2. Understand the scope and effects of the problem.

Background.   Some states now videotape drivers suspected of driving under the influence of alcohol. Law enforcement officials tape the person accused of drunk driving and show the tapes to defense attorneys. The cameras are in police cars and record drivers from the time the officers believe there is probable cause for a DUI citation.

Suggested Activities.
1. Arrange for a local police representative to discuss DUI videotaping. Some have a video presentation that can be viewed along with the presentation.
2. Attend court when drunken drivers are scheduled to appear.
3. List ways that police might discover people who are driving drunk.
4. Discuss how to prevent drunken drivers from (a) ever driving again or (b) getting behind the wheel.

Confiscate Cars

Learning Objectives.
1. Understand the policy implications of confiscating a car after a conviction for drunken driving.

Background.   Politicians continually seek ways to address social problems that would have general community support. "Get tough on crime" usually has the support of the public and a variety of means have been proposed and implemented to get drunken drivers off the road. Confiscating their cars, it is argued, is similar to confiscating drug-acquired assets.

Suggested Activities.
1. Discuss the consequences of laws confiscating the car of drunken drivers.
2. Conduct a poll to determine if this proposal would have community support.
3. List ways to reach the intended consequences of such laws without so adversely affecting violators.
4. Research and report on individuals whose lives have been affected by a drunken driver.
5. Discuss, pro and con, the position of a "right to drive."

BALs to Start Cars

Learning Objectives.
1. Learn how technology may be increasingly called upon to deal with social problems.
2. Understand that no system is full proof and can be abused.

Background.   Electronic equipment can be installed in cars to measure the blood-alcohol concentration of the driver. Drivers would breathe into a tube linked to the vehicle's ignition. The vehicle would not start if the BAL was above a pre-determined level. Both Illinois and Massachusetts have already passed legislation permitting judges to order convicted repeat drunken drivers to install this device in their cars as a condition of probation.

Suggested Activities.
1. Research the available devices and how they work.
2. Discuss ways of circumventing these devices.
3. Discuss ways to keep drunk drivers off the road.
4. Discover how many people in the state have been convicted for drunk driving offenses and how many are in jail.
5. First time DUI offenders generally have their license suspended and are required to attend an educational class. Learn and report on the content of these classes.

Over-the-Counter Nicotine Sales

Learning Objective.
1. Appreciate the policy consequences of selling nicotine over-the-counter.

Background.   Should nicotine substitute products, designed to help smokers to quit cigarettes, be available without a prescription? A variety of drug-distribution products have become available. These provide nicotine through transdermal patches, in gum, and in other oral forms. Proponents argue that making these products more accessible removes the obstacle of getting a prescription. They argue that the dangers from smoking (lung cancer, emphysema and other respiratory ailments, and heart disease) come more from inhaling the toxic substances produced by a burning tobacco than it does from nicotine. Also, nicotine is less concentrated in these alternate delivery forms than through tobacco use. Counterarguments include the facts that nicotine is addicting, affects the brain, and affects fetuses, and the user may simply trade one habit for another.

Suggested Activities.
1. Discuss the attitudes toward the use of nicotine substitutes and their perceived effectiveness from the point of view of people who have used them.
2. Conduct a poll to determine general opinions about whether nicotine should be available only by prescription or should be sold over-the-counter.
3. Discuss the effects over-the-counter nicotine might have on tobacco growers and manufacturers.

Drug Roadblocks

Learning Objectives.
1. Understand possible public reaction to drug roadblock.
2. Appreciate the possible future consequences in terms of expanded police power.

Background.   Should the police set up road blocks and subject cars to inspection by drug-sniffing dogs? Some have established highway check points in high-crime areas, checking driver's licenses while drug-sniffing dogs circle the car of the stopped vehicle. The Supreme Court has ruled that roadblocks to search for illegal immigrants and drunken drivers are constitutional but ruled that drug road blocks are not constitutional. Proponents argue that drug-search roadblocks are consistent with the law. Others content that such police tactics violate the Constitution's Fourth Amendment against unreasonable search and seizure, as well as its guarantee of freedom. They worry that the next step might be having police dogs sniff all pedestrians as they wait at traffic lights.

Suggested Activities.
1. Interview someone who has been involved in a drug roadblock for feelings and reactions to this experience.
2. Discuss in small groups what feelings students might have in experiencing a drug roadblock.
3. Discuss the extent of police powers the class is willing to tolerate to control a particular problem.

Mandatory Sentencing

Learning Objectives.
1. Understand what is meant by mandatory sentencing laws.
2. Appreciate their intent, consequences and possible abuses.
3. Understand how politics affects laws.

Background. Because a political party considered judges "too lenient," Congress enacted mandatory sentencing laws that apply to drug-related offences. In some cases, they carry a life sentence, and in some cases the penalties are harsher than for convicted murderers. As a result of these laws, more prisoners plea bargain and testify in court against friends to avoid harsher penalties.

Suggested Activities.
1. Obtain and view the *Frontline* (PBS, 2001) video on mandatory sentencing and their abuses and consequences.
2. Develop a list of drug-related crimes that should carry mandatory sentences.
3. Develop a list of drug-related offenses that should carry a sentence of life imprisonment.
4. Research the political environment that surrounded the enactment of the drug sentencing laws.
5. Discuss the pros and cons of plea bargains.

Interdiction

Learning Objectives.
1. Appreciate the difficulty in detecting drug smugglers.
2. Understand the consequences and rewards for smuggling drugs.

Background. Cocaine smugglers have used increasingly bizarre methods to smuggle in their product. In 1992, FBI agents found cocaine that had been chemically combined with fiberglass and molded into portable dog kennels. Smugglers have packed cocaine into cans of faked yams, hidden it in shipments of frozen fish, and secreted it in statues of the Virgin Mary. To combat such practices, the U.S. Customs Department uses drug-sniffing dogs and periodic random searches of imports.

Suggested Activities.
1. Determine the penalties for smuggling and discuss the costs and benefits of continuing this illegal activity.
2. Think of ways to smuggle an illicit product into the United States.

Seizing Assets

Learning Objectives.
1. Understand the effects and consequences of forfeiture policy laws.
2. Develop an appreciation of possible future abuse of state power.

Background. States have enacted forfeiture laws that allow authorities to seize property used in the drug trade. They may seize cash, homes, boats, weapons and other valuables, if they can prove these items were used in or resulted from the drug trade. The money resulting from these seizures is distributed to local law enforcement agencies in their continuing battle to combat crime. Subsequently, the Supreme Court has ruled that such practices are constitutional, but can occur only after it has been proved legally that such valuables were obtained through illegal means.

Suggested Activities.
1. Think of ways confiscated assets could be used other than returning the money to law enforcement.
2. Find out how much drug asset money has become available to the local police department in the past year.
3. List possible abuses of this law.
4. Argue, pro and con, whether states should have such sweeping power.

Money Laundering

Learning Objectives.
1. Understand how and why drug money is laundered.
2. Learn how smugglers launder money.
3. Discover ways that the government is trying to stop money laundering from drug traffickers.
4. Understand how bankers, lawyers, and accountants are part of the illicit drug trade and trafficking.

Background. Almost all drug transactions are in cash—usually in 5, 10, and 20 dollar bills, resulting in a huge cash hoard. One million 20 dollar bills weighs about 100 pounds. The federal government enacted a law that requires banks to submit a Currency Transfer Report to the Internal Revenue Service for any deposit, withdrawal, or exchange of currency that exceeds $10,000. A Currency and Monetary Instrument must be completed on any goods or merchandise valued in excess of $10,000 that enter or leave the country. Drug traffickers have hundreds of bales of cash to convert from an illegal to a legal money source (i.e., "launder") or smuggle out of the country.

Suggested Activities.
1. Research ways that money has been laundered.
2. Research laws and steps the government has taken to prevent money laundering.
3. Generate a list of ideas that might stop, curtail, or prevent money laundering

Treatment

Treatment should be compulsory for any drug abuser.

Learning Objective.
1. Understand the effects and consequences of requiring drug abuse treatment for all abusers.

Background.   Drug treatment professionals have produced evidence that treatment for drug abuse is effective. Some have argued that treatment should be mandatory for all drug-abusing patients. Others believe that treatment can be effective only when it is voluntary and not compulsory.

Suggested Activities.
1. List the possible effects on an abuser's life, pro and con, if treatment were mandated.
2. List crimes for which the perpetrators should receive treatment and not punishment.
3. Consider the effects on drug treatment programs, if the courts increasingly mandated drug treatment.
4. Consider the consequences in the Criminal Justice System if drug abusers were mandated to treatment.
5. Consider ways ways to get help for abusers without sending them for treatment.

GOVERNMENT INTERVENTION

Food and Drug Administration Regulation of Tobacco as a Drug

Learning Objective.
1. To develop a position on the regulation of nicotine.

Background.   The Food and Drug Administration proposed regulating cigarettes and smokeless tobacco as drug delivery devices. The FDA is charged with the responsibility of determining the safety and efficacy of a drug before it goes to market. Because nicotine is a drug, they argued that it is within their purview to control it. They called for (1) a minimum age of 18 to purchase cigarettes, (b) a ban on all vending machines, mail-order sales, free samples, and self-service displays, (c) restricting advertising that reaches children to black and white text, (d) banning the sale or distribution of hats, tee-shirts and other items that display the name of a tobacco brand or product, (e) restricting the sponsorship of events to corporate name only and (f) requiring tobacco manufacturers to conduct a public education program to reduce the appeal of smoking to youth. Subsequently the Supreme Court ruled that the FDA may not regulate tobacco, saying that it was up to Congress to do so.

States attorneys sued the tobacco companies to recover health care costs of treating smokers. They argued that the financial and social costs of caring for smokers had become intolerably high and wanted the tobacco companies to reimburse them, because their product had caused the problem. Subsequently, the tobacco companies agreed to pay an enormous sum in the first 25 years, fund smoking-cessation programs, antismoking education and advertising, and agreed to many of the stipulations contained in the original FDA proposal. They also agreed that the FDA could regulate nicotine as a drug but could not ban it until 2009. In return, class-action suits against the industry were dropped.

Suggested Activities.
1. List the "hardships" in the life of an adult or of a teen if the FDA proposal had become public policy.
2. Discuss which of the many initial FDA proposals should have become law.
3. Poll youthful smokers to determine (a) why they started to smoke and (b) why they continue to smoke.
4. Document the health and social consequences of chronic cigarette smoking.
5. Discover the research that tobacco companies have engaged in to develop a "safe" cigarette.
6. Determine why the tobacco companies agreed to this settlement.

Higher Taxes on Alcohol

Learning Objectives.
1. To discover the relationship between taxation and alcohol consumption.

Background.   In principle, microeconomic theory argues that reductions in availability of a drug should increase the price of that drug. To the extent that the demand for the drug is elastic (i.e., sensitive to price), then price increases should discourage drug use. This is the theory behind reducing the supply of illicit drugs on the street. The same argument holds for taxing alcohol. If the price increases, people would only reluctantly purchase it, and overall consumption would decrease. The evidence for this effect is inconsistent, given the modest price hikes on most alcohol intoxicants.

Suggested Activities.
1. Discover the historic statistics on raising taxes on alcohol and subsequent alcohol consumption.
2. Poll community and class to determine, among those who drink, how much more the product would have to be taxed before individuals reduce or eliminate the consumption of alcohol.
3. Find out how alcohol taxes are used in the state and community budgets.

Higher Legal Drinking Age

Learning Objectives.
1. To understand why proponents want to raise the legal drinking age.
2. To appreciate the effects and consequences of raising the legal drinking age.

Background.   To reduce alcohol-related offenses, it has been proposed that states should raise the legal drinking age. This is based on statistics that show that people 18–25 tend to have higher prevalence of alcohol use and also tend to have more alcohol-related criminal offenses (i.e., DUIs, accidents, crimes in which alcohol has played a role, etc.). It is argued that raising the legal drinking age would reduce these alcohol-related offences.

Suggested Activities.
1. Obtain criminal statistics on alcohol-related offenses and convictions in the community.
2. Discuss the pros and cons of raising the legal drinking age.
3. Predict the effects of raising or lowering the legal drinking age.

SOURCES OF INFORMATION

Abadinsky, H. (2000). *Drugs: An introduction.* Belmont, CA: Wadsworth.

Frontline (2001). *America's war on drugs.* Boston, MA: PBS.

MacCoun, R. J. (1993). Drugs and the law: A psychological analysis of drug prohibition. *Psychological Bulletin, 113,* 497–512.

Office of National Drug Control Policy (1998). *Per-* *formance measures of effectiveness: A system for assessing the performance of the National Drug Control Strategy: 1998–2007.* Washington, DC: U.S. Government Printing Office.

Office of National Drug Control Policy (2000). *National Drug Control Policy: 2000 Annual Report.* Washington, DC: U.S. Government Printing Office.

Abadinsky, H., 13, 227
Abraham, H. D., 68
Acierno, R., 147
Adel, E. L., 68
Alarcon, R. D., 68
Alexander, B. K., 174, 189
Allen, J. P., 110, 140, 148
Alterman, A. I., 133, 148
Anisman, H., 69
Anker, A. L., 129, 147
Argeriou, M., 81, 110
Arndt, I. O., 13, 138, 148
Axelrod, J., 68

Babor, T. F., 148
Bachman, J. G., 5, 13
Badger, G., 147
Baekeland, F., 147, 167, 169
Bailey, W. C., 68
Baker, J. M., 207, 210
Baker, S. L., 147
Balter, M. B., 71, 111
Bariansfather, L., 187, 190
Barnatt, L. W., 147
Barnes, G., 19, 32
Barr, H. L., 110
Barredo, V. H., 186, 190
Barry, K. L., 147, 155, 169
Begleiter, H., 27, 32
Bennett, G., 198, 209
Ben-Yehuda, N., 189
Berkowitz, A. M., 27, 32, 186, 189
Berry, J., 68
Bickel, W. K., 129, 137, 147, 149
Bigelow, G. E., 129, 149
Bihari, B., 27, 32
Black, C., 185, 189
Blaine, J. D., 20, 32
Blane, H., 19, 32
Blaney, T., 139, 147
Blatt, S. J., 21, 32
Block, J., 57, 195, 210
Block, R. I., 57, 68

Bokes, P. J., 190
Bloom, F. E., 27, 33, 129
Bond, C. F., 23, 32
Boone, J., 88, 110
Boone, K., 68
Boren, S. J., 190
Bovan, J., 209
Brabender, V., 159, 161, 162, 164, 169
Branch, L. G., 147
Bray, R. M., 208, 209
Brever, A., 68
Briley, E. M., 68
Brill, P., 148
Brown, B. S., 69, 137, 149
Brown, S., 184, 189
Brownell, K. D., 132, 147
Budney, A. J., 137, 147
Bukstein, O. G., 196, 210
Burglass, M., 33
Burk, J. P., 184, 189
Burns, W., 69
Butcher, J. N., 94, 110
Bux, D. A., 203, 204, 209

Cacciola. J., 81, 83, 110, 111, 133, 148
Caebano, R., 201, 210
Campbell, V. L., 94, 111
Carroll, C. R., 68, 131, 147, 169
Caudill, S. P., 88, 110
Cermak, T. L., 187, 189
Cervantes, O. F., 172, 189
Chasnoff, I., 69
Chavez, E. L., 202, 210
Chiang, C. N., 110
Ch'ien, J. M., 134, 148
Cisin, I. H., 71, 111
Clark, C. L., 201, 210
Cleveland, M., 189
Coe, R., 139, 148
Cohen, J., 129, 149
Cohen, S. J., 68
Coleman, E., 172, 189
Colgan, P., 172, 189

Columbus, M., 110
Cone, E. J., 69, 137, 149
Connors, G. J., 148
Cook, B. L., 138, 148
Cotton, N. S., 25, 32
Craig, R. J., 19, 20, 32, 72, 78, 94, 110, 117,
    139, 147, 165, 167, 169, 186, 190
Crowley, T. J., 22, 32, 147
Cruse, J. R., 190
Cummins, C., 134, 147
Czechowicz, D., 69

Daley, D. C., 135, 147
Dahlstrom, W. G., 94, 110
D'Andrea, L. M., 187, 189
Davis, B. L., 68
Dax, E. M., 69, 149
Decker, S., 68
De La Rosa, M. R., 202, 209
Deleon-Jones, F., 33
DeLuca, A., 158, 169
Deren, S., 186, 189
Desmond, D. P., 190, 201, 202, 210
Devane, W. A., 68
Dibb, G. S., 174, 189
Dickinson, W. A., 68
DiClemente, C. C., 140, 142, 148
D'Lugoff, B., 129, 149
Doerr, H. O., 139, 148
Dohn, H. H., 68
Dole, V. P., 32
Donohue, B., 147
Dorus, W., 137, 147
Doweiko, H. E., 68
Druley, K., 111, 148
Dusek, D. E., 68
Dworkin, S. I., 68

Edward, G., 139, 147
Egert, S., 139, 147
Ellis, B. G., 189
Ereshefsky, L., 69
Estes, N., 189, 210
Estroff, T. W., 68
Etinger, A., 68
Evans, F., 110
Eyre, S. L., 68, 69

Fairbank, J. A., 208, 209

Fallon, A., 159, 161, 162, 164, 169
Felder, C. C., 68
Fernandez, L., 172, 189
Finn, P., 26, 33
Fiore, M. L., 68
Fischman, M. W., 68
Fishbein, D. H., 68
Fischer, L., 187, 189
Flores, P. J., 155, 162, 169
Foerg, F., 147
Foote, J., 158, 169
Frances, R. J., 68, 210
Fuller, R. W., 69

Gacono, C. B., 69
Ganger, R., 190
Garvey, M., 138, 148
Gawin, F. H., 68, 169
Gay, G. R., 190
Gelernter, J., 27, 32
George, R. L., 190, 191
Ghoneim, M., 68
Gibson, D., 68
Gierymski, T., 190
Girdano, D. A., 68
Glantz, M., 15, 32
Glassroth, J., 69
Glatt, S., 68
Gluck, B. C., 148
Gold, S., 68
Goldberg, R., 68
Gomberg, E. S., 33, 198, 210
Goodwin, D. W., 25, 26, 32
Gordon, J., R., 132, 134, 147
Gordon, L. T., 169
Grabowski, J., 68
Graeven, D. B., 68
Graham, J. R., 94, 110
Grant, I., 68
Grauch, A., 158, 159
Greenfield, S. F., 133, 147, 158, 169
Griffin, D., 68, 81, 83
Griffin, M. I., 133, 149, 171, 190
Griffith, J., 83, 110, 111
Girsham, K. J., 210
Grissom, G. R., 81, 110, 140, 148
Gruber, A. J., 57, 69
Gurnack, A. M., 205, 210
Guthrie, S., 139, 147

Haetrzen, C. A., 69, 137, 149
Halikas, J., 69
Hall, W. C., 69
Hallmark, R., 94, 111
Hanus, L., 68
Hansen, H. J., 88, 110
Hansen, N. D., 187, 190
Harbin, H. T., 174, 190
Hardwick, C. J., 187, 190
Harris, L. S., 147
Harrison, P.A., 1, 196, 210
Harrson, T. C., 69, 187, 189
Hatcher, R., 69
Hawker, A., 147
Hawks, R. K., 110
Hawthorne, J., 129, 149
Heard, D. B., 190
Heinemann, M. E., 189, 206, 210
Henley, G., 210
Hensman, C., 147
Herjanic, B. M., 186, 190
Herjanic, M., 186, 190
Herning, R. I., 69, 149
Higgins, S. T., 137, 147
Highes, J. R., 147
Hinkin, C., 68
Hoffman, N. G., 196, 206, 210
Hoffman, A. L., 206, 210
Hoffman, P. L., 26, 27, 33
Hogan, I., 172, 190
Householder, J., 69
Hubbard, R. L., 12, 13
Hufford, C., 133, 149
Hull, J. G., 23
Hughes, A., 137
Hunt, W. A., 147

Imhof, J., 110
Itkomen, J., 69

Jaffe, J. H., 148
Jalali, B., 172, 190
Janzen, C., 171, 190
Jellinek, E. M., 24, 24, 33
Johanson, C. E., 27, 33
Johnson, L. D., 5, 13
Jones, C., 69
Judd, L. L., 68
Julius, D., 20, 32

Kabasakalian-McKay, R., 133, 148
Kadden, R. M., 133, 148
Kaemmer, B., 94, 110
Kaminer, Y., 196, 210
Kaufman, E., 190
Khalisa, J. H., 202, 210
Khantzian, E. J., 20, 33, 69, 78, 110
Kinney, J., 69
Kirschner, S., 190
Kissen, B., 27, 32
Kleber, H. D., 22, 33, 68, 69, 78, 83, 111, 172, 190
Kleiman, J. I., 190
Kogan, E., 147
Kokkinidis, L., 69
Kosten, T. R., 21, 33, 69, 83, 138, 148, 172, 190
Kron, R., 111
Ksir, C., 69
Kushner, H., 81, 110

Lawrence, C., 129, 149
Lawson, G. W., 69
Lee, J. M., 26, 27, 33
Leonard, K. E., 19, 32
Leaton, G., 69
Lettieri, D. J., 33
Lex, B. W., 195, 199, 201, 202, 207, 210
Lichtenstein, E., 69, 132, 147
Liebson, I. A., 129, 149
Lipscom, B. S., 190
Litt, M., 140, 148
Longbaugh, R., 140, 148
Luborsky, L., 81, 83, 110, 111, 140, 148
Lundwall, L., 147, 167, 169
Luthar, S. S., 171, 174, 175, 190
Lyden, S., 69

MacCoun, R. J., 219, 227
MacDonald, B. I., 69
Madanes, C., 190
Maddux, J. F., 190, 201, 202, 210
Magura, S., 158, 169
Mandelbaum, A., 68
Marlatt, G. A., 84, 111, 131, 134, 147
Marsden, M. E., 84, 111, 131, 134, 147
Martinez-Raga, J., 133, 149
Mattson, M. E., 140, 148
Maziar, H. M., 174, 190

McAuliffe, W. E., 134, 148
McDonald, C., 21
McEntee, R., 191
McGahan, D., 81, 111
McKay, J. R., 133, 148
McKie, K., 68
McLellan, A. T., 13, 69, 78, 81, 83, 110, 111, 138, 140, 148
McWilliams, S. A., 69
Mechoulam, R., 68
Mello, N., 148, 210
Mendelson, J., 148, 210
Meltzer-Brody, S., 33, 148
Menicurri, L., 172, 189
Metzger, D. S., 13, 81, 110, 138, 148
Meyer, R. L., 148
Michael, J. L., 171, 190
Michaelson, B. S., 69, 149
Miller, M., 68
Miller, S. I., 210
Miller, W. R., 84, 111, 148, 158
Millon, T., 94, 110
Milosky, E. S., 33
Minkoff, K., 210
Mirin, S. N., 171, 190
Mitchenson, M., 147
Mohans, L., 68
Mora, L., 202, 210
Morse, C., 69
Moss, P. D., 33
Mowatt, D. T., 190

Nagy, P. D., 155, 169
Najavits, C. M., 158, 169
Nich, C., 169
Nickless, C. J., 140, 148
Nieberding, R., 94, 111
Novak, P., 172, 190
Norcross, J. C., 142, 148
Novelly, R. A., 69
Noyes, R., 138, 148
Nurco, D. N., 71, 111
Nyswander, M. E., 32

O'Brien, C. P., 13, 69, 78, 81, 83, 110, 111, 140, 148
O'Malley, P. M., 5, 13
Onken, L. S., 190
Oppenheimer, E., 147

Orford, J., 139, 147
Osnos, R., 171, 190
Otto, M. W., 137, 148

Pattison, E. M., 139, 148
Pearson, H. W., 33
Pease, S. E., 68
Peele, S., 148
Perkins, H. W., 186, 189
Perry, D. J., 138, 148
Pertwee, R. G., 68
Peters, R., 81, 110
Peterson, J., 26, 33
Pettinato, H., 81, 114
Pickens, R., 15, 32
Pihl, R. O., 26, 33
Platt, J. J., 69
Polich, J., 27, 33
Pollack, M. H., 27, 148
Pollock, V. E., 33, 137
Pope, H. G., 57, 69
Porjesz, B., 27, 32
Powell, D. J., 69
Prochaska, J. O., 142, 148
Pumphrey, E., 138

Rado, S., 19, 20, 33
Randall, D., 140, 148
Rawson, R. A., 138, 149
Ray, O., 69
Reitan, R. M., 68
Reiter, S. R., 137, 148
Rhodes, R. J., 139, 148
Riley, P., 190
Ripple, C. H., 171, 174, 175, 190
Rosenbaum, J. F., 148
Rosenblum, A., 169
Rounsaville, B. J., 21, 33, 68, 69, 83, 111, 169
Rouse, B., 202, 210
Rouse, S. V., 94, 110
Rutherford, M. J., 133, 148

Sachs, S. R., 137, 148
Saito, T., 26, 27, 33
Salmon, R., 33
Salmon, S., 33
Sayers, M., 33
Scheidt, S., 191
Schindel, B. J., 189

Schnoll, S., 69
Schuckit, M. A., 26, 33
Schuster, C. R., 27, 33
Schwartzman, J., 190
Scott, S. M., 191
Seecof, R., 138, 149
Shadish, W. R., 190
Shaffer, H., 33
Sharp, J. G., 68
Shedler, J., 195, 210
Sher, K. J., 184, 189
Shontz, F. C., 69
Shugart, G., 190
Siegel, R. J., 69
Simpson, J. T., 68
Skinner, H. A., 139, 148
Sorensen, J. L., 172, 189
Spotts, J. V., 69
Stahl, S., 179
Stanton, M. D., 174, 190, 191
Stark, M. J., 117, 149
Starrsman, R. J., 69
Steinman, L., 68
Stevenson, L. A., 68
Stitzer, M. L., 129, 149
Stoval, G., 186, 190
Strabenav, J. R., 148
Sugarman, A., 21, 32

Tabakoff, B., 26, 27, 33
Taylor, C., 147
Taylor, S. D., 171, 190
Talbert, R. L., 69
Tarter, R. E., 196, 210
Telegen, A., 94, 110
Tennant, F. S., 138, 149
Terenzi, R. E., 110
Todd, T. C., 190
Tomelledi, C. J., 186
Treece, C., 69, 78, 110
Trimpey, J., 126, 149
Tuttle, R. J., 69

Vaillant, G. E., 33

Van Duesen, J. M., 190, 191
Van Gorp, W. G., 68
Vardy, M. M., 69
Venturello, P., 69

Wallace, B. C., 158, 169
Wanck, B., 189–191
Warner, A., 169
Warner, P. D., 33
Watkins, C. E., 94, 111
Weddington, W. W., 69, 137, 149
Weinberg, D., 110
Wegsheider-Cruse, D., 185, 191
Weiss, R. D., 133, 149, 158, 169, 171, 190
Weissman, M. M., 22, 33, 69, 78, 111
Weller, R., 69
Wellish, D. K., 191
Wermuth, L., 172, 189, 191
Westermeyer, J., 207, 210
Wikler, A., 22, 33, 69, 78, 111
Wilber, C., 21, 32, 69, 78, 111
Wilbur, M., 78, 171, 190
Wilkins, J. N., 68
Willard, B., 27, 33
Williams, T., 190
Wilson, G. T., 132, 147
Winick, C., 28, 29, 33, 205, 210
Winters, K. C., 111, 210
Winters, W., 69
Wirtz, P. W., 140, 148, 169
Wolf, E., 68
Woody, G. E., 13, 69, 78, 83, 111, 138, 140, 148
Woolverton, W. L., 33

Yalom, I. D., 156, 169
Yorke, C., 19, 33
Young, T., 69
Yurgelum-Todd, D., 57, 69

Zanis, D., 140, 148
Zucker, R. A., 33

Acceptance, 120, 158
Acetylcholine, 38
Acting out, 117
Active listening, 118, 119
Addict games, 145, 146
Addiction Admission Scale, 94, 299
Addiction Potential Scale, 94, 209
Addiction Severity Index, 81, 83, 84, 97–109
Addictive personality, 19
Adolescent substance abuse
  interviewing, 196
  problems in treating, 196–198
  problems with diagnostic criteria, 194, 195
  stages of use, 194
Advice, 84, 87, 120
Adult Children of Alcoholics (ACOA). *See* Co-dependence
African American substance abuse, 31, 193, 201
Aftercare, 114, 137, 158
Aggression, 20, 21, 23, 44, 57, 63, 74, 163
AIDS, 12, 51, 54, 80, 87, 96, 115, 158
Alcohol
  dependence, 42, 54
  detection of, 41, 91
  epidemiology, 4, 5
  intoxication, 41
  main effects, 41
  medical problems with, 42
  public health problems, 42, 43
  tolerance, 41
  withdrawal, 42
Alcohol epidemiology, 2
Alcoholics
  daughters of, 26
  sons of, 25–27
Alcoholics Anonymous (AA), 30, 49, 76, 124–126, 139, 140, 143, 155, 158, 160, 161, 173, 197
Alcoholism
  disease concept of, 23–27
  familial incidence of, 25

familial type, 25, 26
stages of, 24
types of, 24, 25
Alpha alcoholic, 24
Altruism, 156
Amenorrhea, 80
American Medical Association, 23, 215
American Psychiatric Association, 23, 44, 63, 95
American Society of Addiction Medicine, 24
Amotivational syndrome, 57, 58
Amphetamines
  adverse reactions, 45, 46
  dependence, 44
  detection of, 44, 88, 91
  main effects, 40, 43, 44
  medical uses, 44, 45
  psychosis, 45
  route of administration, 44
  tolerance to, 44
Analgesics, 19, 35, 52
Anger, 20, 21, 45, 47, 163, 184
Anorexia, 61
Antabuse (Disulfiram), 32, 76, 130, 138
Antisocial personality disorder, 17, 26, 54, 78, 165
Anxiety, 48, 55, 62, 78, 95, 132, 186
Asians, 26
Association theory, 28
Asthma, 61
Ativan, 41
Attention Deficit Disorder (ADD), 17
Aversive conditioning, 130
Avoidance conditioning, 128

Balanced placebo design, 23
Barbiturates
  dependence, 40, 47
  detection of, 47, 88, 91
  main effects, 47
  route of administration, 7
  tolerance to, 47

public health problems, 47, 48
  withdrawal, 47, 137
Behavior therapy, 127–131, 139
Behavioral contracting, 129
Benzedrine, 43
Beta alcoholic, 24
Biological markers, 23
Bipolar disorder, 17, 208
Birth defects, 42, 59
Blackouts, 24, 30, 43, 126, 180
Blood-alcohol, 2, 38, 41, 88, 92, 93, 129, 221
Breathalyzers, 38, 88, 198
Brief therapy, 141, 142
Buprenorphine, 138

Caffeine
  dependence, 48
  main effects, 48
  medical uses, 49
  route of administration, 48
  side effects, 48
  tolerance, 49
  withdrawal, 48
Cancer, 43, 60, 64, 67, 205
Cannabinoids, 40, 55
Carbon monoxide, 64, 67
CARF, 118
Catecholamines, 43
CAT scan, 59
Catharsis, 157
Change, stages of, 142, 143
Child abuse, 73, 80, 168
Children of Alcoholics (COA)
  roles, 184–186
  treatment, 187
Chloral hydrate, 41
Cirrhosis, 42
Clinical Interview, 74–81
Clonidine, 136
Club drugs, 62, 63
Cocaine
  addiction, 50
  detection of, 50, 88, 91
  epidemiology, 5–7
  half-life, 49
  main effects, 39, 49
  medical problems, 51
  medical uses, 50, 51

psychological effects, 50
public health problems, 51
tolerance, 50
withdrawal, 50
Codeine 41, 52, 89, 91
Co-dependence, origins of, 171, 178, 179, 187
Co-dependent
  counseling of, 183, 184, 189
  roles, 182, 183
  traits, 179–182, 187, 188
Comorbidity, 78
Comprehensive Drinker Profile, 81, 84
Conditioning
  classical, 22, 49, 130, 131
  operant, 22, 66, 130
Conduct disorders, 17, 131
Confidentiality, 72–74, 118, 168, 196
Confrontation, 120, 121, 143
Contingent reinforcement, 129
Coping response, 133–135
Counseling
  preparation, 117
  problems in, 115–117
  techniques, 118–124
Counter-conditioning, 128, 129
Countertransference, 73, 74
Craving, 24, 65
Criminal justice system, 10, 114
Criminality, 18, 57
Crystal methamphetamine, epidemiology of, 46
Cultural assessment, 79, 80

D2 receptor, 27
Defocusing, 144
Delerium tremens (DTs), 30, 42, 136
Delinquency, 18
Delta alcoholic, 45, 47, 74, 164
Demerol, 37, 41, 52, 89
Denial, 117, 121, 179, 181, 206
Dependent personality, 55, 78
Depression, 19–21, 45, 50, 52, 62, 78, 93, 132, 179
Detoxification, 114, 136, 137
Dexedrine, 41
Diabetes, 54, 161
Diagnosis, 71, 85, 96
Dilaudid, 41, 52

Disulfiram. *See* Antabuse
Dopamine, 38, 43, 49
Doriden, 37, 41
Dosage, 35, 44
Dose
   main effects, 35
   peak effects, 36
   potency, 36, 40
Dose-response curve, 35, 36
Drug
   additive effects of, 37
   antagonist effects of, 37
   interactions, 37
   synergistic effects, 37
Drug abuse, theories of, 18–31
Drug abuse epidemiology
   arrestee urinalysis data, 3
   DAWN, 3, 6
   drug seizure data, 3
   high school senior survey, 3
   National Household Survey on Drug Abuse, 4
   treatment surveys, 3
Drug courts, 1
Drug Enforcement Administration (DEA), 3, 40, 214, 215
DSM-IV, 26, 95, 118
Dual diagnosis
   assessment, 208, 209
   treatment, 158, 209
DUI, 30, 77, 93, 220, 221

Ecstasy, 7, 62, 91
Education, 121, 158, 161, 177, 197
Elder abuse, 73, 168
Empathy, 85, 119
Employee Assistance Programs (EAPs), 77
Enabling behaviors, 78, 171, 176–178
Endocarditis, 54
Endorphins, 38
Environmental manipulation, 127
Enzyme Multiplied Immune Assay (EMIT), 90
Epidemics, 20
Epidemiological data, sources of, 2
Epilepsy, 45, 46, 61
Epinephrine, 43
Epsilon alcoholic, 24
Erectile dysfunction, 20

Expectancy theory, 19, 23
Expectations, 39
Exploration, 121

Families of substance abusers, characteristics of, 173, 174
Family
   antisocial behavior in, 18
   assessment, 77, 78
   counseling, 171, 172
   disruption, 174
   divorce, 18, 174
   rules, 176
   structure, 174–176
   substance abuse in, 18
   therapy, 29, 135, 172, 173
Federal Bureau of Investigation (FBI), 215
Fetal Alcohol Syndrome (FAS), 42, 201, 207
Flashbacks, 52
Food and Drug Administration (FDA), 36, 45, 56, 138, 213, 215, 225, 226
Free-basing, 49–51
Free radical assay, 90

Gamma alcoholic, 24, 25
Gas liquid chromatography, 89
Gastritis, 42
Gay and lesbian substance abuse
   etiological factors, 203–205
   risk factors, 203
Genetics, 171
General systems theory, 163
Geriatric substance abuse
   epidemiology, 205, 206
   manifestations, 205, 206
   treatment of, 206, 207
GHD, 62
Glaucoma, 61
Grandiosity, 20
Group cohesiveness, 157, 160
Group therapy
   curative factors in, 56–158
   problems in, 167–169
   selection of patients, 164, 165
   stages of, 159–161
   systems theory, 158, 159
Guilt, 21, 24, 185, 187

Hair testing, 91, 92
Hallucinations, 7, 8, 19, 40, 45, 51, 58, 62, 164
Harm reduction, 115
Hashish, 55, 91
Hazelton, 135
Heart disease, 42
Hemagglutination inhibition, 90
Hepatitis, 30, 42, 51, 54, 77, 115
Heroin
  dependence, 27, 53
  detection of, 53, 91
  main effects, 7, 8, 40, 52, 208
  medical consequences of, 40, 52–55
  mortality, 55
  route of administration, 52
  tolerance, 53
  withdrawal, 53
Heroin addiction, metabolic disease, 27, 28
High risk situations, 133, 134
High risk studies, 26
Hispanic substance abuse, 202
HIV. *See* AIDS
Hostility, 21, 44, 47
Humor, 121, 122, 186
Hyperactivity, 45, 49, 55
Hypnotics, 19

Immunoassays, 89, 90
Impotence, 80
Impulse control disorder, 115
Impulsivity, 17
Inhalants, 40, 202
Insomnia, 44, 47, 48, 53, 62
International Classification of Diseases (ICD),
  95
Interpretation, 122
Interview
  format of, 74 – 81
  reliability of, 72
  taping of, 73
Intravenous (IV), 52, 53
Introspection, 116

JCAHO, 118
Journal of the American Medical Association, 27

Ketamine, 63
Korsakoff's psychosis, 42

LAAM, 121, 131, 138
Laboratory tests, 88
Learning, 19, 22, 131, 157
Learning disabilities, 51
Legal assessment, 77, 95
Lidocaine, 46
Liver damage, 42
Look-alike drugs, 46
Loss of control, 23–25
Low frustration tolerance, 19, 116
Low self esteem, 17, 20
LSD
  depression and, 52
  flashbacks, 52
  main effects, 40, 41, 51, 52
  tolerance, 52
  withdrawal, 52

MacAndrew Alcoholism Scale, 84
Major depression, 17
Malnutrition, 45
Manipulation, 116, 121, 144
Marijuana
  abuse, 55, 135, 136
  criminal behavior and, 57
  detection of, 56, 91
  epidemiology, 8
  issues, 56–60
  learning and, 57
  legalization/decriminalization, 60
  main effects, 55
  medicine and, 60–62
  motivation and, 57
  physical problems, 58–60
  psychopathology, 58
  route of administration, 55
  tolerance to, 56
Marinol, 61
Mass spectrometry, 90
Maturation theory, 29
MDMA. *See* Ecstasy
Medical therapies, 136–139
Mental status, 75, 82
Mescaline, 40, 41, 91
Methadone, 88, 91, 137, 138
Methadone maintenance, 12, 27, 76, 114, 131,
  137, 138
Methadrine, 43

Methamphetamines. *See* Amphetamines
Michigan Alcoholism Screening Test (MAST), 95
Millon Clinical Multiaxial Inventory (MCMI), 94, 208
Minnesota Multiphasic Personality Inventory (MMPI), 94, 208
Minor tranquilizers. *See* Barbiturates
Monitoring the Future, 4
Monoamine oxidase (MAO), 26, 64, 130
Morphine, 40, 41, 52–54, 88–91
Motivational enhancement, 135, 140
Motivational interviewing, 84–88, 135, 140, 145, 158
Multiple sclerosis, 61

Naltrexone, 37, 130
Narcan, 138
Narcissism, 21, 54, 156
Narcolepsy, 45
Narcotic antagonist, 137, 138
Narcotics Anonymous (NA), 76, 139, 143, 155, 158, 160, 161, 197
National Center for Health Statistics, 2
National Drug and Alcoholism Survey, 3
National Drug Control Strategy, 6–10, 199, 212, 215
National Highway Traffic Safety Administration, 2
National Household Survey on Drug Abuse, 4, 7, 199
National Institute on Alcoholism and Alcohol Abuse (NIAAA), 2, 4, 10, 199, 210
National Institute on Drug Abuse (NIDA), 3, 4, 10, 12, 56, 113, 138
Native American substance abuse, 193, 207
Needles, 199
Nembutal, 46
Neonatal addiction, 54
Neuropsychology, 51, 54, 59
  neuropsychological markers, 26, 27
Neurotransmitters, 38, 43
Nicotine
  effects of, 64
  epidemiology, 8, 9, 49
  medical problems, 66, 67
  pregnancy and, 67
  reasons for smoking, 64

reasons for stopping, 65, 66
social problems, 67
withdrawal, 63, 64
Norepinephrine, 43
Nutrition, 39

Object relations, 162, 163, 187
Opiate receptors, 53, 138
Opium. *See* Heroin
Oral stage, 19
Overdose, 47, 48, 51, 54, 55, 76
Pancreatitis, 43
Panic reactions, 39, 46, 58
Paraphrasing, 122
Paregoric, 41
Paranoia, 62
PCP, 31, 40, 51, 63, 91, 202
Pentobarbitol, 41
Personality disorder, 54, 78, 165, 208
Pharmacokinetics
  absorption, 37, 38
  distribution, 38
  excretion, 38
  metabolism, 38
Pharmacotherapy, 130
Phenobarbitol, 41
Phenylpropanolamine, 46
Physical dependence, 23, 24
Posttraumatic Stress Disorder, 17
Power motivation, 19–21, 44
Preludin, 43
Procaine, 46
Project Match, 140, 141
Protective factors, 15
Psychiatric disorders, 19, 20
Psychoanalytic models, 78
Psychological markers, 26, 27, 78
Psychological tests, 20, 92, 94
Psychopathology, 26, 54, 58, 132, 163, 172
Psychosis, 45, 51, 58
Psychotherapy, 76, 163, 183
Public policy
  government interventions, 225–227
  law enforcement, 219–225
  national policy, 211, 212
  social interventions, 212–219

Questioning, 122, 123

Radioimmunoassay (RAI), 90
Rational Recovery, 126, 127
Reassurance, 123
Receptors, 53
Recovery, 11, 49, 115, 135, 155, 172, 183
Recreation, 78
Reflection, 123, 143
Reinforcement
  negative, 22
  primary, 22, 65
  secondary, 22, 129, 130
Relapse, 49, 63, 66, 88, 131, 135, 143, 161
Relapse prevention, 114, 131–135
Resistance, 85, 86, 131, 144
Risk factors, 15–18
Ritaline, 43, 45, 49
Roach clips, 58
Role deprivation, 28
Role playing, 134
Role theory, 28, 185
Route of administration, 36, 37, 44, 47, 52, 55

Schizophrenia, 45
Seconol, 46
Sedatives, 19, 46
Seizures, 47, 48, 137
Self-disclosure, 123, 124
Self-efficacy, 85, 87, 133, 143
Self help, 158
Self image, 116
Self medication hypothesis, 20, 132
Sentencing laws, 223
Separation anxiety, 160, 161
Serotonin, 38, 62
Sexual abuse, 180, 186
Sexual disorders, 80, 95
Sexually transmitted diseases, 51, 115, 158
Sherman sticks, 7
Sidestream smoke, 67
Silence, 124
Skills training, 130, 131
Social assessment, 77, 78
Social pressure, 65, 66, 133
Sodium pentothal, 46
Spectrometry, 89, 90
Spectrophotometric technique, 90
Speedballing, 44
Spirituality, assessment, 79

State-dependent learning, 43, 45
Status theory, 28, 29
Stepping stone hypothesis, 57
Stimulants, 40, 43–46, 62
Substance abuse
  epidemiology, 1–13
  etiology of, 15
  interview, 72
Suicide, 47, 55, 73
Summarizing, 124
Supreme Court, 212, 213, 224

Teen pregnancy, 18
Thematic Apperception Test, 117, 186
THC, 40, 55, 56, 58, 60, 61, 91
Therapeutic community, 12, 76, 96, 139, 202
Thin-layer chromatography, 89
Tobacco. *See* Nicotine
Tolerance, 24, 41, 43, 47, 48, 50, 52, 53, 56,
  62, 63, 75
Tranquilizers, 40, 136
Trazadone, 44
Treatment
  categories (modalities), 124–138
  cost effectiveness of, 11, 112
  plan, 72, 76, 82, 114, 118, 137, 151–153,
    197
  principles, 113–115
Treatment matching, 139–141
Tuberculosis, 54
Tuonol, 37
Twelve-step program, 125, 141
Twin studies, 25

Ulcers, 43, 53, 180
Urinalysis, 53, 56, 88, 91, 92
  error rates, 88
  sensitivity, 89
  specificity, 89

Vaginismus, 80
Valium, 31, 41
Veterans Administration (VA), 1, 94
Viet Nam, 1, 28
Violence, domestic, 43, 77
Vistaril, 37
Vocational assessment, 76, 77, 95

Wernicke's encephalopathy, 43
Withdrawal, 22, 24, 42, 47, 48, 52, 53, 56, 62–
  64, 66, 75, 76, 131, 132, 136, 137, 195
Women substance abuse
  drug and alcohol use, 198, 199

etiology, 200
World Health Organization (WHO), 44, 65, 95

Xanax, 41, 138